AMERICAN LADY CREATURE

(MY) CHANGE IN THE MIDDLE EAST. A QATAR MEMOIR.

L.L. KIRCHNER

ABOUT THE AUTHOR

L.L. KIRCHNER is an award-winning screenwriter and author. She lives in Florida with her favorite husband.

If you enjoyed this book, please leave an Amazon review.

Her debut historical fiction novel, **Florida Girls** (the first book in The Queenpin Chronicles) will be out in May. Get an audio version of the prologue here and you'll be the first to know when the books are available.

Get new stories, craft and publishing tips in her newsletter, Ill-Behaved Women.

More at LLKirchner.com.

On socials everywhere @llkirchner_.

ALSO BY THE AUTHOR:
Blissful Thinking: A Memoir of Overcoming the Wellness Revolution, a 2023 Pushcart nominee

CONTENTS

FOREWORD TO THE NEW EDITION

ST. PETERSBURG, FL
December 2021

WHEN THIS BOOK WAS first published by Greenpoint Press in 2014 as *Hello American Lady Creature: What I Learned as a Woman In Qatar*, I imagined a future edition that might coincide the FIFA World Cup, already on the schedule for Qatar in 2022, and already controversial for graft, corruption, and abuse of migrant workers.

While this is the personal story of my divorce—finalized in November 2006 when I was living in Doha—it's also a collision of historic events and cultural norms. This chronicle of that particular time and place—Qatar in the early aughts—is from my perspective as an outsider. And while I have made edits for clarity (such as the title; I've always loved my original—extrapolated from the thought cloud I pictured in my assistant's head each time he looked at me—in the seven years since this book originally came out, that title has tripped on every tongue), I have not changed the book's essence.

I wrote the book because living in Qatar showed me how I'd

internalized misogyny. That's not the plot, and those words don't appear in the text. And this isn't only because, when this book first came out feminism was still considered a negative term, but because I think the most effective stories don't *try* and teach.

In the years since this memoir was first published, the Qataris have taken steps to improve labor conditions in much the same way that we in the U.S. have experienced a shift since #metoo. In other words, they've made a good start, but there's a long way to go.

As you'll see, the worst treatment and discrimination I faced over the course of events described herein came at the hands of Western expats. And yet, these are not the worst exemplars of misogynistic behavior I've experienced. Even so, if I hadn't been living in Qatar, I don't think I'd have seen the ways I behaved based on my adoption of certain norms of patriarchal culture.

My hope was (and is) that by exposing my foibles in dramatic fashion, others might see how they might do the same kinds of things. I use humor to keep it compassionate, because I believe people can change if we're gentle enough. Or maybe that's why change for me has been incremental and maintained only with regular updates. This is largely the topic of my follow-up book, *Blissful Thinking: A Memoir of Overcoming the Wellness Revolution.*

What prompted me to write this book in the first place was how, on my return to the States, everyone was talking about Hillary Clinton and Sarah Palin as if they were both presidential candidates, which they were not. Against this backdrop of prominent women painted as bitch and bimbo, people seemed hyper-aware of the female struggle. Yet ironically, the most common refrain I heard upon saying I'd just returned from the Persian Gulf was, "How could you stand it there? They treat women so badly!"

And we were doing so much better?

I'm not trying to defend Muslim culture, but neither do I wish to villainize it. If anything, in my experience their overt discrimination made the rules clear, and thus easier to subvert.

As someone who grew up saying, "I'm not a feminist, *but—*" and then proceeded to list all the ways I was in fact a feminist, I suffered for years under the illusion my interest was in *human* rights.

Clearly, I've always been a feminist. And as I now know, it's possible to be a feminist and a humanist. But the words, the labels... they matter. I will always have work to do. A level playing field is not natural, but a by-product of civilized society, itself a label, an idea. Something to seek.

Books have always been my best window to learning, and so I offer mine. Thanks for looking through.

PROLOGUE

Salaam oulaikoum:
"The peace of God be with you," is the standard greeting in the Arab world. Wa alaikum as-salaam is the somewhat standard reply, meaning, "And also with you." Or that's my Catholicism-influenced interpretation anyway.

DOHA, QATAR
February 2006

M Y EYES AREN'T YET open and already I have that desperate feeling. I am *desperate* for a shag. It is true what they say about women in their late 30s and teenage boys. Sadly, libido is not all we share. Despite the advantages I should've accrued, I'm not getting any either.

Forget about sex, here in Qatar dating is illegal. For everyone: even a green-eyed, blonde from Pittsburgh who wasn't raised with words like "shag." Not that I'm looking for a date; I miss my husband. This is so not what I had in mind for the

Persian Gulf when I took the job of heading up marketing efforts for Carnegie Mellon's branch campus in Doha.

Ostensibly we'd moved to set up my beloved in a safe and centrally-located country in order to pursue his dream of covering international news. In truth, *I'd* moved to make our relationship bulletproof. I'd long been the primary breadwinner, something I didn't think was good for our relationship, not if we were going to have children. This was also because of what I wanted, to be the one to stay with our children.

Then the whole journalism thing didn't pan out. He'd returned to the States recently to look for work.

I blame Qatar as I paw the nightstand for my vibrator. Thank God the guys at customs are afraid of anything stuffed in a box of tampons. The batteries are dead. It hasn't even been a month since Geoff went home to look for work. Have I been using this thing that much?

When I can't pretend to lie still anymore, I reach to find the time on my mobile, another Briticism that's crept into my vocabulary in this country of very few American expats. It's 5:35 a.m. I might be a morning person, but this is ridiculous. It's Saturday. There is no alarm, no one to see, nowhere to be, and I am wide awake. I've been backsliding on sleep since Geoff left. Please God don't let it get as bad as our first year in Qatar. Not even Sophie or Grandpa stir as I push out of bed, until they hear the food hit their bowls.

While waiting for the coffee to brew, I notice the harmonica I'd given Geoff for Christmas. It's in a basket on the counter in plain view. I must've been seeing it every day these past three weeks, I just haven't actually seen it. No wonder he left it behind. I lift it to my nose, hoping for a drag of my beloved; it smells like metal. I tuck the instrument into my robe, thinking I'll surprise him with it when I see him. In just ten days we're going to rendezvous in the U.S., the first of two such trips I've planned during our time apart. Maybe I should look around and see what else he's forgotten. Start the process of deciding what to keep and what to give away.

When the school year ends, I plan to pack up, join my partner of seven years and never look back. Coffee in hand, I pad back up the stairs. This time, Sophie and Grandpa are right behind me. Somewhat tentatively I push open the door to the third bedroom, Geoff's room that I haven't been in since he left. Not that I went in much when he was here. We'd shared the master bedroom, the second room was my closet, and this had been his. *What a godsend.* I might have to rearrange our house in Pittsburgh like this; he should always have his own space to be messy in, and I should always have my own bathroom. Will we ever have the luxury of separate baths again? Or even move back to Pittsburgh? My other half is in Buffalo working at the same newspaper he'd been at when we first met. He says it's temporary, but I wasn't happy about it. It's a job that won't pay the bills, and meanwhile, our house is sitting empty. The house we just renovated. All that scraping, the re-wiring, moving walls...

But now is not the time to go down that road. Geoff and I had decided that these six months apart were practical if not ideal. His journalism career — which we thought would soar merely by being at the center of world news — had stalled. He was not a natural freelancer. Much as I looked forward to getting back to it — freelancing — I couldn't up and quit my job just now. I'd only recently hired my team and they needed to be trained. Besides, somebody had to pay the mortgage on that heat-leeching Victorian. There had been plenty of times I couldn't shut off my doubts, but Geoff reassured me, "It's only temporary, and you'd be miserable in Buffalo over the winter."

I slide back the closet door and start flicking through the

hangers. Sophie and Grandpa track the movement, eyes and heads drooping. I hear one of them snore.

Then I make contact with Gortex.

Pushing the clothes apart I spy my husband's winter coat, the first pricey gift I ever gave him, a present while we were dating. At the time we lived in separate states, he in New York, I, Pennsylvania. To offer him something more substantive than his thrift store wool overcoat gave me a secret thrill, as if I could protect him even when I wasn't there. Now the jacket looks lost and forlorn, not even encased in plastic. I reach for its sleeve, relating I've felt equally out of place in this sweltering desert. I'm going to put it in the "take to Pittsburgh" pile. Then it hits me. I stop.

It's February. My other half has just left our desert home in Doha for the North American tundra that is Buffalo, New York. My beloved might not be the most thorough of packers, but how could he possibly have forgotten this? It's his only winter coat.

Panic washes over my body. Is this a sign?

But it can't be. Despite my disappointment over his employment choices and our subsequent fight, he'd just sent an e-mail saying he loved me and couldn't wait to hear the sound of my voice. I don't want to take my crazy to him. Again.

A self-diagnosed "friend-dependent"—I can barely figure things out without talking them over with friends, a group I call "My We"—life in Doha has been rough. The only Americans I know, and thus, those with whom I can share cultural references and irony, are co-workers. Not people I want knowing about the details of my marriage. But I have carved out a few cohorts. Unfortunately, this group includes only one female friend who also has a "trailing spouse"—a financially dependent husband in this, one of the most patriarchal cultures in the world — and she's in Singapore for work. So I call my friend Paul, a guy who not only knows me, he's spent time with Geoff and I as a couple. He'll have the perspective I'm lacking.

"I can't even tell you what just happened. It's so trivial it's embarrassing, but I'm going a little crazy and could really use your advice," I explain.

I ask him to meet me at the City Center Mall, not my favorite of Doha's eight cavernous shopping malls, but then, I don't like any of them. It baffles me that eight malls are required in a city with barely 400,000 people, which is roughly the size of Tulsa, Oklahoma. "It's on three. You have to walk past the skating rink," I guide him. "Not toward the movie theater or the children's, you have to go to that weird, outer perimeter."

He needs the directions because I've asked him to meet at the Starbucks less traveled, the one on the third floor, where locals ward off the expats with their cologne and cigarettes. Not only can I bum a smoke up here, I can huff it down without being seen. I'd recently started teaching yoga and I don't want my students to see me smoking. There are "no smoking" signs, of signs up here. Just like at the Starbucks on the first floor. We ignore them.

When Paul arrives I tell him about finding Geoff's coat in the closet, needing him to confirm that my "evidence" is inconclusive at best. After listening thoughtfully, he says, "I'm sorry you lost your husband."

Then Paul starts laughing and I get it. Joke. This is exactly why I'd called him.

Paul knows this is part of our plan, the plan whereby I took a job I didn't really want so that my husband might advance his career. So that eventually he might take the financial reins. None of it had worked, in fact, until now. He had taken charge by leaving for the States to find employment. Though lately he'd been working at his "temporary" job in Buffalo so hard, I couldn't imagine how he'd have time to look for other work. Or how he'd get away to help me move our stuff back to the States.

When we stop laughing, I agree with Paul. "He never thinks about the cold, not like me. That's just how he is. It's like that one-sentence email he sent me on Valentine's Day..." I trail off for a moment, remembering his words: Hi doll, I'm sorry I've been such a jerk.

"He's like an absent-minded professor," I go on. "Really, I'm more surprised at how little he did leave behind. He's usually not quite so... thorough." Ultimately, the Pittsburgh pile I'd put together that morning consisted of only three items —the coat, a harmonica, and Geoff's college diploma.

"Everything turns out fine in the end," Paul reassures me without, I'd realize much later, actually assuring me of anything. "If it's not fine, you're just not at the end yet."

I was nowhere near the end, and I didn't even know how I'd gotten to this place. I needed to go home and smoke and try to figure this out, retrace my steps. From the beginning.

PART I

ONE
AN ANNIVERSARY TO FORGET

Qatar:
Sheikhdom in the Persian Gulf (or Arab Sea if you're in the GCC). Mispronounced by all: Americans, CUT'er; Canadians, CATTer; and the Brits, q'TAAR.

The Gulf Cooperation Council/GCC:
A political and economic union including Qatar, Saudi Arabia, Oman, the United Arab Emirates, Bahrain and Kuwait.

PITTSBURGH, PA
February 2004

"Qatar," I HEARD CARNEGIE MELLON'S head of media relations say. "We've got to peg this place in people's minds. We should put up top that it's in the Persian Gulf."

Luckily for me she was simultaneously passing around a stack of press releases titled, "DRAFT: Carnegie Mellon Launches Undergraduate Branch in Qatar." Otherwise I'd have had no idea what she was talking about. Prior to this conversation I'd never even heard of "CUT'ter," as she pronounced it. I'd always thought it was called "q'TAAR."

The director looked around the room, then focused on me. "You lived in the Muslim world before, Lisa. What do you think?" At the time I was living in Pittsburgh with my husband of two years. I was a freelance PR and branding consultant, while he was the editor of a local newsweekly.

Typically I consulted from home, but on that day I was working out of their main PR office, a converted space on the first floor of an old Victorian house on campus. The university had been a client of mine for a couple of years at that point, and while I'd made it known I'd been a volunteer with the Peace Corps in Tunisia; I never mentioned I'd been kicked out. Sensing potential new business, I wasn't about to mention it now.

Agreeing most Americans were geographically challenged, I Googled Qatar. The first thing I clicked on was a map. So that's *where it is*, I thought, looking at a narrow peninsula nestled between Saudi Arabia and Dubai. The map also indicated that the country was home to the U.S.'s largest offshore military base, Central Command, CentCom for short. According to the release, the school was about to announce the opening of a new campus in the country's capital city of Doha, alongside the likes of Weill Cornell and Georgetown. This would be their first undergraduate branch outside the main campus in Pittsburgh, PA.

"We should put in that Al Jazeera's there too," I added, pleased when no one else in the room knew this fact. Or was able to type faster than me, anyway. I never would have imagined that three months later, I'd be living there.

T wo weeks later...
    My cell phone rang. I fished it out of my pocket and squinted at the number. No idea. If I'd been back home I probably wouldn't have picked up, but I was in Barstow, CA, working media for Carnegie Mellon at the DARPA Grand Challenge, an autonomous vehicle race backed by the U.S. government to further military research. This event brought the tech-geek journos out of the woodwork. It was probably one of them from God knows where calling with some fancy gadget. A cloud of dust kicked up in front of me as an unmanned motorcycle fell over in the dirt.

    "Happy second anniversary, baby," I heard over a scratchy line. Geoff! How he'd managed to get his hands on a satellite phone I couldn't imagine; he was in Iraq. Best anniversary present ever. *Everyone should have a Geoff.*

    While part of me would have liked to have been the kind of wife who could successfully protest her husband's absence for this annual celebration of matrimony, I was the kind who hadn't even tried. By the time my other half arranged his trip, I already had plans to take this gig. The irony wasn't lost on either of us. He'd be off pushing peace, while I'd be promoting warfare technology. This was the crux of our love, I thought. A mutual ability to support one another.

    "I just wanted you to know before you heard about it on TV," he went on. "The huge bomb that just went off was the hotel next door. Not my hotel. I'm fine. We're all fine."

    It was March 2004, one year since Bush had given his "Mission Accomplished" speech aboard the aircraft carrier the *USS Lincoln*. Despite Bush's proclamation of victory, U.S. media had stopped talking about "the end" and now simply referred to "the war." But the speech's anniversary did not go unnoticed by Al Qaida. They used the occasion to ramp up attacks against foreigners, especially journalists like my spouse. They could not have known he was there on a volunteer mission, aimed at proving the war was far from over.

Of all the horrible scenarios I'd imagined since he'd announced this junket, incidental bombing was one I'd refused to think about. My imaginings ran more along the lines of his being taken hostage, and then released once the kidnappers realized what a decent human being they'd captured.

"This is where the world news is happening," he went on, sounding more excited than he had in a long time. "It would be so great to live out here. Become a foreign correspondent."

Many people, on hearing their partner express such a whim, might murmur politely and change the subject. But I'd grown up in a family where geographic change was the norm. By the time I was 12 we'd moved nine times. In my experience, once the desire to relocate was announced, you were as good as gone. I couldn't sit back and watch him go without me.

Prior to this call, I'd been thinking of the new Qatar campus as an opportunity to get some more work and maybe rack up the frequent flier miles, but *moving* to the region could be Geoff's ticket to the next rung on the career ladder. As the editor of our town's alternative newsweekly, he'd already reached the pinnacle of success. It was not financially viable. Not if we were ever going to have a family. The university was offering three-year contracts, which would give him plenty of time to establish himself in his new career, and I'd just have turned forty; the ideal conditions for us to start our family.

In the course of that conversation I didn't miss a beat. "What would you say to Qatar?"

Three months later, I was living there. Yes, *I*.

W e spent far more time rationalizing our decision to leave the country than we had making it.

"You've got to be kidding me," was how my mom responded. Though it was not shocking neither of my Fox News-loving parents wanted to see their youngest daughter move to a post-9/11 Persian Gulf, Mom was referring to my earlier stint in the region.

"Mom, please, it's nothing like Tunisia. Qataris one of the richest countries in the world," I said. "They don't even have Peace Corps volunteers."

Though I had found some similarities between Tunisia and Qatar — both had shaken off the shackles of colonialism and were described as progressive — when it came to keeping a population under control, the divide was enormous. Whereas Tunisia's GDP put them at poverty level, Qatar had the second highest per capita income in the world. By virtue of its natural gas wealth, the ruling Al Thani family was able to provide each of its 250,000 citizens with a paycheck for simply being a national. The rest of us, the remaining 750,000 majority? We were imported to work. The criminal, the diseased, the unemployed... they weren't allowed in. If you didn't play nice in Qatar, you got deported, and no GCC country would hire you ever again.

Didn't the campus itself say a lot about the country? Begun to educate women, the unfortunately named "Education City" now housed co-ed undergraduate branches from several American universities, with plans for ten more in the coming years. The whole thing was headed up by Her Highness Sheikha Mozah bint Nasser Al Missned. A *woman*.

I didn't mention to my mother that she was but one of His Highness' three wives. A stay-at-home housewife herself, Mom had made it clear she didn't want either of her daughters becoming, well, stay-at-home housewives. She'd taught us to be independent. I was around five when I started to cook. When I took her my first creation—an experiment with salt and flour and baking soda—she took one look and hissed at my father, "Bob, she's making cake."

The next toy I got was a microscope.

"It's not like I'll be in Saudi Arabia," I finished. "I don't have to cover. I'm allowed to drive."

"*Allowed* to drive," Mom said. "Kid, you're gonna drive me up a wall."

I t wasn't the first time I'd lived in the Muslim world; I'd come to pray it would be the last.

TWO
MARHABA!

Marhaba:
"Hello." Secular and vaguely unfriendly, not a good substitute for salaam alaikoum.

DOHA, QATAR
June 2004

QATAR GREETED ME WITH a wall of sticky sea air so intense it took my breath away. I'd done my research; this was a business trip after all. I wasn't surprised when the captain announced the temperature — 110 degrees, ideal for melting chocolate — but until I tried to suck it in, I had no idea what that kind of air was like. Qatari peninsula is so narrow in some spots you can drive across it in about 45 minutes. Air traveling over that sand doesn't have time to drop its moisture. It was practically sweating; I know I was. No wonder the locals on the plane had begun to douse up on heavy cologne as we cleared for landing.

The chilled black Mercedes that shuttled us from the tarmac to the terminal offered welcome respite for the entire ten seconds it took to beeline it to the entrance. Then the waiting at customs, then another Mercedes. I couldn't wait to experience the exotic landscape I'd been imagining. Ah, *Q'taar*, a word that evoked a whiff of incense and the rustle of a belly dancer's scarves, so long as I ignored the correct pronunciation, CUT'ter, which would turn out to be more telling.

We'd landed around midnight so my new home remained shrouded in mystery as we sped from the airport to the hotel. Immediately obvious, however, were the waves of nausea that swept over me. For the first time in my life, I was experiencing car sickness.

Traffic in Doha did not meet at four-corner intersections, but roundabouts, ginormous circles that divided the world into two types of drivers: the enraged and the terrified. The former seemed hell-bent on passing through these crossings without slowing down, whereas the latter, which our driver turned out to be among, lacked the requisite aggression to exit. This meant we sloshed around multiple times before being spit out in another direction. By the time we got to the hotel, I had no idea where I was in relation to the airport.

Alighting from the vehicle led to instant, if short-lived, relief, as that wave of hot air hit us again. "This is unbelievable," Kyle, my boss and companion for this trip, said as she pushed a wisp of frosted blonde hair off her forehead. "I thought it would be a dry, desert heat."

I watched as she adjusted her bracelets and rings and necklaces, all sticking to the sheen of perspiration that had broken out. Somewhere in her 40s, Kyle worked harder than most 20-year-olds I knew. I wondered how — in addition to the job, the daughter and the husband — she found the time to put together trendy outfits, complete with exotic jewelry. The only thing I had the time for was the business end of The Gap, looks I accessorized as sparsely as the clothes demanded.

"Now I get why Lonely Planet says the best time to visit was the Ice Age," I said. "It feels like we're standing in front of an open clothes dryer."

The reception desk inside was another story; it felt like the inside of a meat locker. I was glad I'd been warned to dress conservatively, covering my elbows and knees at all times, but made a mental note to ask my husband Geoff to bring some sweaters out of storage. I'd be needing them if I was going to live here. Not that the university had offered me the marketing director job. But so long as I could convince them to create the position I was proposing, I would be taking the post and we would be moving to Doha.

Though it wasn't yet public knowledge, the newspaper where Geoff worked had just filed for bankruptcy. The industry outlook was grim, newspapers simply weren't hiring. A post-9/11 Persian Gulf, however, surely offered stories for the taking. He could find and report on news that papers would want and wouldn't otherwise have access to. Rather than having a lull in his resume while he looked for work, he could become a free-lance foreign correspondent and catapult his career. Secretly I imagined him on television, grainy and small. It didn't matter that he'd never worked in broadcast news. I knew that once he got rolling there would be no stopping him. For God's sake, not only was he brilliant, he was gorgeous. He *should* be on camera. He claimed to be shy, but surely any man that could woo me and run a paper had more than enough nerve to go on television.

As for me, professionally the move was lateral. But once the three-year contract (they hadn't yet offered) was up, I'd get to take some time off and work on my writing. He'd have become so successful, I could step back from the financial reins and get started on that family. We were perfect partners like that. In the meantime, I had to impress my boss-to-be. Not an easy task.

Kyle's enthusiasm for work made me feel like a slacker.

Since being dot-bombed out of a marketing director's position with an internet company three years earlier, I'd launched a communications consulting business. Simultaneously, I was the religion editor for a gay and lesbian newspaper, the bridal editor for a society rag, and the dating columnist for an alternative newsweekly. I was used to working hard, I just wasn't used to getting out of my pajamas before 10 a.m. On any kind of a regular basis. For instance, I would've thought a lie-in was in order the morning after we arrived, but Kyle wanted to meet in the lobby at 8 a.m. This would turn out to be the latest start time during our trip. usually, we met over breakfast and crawled home after a late supper. Not that I was without blame. I'd helped Kyle put together such ambitious plans for the campus, they'd have to hire a team to implement them.

The university brass originally thought the marketing and communications position could be done by an admin. Part-time. In addition to their other duties. I'd encountered opposition to my field in other jobs, but the university was particularly adverse to marketing. God forbid we discuss the "brand value" of a university. It might turn education into some kind of commodity. But going to a campus far away was an opportunity to change that. I put "dim view of my profession" on my list of things to turn around. Right after "female oppression." And "spouse's career."

I imagined leading a team to renovate the dean's residence, analyze market research, and establish a media presence for Carnegie Mellon, which had no name recognition in the marketplace. But Qatar had no built-in talent pool to do the work involved.

For most of recorded history, the place had been an uninhabitable no-man's land. The rare settlements that did form near wells were ransacked or abandoned. This Lord of the Flies-like environment spawned pirates so fierce they managed to beat back the ottoman empire in the Arab sea. That same family — the pirates — still runs the country today; displaying a kind of Machiavellian instinct I find alternately impressive and shocking. Take, for example, the CentCom/Al Jazeera dichotomy. Imagine for a moment the delicate balance these leaders must keep, appeasing their conservative brethren while pushing for change. They had money to begin with, what with the pearling and the oil, but what changed everything for Qatar was the discovery that they sat atop one of the world's largest reserves of natural gas. In less time than it's taken me to grow up, they have transformed their country from a backwater nation into a major player in the global economy. That meant importing people. Lots of people.

When I arrived in 2004, there were about a million souls in all of Qatar. Out of that, only about 250,000 were actually Qatari. The rest of us had been brought in to work. First up were engineers and gas drilling types. Then there were roads and houses to be built. And, of course, there was the whole barren wasteland thing. They needed groceries and doctors before graphic artists and printing presses. Kyle and I shot an advertisement during our trip, and to get it done we had to bring in not only our photographer from Bahrain, but also models from Dubai. As for the extraordinary expense and effort to open an undergraduate branch campus? After bringing in everything from a school nurse to professors to building the actual campus, our inaugural class was comprised of 48 freshmen.

We were there as part of an initiative called Education City, which existed thanks to the current Al Thani leader, who'd taken power in 1997 in a move that was always referred to as a "bloodless coup." From all accounts, the son took power while dad was vacationing in France. There's no telling if said coup was planned or not, but one thing is certain, the changes since have been massive and rapid-fire. The vibe that greeted me was

Wild West meets American mall culture, with SUVs taking the place of horses and guns. It took me a while to understand how lawless such a strict society could be; particularly, in light of my first experience in the region, when I was a Peace Corps volunteer.

About here is as good a place as any to describe what happened during my tenure in Tunisia, because I'm not the kind of person you meet and think, *Hey, I could see this one as a Peace Corps volunteer*. If I mention it, I often get an inquisitive, "Really?" My pragmaticism doesn't jive with the program and the people in it. My foray into idealistic hippie culture was part of a lengthy crisis.

Growing up, my dad moved my mom, my sister and me nine times by the time I was twelve, going from one rust-belt suburb to the next. My father was a metallurgical engineer; not a profession associated with frequent relocation. But he was a man ahead of his time. When he did ditch the steel industry in 1979, it was to buy a health club. I loved it, going to new places, meeting new people and seeing new things. It wasn't until I was an adult that I realized, I had no idea what it meant to stay. And then, only thanks to my first love, Jeffrey (yes, same name as the husband, but a different man and a different spelling).

The first Jeff taught me what it meant to fight with someone and still love them. How to accept another person's shortcomings. The enduring nature of love. But our forever lasted only five years. In June of 1991 he drowned. Just like that, he was gone forever. I was twenty-four and knew no one would ever love me like that again. I went through the motions, going to work, even dating, but I no longer wanted to be in the same place. I wanted my outsides to match how I felt inside, torn apart. This time the move needed to be especially dramatic, and so I joined the Peace Corps.

Jeffery and I had met in sober recovery. Following his death,

I set my sights on getting into one of the then-newly opened eastern-bloc countries, a — stan or a — slav something. Though the Peace Corps sent me to Tunisia, I began to drink like a good Eastern European anyway. This behavior did not go over well in a country where drinking is *haram*, or forbidden by the Quran. After three short months, I was "medically evacuated." Looking back, I'm horrified by my antics, and damn curious as to how I lasted three months. On our first night together, we volunteers gathered in a hotel lobby in Tunis. It had to be at least a four-star place (one of the ways they restricted consumption was by making it too expensive for locals to drink) because they served alcohol. Despite the rating, the interior — like so many places around the world that try to emulate Western-style elegance — was dilapidated. The lobby held a long sofa on one wall, fronted by a low table where we pulled up a few mismatched chairs in a loose circle. My fear of not fitting in was on high alert as I read the situation. There was me, and then there was this group of earnest, fresh-from-college graduation individuals. I didn't believe we were going to spread peace, love and/or harmony. Joining the Peace Corps had simply been my last, best escape option, a way to get my life off the track it was on, and start over. A way to gain experience instead of going to grad school.

I don't know whose idea it was to start up a game of Suck & Blow, but once it got going I was all *game on*. The idea was to pass a deck of cards around a circle without using your hands. You inhaled a card to your mouth, then exhaled to pass that card to the player beside you. Should the card fall a penalty shot was imbibed, once mouths could be pulled apart. As far as I was concerned, this Suck & Blow was the perfect way to get to know my fellow recruits. Especially, my insta-crush Dave. That I was engaging in this behavior in a public venue in an Islamic country absolutely blows my mind now, but at the time I thought, *At last! The chummy college years I never had because I was too busy being sober.*

Interestingly, I wasn't the only one to pack it in on Tunisia. Shortly after I was booted, the Peace Corps canceled its program there and phased out the volunteers. This enabled me to mention my service freely. It rarely led to follow-up questions, and if it did the conversation mostly went like this:

"Really?" the person listening would usually say. "How long were you there?" (Mysteriously, this is the most frequently asked question.)

"Only three months," I'd say. "They canceled the program while I was there."

It's not exactly a lie, and I've often doubted I'd have lasted the whole three years. One of the volunteers had been raped shortly before we got there — an event I was shocked the Peace Corps failed to mention prior to our arrival. The suggested safeguard was that we travel together in groups at all times, a strategy that did not always work. One day at the beach, a group of us were surrounded in the ocean by some young Tunisian men. The only way through was to break free. I will never forget the feeling of hands groping me underwater as I swam for the shore.

Thus, ten years later, as I contemplated living in Doha, one of the things I feared most about making the move was losing my freedom. In Tunisia, no matter how tattered or shapeless my outfit, I was regularly asked for money and called a "whore." Meanwhile in Qatar, the first thing I noticed was that, far from feeling harassed, I was ignored. This was not just my imagination, as I learned from the university's Chief Operating Officer, Mohamed.

One afternoon in his office, we —Mohamed, decked out in Dockers and an Oxford; Fawzi, our admissions counselor, sporting the full-on starched white thobe and red and white checked *ghutra*; Kyle in a long, colorful, fitted Missoni dress; and me, in a size-too-large black linen pantsuit — were reviewing the ad campaign for the school's launch.

"I don't think we want to run that," Mohamed said, shaking his head.

"Could you be more specific?" Kyle asked.

Despite how American Mohamed looked compared to Fawzi, both men were from Yemen. The difference was that Mohamed had been raised in Seattle, whereas Fawzi had grown up in Qatar. But they both objected to the ad's central image, a picture of young men and women in a classroom. Together.

In Qatar, male/female segregation was a way of life. Restaurants had separate eating areas, banks had separate lobbies, and schools had separate buildings. But unlike VCU's, our campus — as per the ruling Al Thanis, who intended to bring their country into step with modern times — was going to be co-ed. Not that we were the first. Texas A&M and Weill Cornell Medical College already had integrated campuses at Education City.

"Guys," Kyle said, looking from Mohamed to Fawzi. "If we show only single sex classes, don't you think that's kind of misleading?"

Fawzi promptly left the room.

"What was that about?" Kyle asked, looking from Mohamed to me.

"Don't worry about it, he'll get over it," he said.

"Get over what?" I asked.

"I'd say he didn't like having Kyle look directly at him like that," Mohamed said, looking me square in the eye. "It's *haram* for a man to look directly at a woman he isn't married to."

"You've got to be freaking kidding me," I said, eliciting a scowl from Mohamed. I knew *swearing* was considered impolite in this culture, but imposter curse words, too? More to the point, no *looking*? So that's why I'd felt like everyone was looking right through me. They were!

This assignment is going to be way easier than I imagined, so I thought at the time. That feeling of being invisible, however, would eventually turn into a crushing loneliness. Until I realized I could get away with almost anything.

THREE
THE WEDDING

Habibi/Habibti:
Masculine/feminine term of endearment meaning "dear one,"
as a Baltimore waitress might use the word "hon."

DOHA, QATAR
June 2004

I T WAS GROWING DARK as Kyle and I left
Mohamed's office and headed back to our hotel, but I
peered into the fading scene.

What struck me about this new place, what was visible
whizzing past the car's plate glass, was how little there was to
see. Roads stretched between roundabouts, populated with
single-story shops topped by garish plastic signs. But no people,
except in other cars. Beyond these roads were vast expanses of
nothingness — just desert, flat and interminable looking. It
called to mind a moonscape, or what I imagined the moon
would look like if it came in shades of beige. I wondered if
Qatar's ruling family ordered that even the buildings should be
tan, but later understood that anything left outside was leeched

of color by the unrelenting sun and the sand dust that never washed away. The most significant aspect of the landscape was the construction. The closer we got to the Bay of Doha the denser it became. Cranes and scaffolding dotted the sky — everything poised on the verge of enormous change, an effervescent frenzy of becoming. Little did I know, this included me.

"Hey, look at that," Kyle said, as we headed to our rooms. She was pointing to an easel announcing the graduation ceremony for Virginia Commonwealth, another undergraduate university in Qatar. "Let's go snoop."

We'd been at it since a 6:30 a.m. breakfast meeting and it was now almost 8:00 p.m. That our school was not yet open, and it would be a good four years before we had any graduates, did not deter Kyle. We'd just tacked another week onto our stay. I missed my husband. What I really wanted to do was slink away for a surreptitious cigarette.

"Great idea," I smiled. "I'd love to see it."

It wasn't a total lie. I *was* curious about what went on under those *abayas*, the long black robes worn by women in the Gulf, and since VCU's enrollment was all-female, at least we were in for a display. Jewels and flashes of color poked out from under those black robes, and I knew somebody had to be shopping at the plethora of designer stores in Doha. Women everywhere were eager to show off their purchases to other women, but here, the only time it was acceptable to do so was in their exclusive company. And so we peeked inside the set of massive doors to find about 700 people sitting stock still as speakers droned. Unfortunately, the gathering included fathers, husbands, brothers and sons — decked out in their starched white thobes and red-and-white checked headgear — so the women stayed under wraps.

"Looks like commencement," Kyle said with a smirk.

Just as we turned away, the sound of Arabic pop music

wafted down the hall. "Ha-beeeeb-teee (*habibti*, dear one)," we heard as a clutch of robed women disappeared behind another set of ornate, oversized doors.

Kyle and I looked at each other. We'd just pitched the idea of a getting-to-know-you event for the dean to Mohamed, and he'd warned against it. "It has to be about the family or they won't come. Women don't want to be seen at places where they serve alcohol."

The woman's appearance could only mean one thing. "A wedding!" we cried in unison, rushing toward the sound to see if we might get a glimpse inside. Weddings were definitely segregated affairs. An older woman was shutting the door but stopped. To our surprise she beckoned us in with the universal Asian hand gesture— palm down, fingers bending at the knuckles.

"Come come!"

Inside, I practically had to shield my eyes. The gold lame trimmings. The exotic flower arrangements. The outfits.

Since men have their own connubial shindig, those black wraps were *off*. I didn't have to wear an *abaya*, but looking conservative at all times for a non-shopper such as myself meant I basically sported business casual when I wasn't wearing a full-on suit. That evening I had on a brown silk jacket with three-quarter-length sleeves, tan Capri pants and black flats. For the first time in Qatar I felt underdressed *and* over-clothed. The over-the-top couture styles made me feel like I'd invaded a runway show during fashion week. And the makeup was as thick as the gold jewelry.

What struck me the most, however, was the sound the women made in conversation. Most of the people I interacted with — at the office, in shops, in cabs — were men. Their Arabic had a sharp, guttural tone. But here in this room, speaking the same language, the sound was entirely different, delicate and feminine. Not that anyone was talking to us exactly. Very quickly, I began to feel exactly like I'd felt at so many other weddings. Awkward.

We edged to the back of the room toward a pile of sticky sweets — *just like the cookie tables at Pittsburgh weddings!* — when I heard a very American sounding woman who was not Kyle say, "Have one!"

I whipped around and saw this chick made up like a belly dancer, in what would have been a wildly, revealing Halloween outfit back home. But here she was tame.

She introduced herself as Hend, and told us she'd just graduated from Duke. I asked if it was normal to invite strangers to weddings.

"Oh yeah. The more people the better. They're totally public and totally fun. Unless it's your wedding. I know I'm not looking forward to it."

So I asked when she was getting married.

"Oh I don't know. But they're all the same. See that platform up there?"

Sure enough, at the front of the room was an elevated dais, high enough it looked like the jump off for a high dive than a "platform."

"We'll go up and talk to her, like in groups, but the bride has to hang out up there the whole time. Then the groom will come, and we'll take pictures."

Wait, weren't men forbidden? And pictures, too?

"We'll cover, but like, they are married. They already signed the papers, you know."

I did not. But now I was damn curious, and trying to think of the least rude follow-up question when she started waving across the room, smiling beatifically.

"Ugh," she said through clenched teeth. "It's my Aunt Fatima. She totally wants to talk to me about my cousin. My mom better tell her pretty soon I'm going to grad school, and he better be married before I'm back. He's cross-eyed."

I looked at Aunt Fatima. She was giving Hend the beckoning *come-come* gesture.

"Gotta scoot. Laters."

Then she was lost to Fatima.

Despite my professed lack of idealism, part of my mission in Qatar, both personally and professionally, was to build cultural bridges. Learn. Love. Kumbayah. Hell, I'd written a press release about it. I knew that in Qatar, marriages weren't based on romantic love, or even attraction, but on keeping the family line pure. At the time, I had conflicting feelings about calling myself a feminist. Caught between the '70s and '80s, I'd learned that "a woman needs a man like a fish needs a bicycle." Also, "girls just wanna have fun."

It was a highly confusing time.

I grew up saying things like, I'm not a feminist... but I believe in equal pay. Or, I'm not a feminist... but birth control should be covered by insurance. And my favorite: I'm not a feminist... but a woman shouldn't have to sleep with her boss. Unless she wants to. *Wait, what exactly is a feminist?*

Though I was one hundred percent a feminist, I feared that too much independence smacked of sprouting unwanted hair and never attracting a man. Where was the fun in that? Not wanting the fairy tale was not the same as not wanting love.

In this scenario, however, I had zero confusion.

I looked at Kyle. "Did she just say she has to marry her cousin? That is fucked up."

"Come on, let's go get something to eat," Kyle said. "That thing I just ate is sitting in my stomach like a rock."

There was one last deal breaker to investigate.

Geoff and I had decided to move to Qatar (for the job I had yet to be offered) before I visited, with a couple of caveats. With the feeling of being restricted as I had been in Tunisia off the list, there was but one more item to check. Since that fiasco I'd amassed eight years clean and sober, but I still relied on a community of like-minded people to maintain a happy, joyous, and free state of sobriety. Online, I'd found just such a recovery group in Doha, but I wanted to check them out in person. Between meeting media people and colleagues and liaising with the team back in Pittsburgh however, I couldn't get any time to myself. Merely taking my leave seemed impossible, and I didn't have the energy to lie. Though it was not my habit to tell colleagues (and certainly not supervisors) that such gatherings were how I spent my spare time, I approached Kyle one evening after I'd found a meeting I wanted to attend.

"I need to..." I started. "Tonight I..."

Smoothing her leopard print pashmina, Kyle was looking at me over the desk in the office we were sharing. She'd just asked if I wanted to go to the gold souq.

I started over. "You know I don't drink right? Well, tonight I was going to get together with..."

Before I could finish stammering it out, Kyle took over. Apparently she'd been sober more than a dozen years herself. And she asked if she could come along. How had I never noticed she didn't drink? Here was another opportunity I missed to note how much I was missing. Instead I thought, *Damn, there goes my chance to complain about work at the meeting.*

The meeting was in a hotel at the center of town. Far seedier than the five-star corridor I'd experienced thus far in Doha, it was nonetheless a massive step above many other rooms

I'd gathered in over the years to discuss the relative merits of sober living. There was a tea service for chrissakes. Yet, as groups go, ours was painfully small. Other than Kyle and me, the gathering consisted of Paul, John, Malcolm, and Steve. No one among this bunch of old, white guys was looking like a candidate for my new support crew. And then in walked Michelle, late because of her high-powered job. Sporting a Navy blue suit with low heels, her hair was perfectly coiffed in a French chignon. She shared her frustrations with her job, her kids and her house husband. Michelle was my new best friend. I was all ready to sign up.

Until I got the actual offer.

The university wanted to pay me less than what I billed them in the States, not to mention my other clients. I phoned Geoff. "Oh baby, go ahead, sign it," Geoff said. "We can live on that."

The conversation reminded me of one of the first talks we'd ever had about finances.

Me: "You're moving in soon and we haven't even talked how we're going to handle the budget."

Him: "Oh, money will work itself out."

His attitude wasn't exactly a surprise or he wouldn't have been about to move into my house, but before either of us carted a single box over the threshold I put together a financial plan based on contributions of equal ratio to our incomes. He never let me down in terms of making his share, nor once complained about my weakness for spa treatments or expensive handbags, but it could irk me how blithely uninvolved he was. Until my mom pointed out the obvious when I called to complain one morning.

"He said he'd clean the gutters today and he's not, and I'm just tired of reminding him," I said. "Why do I have to be that one all the time?"

"Lisa, you'd take his head off if he tried to wake you up on a Saturday morning telling you what to do," she said. "Get over it."

Thinking back on her sage advice, *of course* Geoff wasn't the right person to talk to about this quandary. I called in Mary Ellen, the chief of My We.

"It's a job, not a calling," Mary Ellen quipped. "Come up with a number you can live with and take it back to them."

Her advice reminded me of a project I'd done for the university years ago. I was helping Linda Babcock promote her book titled *Women Don't Ask*. In it, Babcock demonstrates how women themselves, more than any persecutors, create their own income discrepancies because they don't negotiate, and how — over the long haul — this adds up to enormous differences in salary. In the end, I wasn't thrilled with the agreement we came to, but I was glad I asked. When I signed, I truly believed I had the absolutely perfect background for this job, and that by setting up my spouse for his next career move I was putting a stake in my happily ever after. But nothing in my history, not the 15 years I'd spent in marketing and communications, not my previous experience in the Middle East, or even the death of my first love, had prepared me for what was to come.

FOUR

MAFI MUSHKILLA

Mafi mushkilla:
Literally, "no problem." Words that in English sound like what you might prefer— the swift blow of a hit man— as opposed to the lack of action that's about to transpire.

DOHA, QATAR
July 2004

I HIT THE GROUND running. The ground hit back.

Despite that I was the first person in my department, my higher-ups at the university appointed my assistant director for me, a man named Fadhel. We'd met on my pre-employment/business trip, but he was so soft-spoken and shy I was shocked to learn he even wanted a communications position. And it turned out, he didn't have any marketing and communications experience. Not only was he in my department, we shared an office.

That first day I crossed the threshold to find Fadhel already ensconced. He practically blinded me with his smile. Not that this stopped me from noticing he'd taken the lion's share of the space, leaving me with the smaller desk that was wedged between the door and a credenza. The natural spot for a receptionist. In his action I did not read malice. What I saw was something more menacing, something more, "Hello and welcome,   naturally-subordinate-American-female-lady-creature!"

I was stressed enough about navigating the politics of an overtly patriarchal work culture. To learn I'd be *supervising* a Muslim man sent me flying to the computer, but the only advice I could find applied to interfaith marriage, which by the way looked grim. Near as I could tell, if we were alone, I could not remove my jacket, or close my office door. I'd been worried enough about my Tourette's-like need to curse while working. Now this guy was going to be in my office?

There was some comfort in the fact that he was from Bahrain, the liberal-ish country next door to Saudi Arabia where the Sauds went to party. Also, he sported Western garb —shiny shoes (as opposed to sandals), dress pants tightly cinched at the waist, paired with a crisp button-down shirt (not the bright white *thobe*), and a beard he kept precisely trimmed (instead of shaggy). But on the first day my strategy was avoidance.

I bid a quick hello — an egregious faux pas — then dropped my bag and sunglasses, and spent the rest of the day by roaming the halls, meeting my new colleagues. No easy task in itself.

Like all structures at Education City, our building had been designed by one of the world's leading architects. In this case, a sadistic Japanese fellow who found it logical that corridors and stairways might cross mass expanses yet lead nowhere, or that doors should push open from the outside but lock on the inside ends of a passage. How was it possible we were tight on space? At one point I had to use my cell phone to call for help, thank God one had been tucked into my hand that morning or my corpse might still be rotting in the long hallway between student services and administration. "When you get your ID badge," the office manager Cindy told me, when she arrived to rescue me, "You'll just swipe it here." Great.

I called Geoff as soon as I got back to my hotel (he was in Pittsburgh closing his newspaper and packing up our house; one condition of my employment offer was immediacy) but he was asleep. "Eat something, sweetheart. I'm going back to bed."

Damn the eight-hour time difference!

He was also right; I was starving. I ordered a club sandwich from room service, but the hotel's weird roast beef and egg combination made me long for the comforts of home even more. (I wasn't yet aware, there was no bacon allowed in Qatar, at all.) I called Mary Ellen, Chief We and night owl.

"Anyone casually walking by our office would look in the room and think I was the assistant," I complained. "Living with Fadhel's setup will send a signal that I can be bullied, but if I ask him to move, don't I look like the bully?"

"You're thinking too much, hon," she yelled into her headset, being one of those people for whom the greater the distance the louder it seems necessary to speak, especially when on a cell phone. "You just have to show him who's boss. You're the boss. Be the boss. Tell him to move."

We spent an hour rehearsing this.

The next morning I got in early and beat Fadhel, hitting with a blinding smile when he got in. "Good morning!

"Fadhel, this office set up?" I continued, before he had a chance to sit, "it's not working for me."

"You want I should move?" he replied. Not a response we'd practiced.

Fadhel and I switched places immediately, our first and last cooperative effort. I didn't swear. Loudly. I certainly didn't remove my jacket. At least not when he was in the office. And I didn't close the door. Also when he was in the office. As I would soon learn, Fadhel wasn't in the office all that much. He just seemed to disappear. I had to function as the marketing department on my own. My deficiencies for this task began to glare.

Since we bunked with Weill Cornell — our building was not yet built — the house where the dean was to live was the sole piece of university property in Qatar. Thus, it was the only place we could really "brand" and, according to Mohamed, was where we should be hosting events.

Like most things in Doha, the house was brand new, all marble floors and white walls. No furniture. A blank slate. One Saturday, while the dean was back in the States helping organize his family's move —a courtesy I was not afforded despite having a house to pack up — I went to his residence to oversee the installation of curtains.

The neighborhood was a construction zone, roads and houses unfinished. I flipped on the ACs and automatically checked the refrigerators. Nothing in the kitchen upstairs or down. *I don't have snacks*, I thought, panicked. *Or water!* I plugged in my laptop but, of course, no internet. At least there was electricity.

I calmed myself with the thought I wouldn't be there long. About a half-hour later, four Indian men arrived in a truck. I described where and how the curtains should be hung to a fellow in pants and a button-down shirt, who turned around and relayed the directions in Hindi to the other three men, all of whom wore blue jumpsuits. Satisfied, he retreated to a corner and promptly lost himself in a Thermos of tea and a sandwich. The men in blue proceeded to talk amongst themselves for a bit. At last they removed the curtain rods and finials from their boxes, inspecting the items as if they'd never seen such things. Then they turned their attention to the wall. One of them pulled out a drill and revved it up.

"Hey, whoa! Time out," I blurted out, which may as well have been in Mandarin, though they did stop.

But how to get what I was thinking across? Was I really the only one worried about this? Figuring a level was too much to ask, I addressed the boss.

"Do you have a tape measure?"

He stared at me from his seat.

Pulling my hands apart in an approximation of using a tape measure hand gesture, I repeated the question.

Then the *Aha!* moment.

"To measure the centimeters," I cried.

"Ah, centimeters. For the hanging of the curtains," the boss said. "Measuring tape!"

It may seem unbelievable that the leap from tape measure to measuring tape was so hard to make, but misunderstandings based on the slightest alteration of words happened all the time. At first it felt condescending to mimic the speech patterns of people with whom I spoke, Inspector Clouseau-style, but there was no denying it worked.

"Yes, measuring tape!" I repeated, pulling my hands apart again, "For the hanging straight."

The boss rose to address his minions, yelling for what seemed like an eternity. I could have sworn I heard the words "tape measure." He pulled out his mobile and began yelling into his phone, marching back and forth across the room, punching the air with his other hand. Suddenly, another man burst in. He was carrying a tape measure, still talking on his phone to the boss he was now in the room with. Where had *he* come from?

No matter.

Big smile. "Wonderful!" I said. "Very good. Thank you."

He handed over the measuring tape and left. The laborers began taking measurements. There was still a problem.

"Pencil?" I asked. "For the marking of the centimeters?"

This did not bode well for the upcoming wallpaper project.

My ability to sleep vanished. I began waking up in the middle of the night, bathed in a pool of sweat, worrying over my to-do list. *Why not crack out my computer?* It was the best time to try and communicate with my cohorts at the university back home. I was so lonely and flummoxed, I made the mistake of confessing my misery. No one wants to hear how lonely and miserable I was flying around business class, living in a hotel and having an office budget so large that you can't imagine what you'll even be able to spend it on.

But at last, Geoff was on his way.

FIVE
MEAT SANDWICH

Vitamin Wa:
More widely known as Wasta, the influence needed to gain and grant favors; an ingredient not found anywhere near a "meat sandwich."

DOHA, QATAR
August 2004

GEOFF ARRIVED AT THE peak of summer. When I saw him come around the corner at airport arrivals, I freaked. He's here. *What now?* Would he find work? Would it be weird to have my husband as an unemployed "trailing" spouse in Patriarchy-R-Us-Ville? He hated the heat like I hated the cold.

But his face broke into a huge grin. He was rumpled and gorgeous and I couldn't wait to get him home. I'd barely seen him in the past three months, and in public like this we couldn't hug or kiss. Not even in the cab (I wasn't able to find my way to the airport yet). *Faster*, I thought for once, as we rode around Doha in circles, edging home.

By now, I'd left the hotel for an apartment building, another temporary stop while we waited for our housing to be built. Geoff took one look at the interior and dubbed it "The Salmon Palace." everything inside — walls, upholstery, even the silken flower arrangements — was a variation on that fleshy shade of pink. How clever and observant and delicious of my husband. We quickly made our way to the bedroom, where I confirmed this was what had been missing. Now maybe I'd settle down, be less cranky. Get some sleep.

"Qatar," Geoff said, smiling at me over a plate of shrimp fettuccini I heated up later in the kitchen. I'd stocked the pantry but run out of time to cook; I'd picked this up at lunchtime. "Who'da thought when we met?"

But was it so unbelievable? It had been the Arab world that brought us together when we met. We were attending the Association of Alternative Newsweeklies' annual conference in Phoenix. As the first day came to a close, I stood outside the Biltmore hotel and watched the fading afternoon light turn the distant mountains purple. It occurred to me I should use the cigarette I was about to smoke as an opportunity.

"Got a light?" I asked one of the editors passing by.

In truth, this moment had begun some four years earlier back when I'd breached the hurdle of thirty still single and begun to worry. I'd confused not *needing* a man with believing I shouldn't *want* a man. The fact that I did felt like a personal failure, so rather than talk about it with friends, I started sneaking into bookstores, thumbing through the self-help titles in secret. *Mars and Venus* said we didn't speak the same language. *Love Languages* told me I needed to decode his lovespeak and use it. *The Rules* said I was a unique creature, and that I was having way too much sex. By the time I hit *Getting to Commitment*, I knew only one thing: relationships should be a trajectory, a steady stream of improvements meant to catapult me into wedded bliss. I did what any writer would do with my newfound well of knowledge, I started a dating column. It wasn't advice so much as storytelling. Each week I'd set a couple up on a blind date, then interview them afterward. Before blogging made oversharing the norm, before Match.com made blind dates acceptable, and before *The New York Times* had a weekly column by the same name, my "Modern Love" offered a weekly peek into the phantasmagoria otherwise known as dating.

Readers loved it. Obsessed as I was with coupledom, so did I. After writing it for a few years, I decided to try and syndicate it. I left my job with Pittsburgh's largest PR firm and started a consulting business so I'd have the flexibility I needed to pitch the column to other papers. I targeted similar cities — small towns with major universities, affording a constantly renewing supply of applicants and an almost certainly gruesome dating scene. And that's how I ended up at that conference in Phoenix, intent on my target.

The man I'd addressed was the editor of a paper in Buffalo. I'd spoken to him a few times during the previous year of planning, and even once earlier that day. If he didn't remember me, I was sure he'd have noticed the swag I'd stuffed into the AAN bags — condoms branded with the column's logo and the tag line, "Modern Love. Go on a blind date without having to go on a blind date."

In a conversation we had before the conference my editor had coyly suggested keeping a handful.

"Please," I'd scoffed, "this is work."

I wasn't about to hook up with someone I met at a conference. That defied all the self-help logic. Besides, I'd just come out of a hideous entanglement; I was nowhere near the right

level on my trajectory for meeting Mr. Right. Even that I'd
started smoking again was in deference to my need for a break
from relationships. If there was anything I'd learned from my
column, not even smokers wanted to date smokers. Asking this
guy for a light was a strategy.

I'd seen the pack of Marlboro Reds poking out of his pocket
earlier when I'd introduced myself. They'd surprised me. His
skin seemed to glow with health, milky yet tan-looking. He
didn't look like a smoker.

Naturally, he lit one for himself and I finagled a seat next to
him on the bus, where I proceeded to flaunt my yenta savvy.
(Despite clear evidence to the contrary, I really believed this.)
had he seen *Mission Impossible II?* No. *I Dreamed of
Africa?* No.

Aha! he must be in a new relationship, those lose-the-world
days. No, he told me, he was new to editing the paper. He
supplied the final pearl: he didn't have a girlfriend. God, he had
killer dimples.

As we entered the party, he touched the small of my back
while

propping the door open, sending a thrill through me. I loved
a man who took charge. But this was work. Work. Work. Work.

Inside we joined an uncomfortable conversational knot, a
group of writers, probably better at dishing out opinions from
behind the safety of a computer screen than in person. Me
included. From nowhere I said I'd been a Peace Corps Volunteer in Tunisia.

As mentioned, I rarely hesitated to invoke the association; I
believed it made me sound worldly and civic-minded. Besides,
no one ever knew anything about the Peace Corps or Tunisia.
Typically, the information proved most effective at making
people's eyes glaze over, or squint and ask, "Tunisia? Where's

that?" Why I'd drop a conversational non-starter into an awkward silence is beyond me, but it changed everything.

"Tunisia?" said my future husband. "Oh, I've been there."

"R emember that?" I asked Geoff now, pushing aside his plate and pulling him back to the bedroom. "Maybe we have some unfinished business here. In fact, I'm sure of it."

Now was not the time to be catching up on my sleep. With my best friend in town at last, I could finally get to know the elusive Doha. Not that I had a great sense of what I was looking for. The only thing like a cultural activity I'd seen was cracked out at special events, musicians and dancers with freshly dusted instruments and costumes. The Qatar that was being built around me had existed less than a decade, since 1995, when the current regime had taken over. A project under construction at the time said it all: Heritage Village. Your heritage. Coming Soon.

T he next day I went off to work, figuring Geoff would spend the time recuperating or putzing in the kitchen. We'd always loved cooking together. But we had no TV or internet, and The Salmon Palace was surrounded on all sides by parking lots. The only escape was by car. My beloved decided to go for a walk.

I came home to a pile of his still-drenched clothes by the door. He'd been so overcome by the heat he'd barely found his way back in time to pass out. We went out and got him a cell phone that night, and from that day on, Geoff drove me to and from work and kept the car during the day. I wasn't exactly sure how to feel about this.

It troubled me that my husband was spending a large chunk of his day ferrying me back and forth, but soon enough I imagined him off on assignments. Having two cars didn't make sense. Besides, I hated driving on those crazy roads, whereas it didn't bother Geoff. I asked Cindy, the office manager who'd saved me from the hallway my first day, if she'd mind giving me rides home sometimes.

"Sure, no problem, love," she said in the long, drawn out vowels of Australia. "Long as you don't mind coming with me to pick up Layla."

Cindy, a partying, Christian, 30-something, was married to a Nigerian Muslim. Layla was their beautiful three-year-old daughter. She was full of life, and a joy to be around; I didn't mind.

DOHA, QATAR
September 2004

On most occasions, a ride with Cindy meant stopping by Layla's school on the way home, but on one particular night we picked her up at the mall. There'd been a birthday party earlier and the kids were at the amusement park near the food court.

"I hate to do this to you, but do you mind hanging out for a bit?" Cindy asked. "I'm famished."

While Cindy picked up a Quarter Pounder, I sat and watched Layla play with some of the other children whose parents had the same idea. The space took on a whole new dimension, less ode-to-consumerism than sheltered playground. Where else are these kids supposed to run around?

Cindy smiled. "We shop a lot, too."

Then the scene changed again. From out of nowhere a man who was not Layla's husband appeared, picked Layla up and started tossing her in the air.

What the?

"Do you see that?" I pointed at the mystery man in the thobe. "Are you just going to sit there?"

"You *are* new here," she said. Cindy had been living in Qatar for five years by this time. "The men here are always like that."

After that I began to notice men, everywhere, publicly showing affection for children in public. And that was something I appreciated about this culture. What a difference it would make to see men, first and foremost, as benevolent father figures. To allow men to be benevolent father figures.

"I found some local fun for us tonight," Geoff said, one Thursday night when he came to pick me up. After the day I'd had — I'd nonsensically fought with human resources over their recruiting brochure thinking that including a list of fast food restaurants would defeat the purpose — my deepest desire was to go home and go to bed. But I also felt compelled to provide companionship to my husband. Doha's expat groups and their activities — knitting circles and spa trips — were designed for the trailing spouses known as wives. There was nothing for him to do. In his shoes I would've been crazed. Besides, local fun was something I'd ostensibly been longing for.

"Awesome," I said. "I hope it starts with food. Just not McDonald's. Or Taco Bell. Or Kentucky Fried Chicken..."

"I believe the correct term is KFC," he said, laughing at my laundry list. Then he went serious. "But it kinda does."

In addition to Doha's smorgasboard of Western eateries, there were a number of exquisite Turkish and Lebanese places. You could also get a lovely Italian meal at the Ritz-Carlton, but these options weren't exactly local. What the hell did people eat before airplanes brought in shitakes and fresh water? What I was about to discover would blow my mind.

We lived on an enormously busy street called Al Saad. Stretched between two roundabouts, in addition to apartments, was a wall of single story, nondescript retail spaces—cell phone stores, banks, car outlets and the like. Not being much of a shopper, I hadn't examined the offerings too closely.

Apparently, behind the store lineup was a warren of shops I never knew existed. Geoff had discovered another world, one that did merit exploration—tailors and grocers and coffee sellers. A mall behind a strip mall, where the shops were a jumble, and everywhere were people, out and walking around. On the streets. *People!* The real Doha had been hidden in plain view all along, but I'd been so busy just getting to and from work, I hadn't noticed.

Geoff pulled into this maze and in front of a place called Hot Chicken. I'd seen similar places along other roads, single-door-wide eateries that catered to Doha's blue-suited laborers. The kind of place I'd been curious about but wouldn't dared have gone into without a male companion. *Jackpot!* Fast food-like as such a café was, it seemed like a genuinely local option. As we approached I anticipated the wacky delicacies we might find inside.

A dozen pairs of men's eyes trained on me as we entered, I was the only woman. These weren't nationals in thobes with a moral code against looking at me, and they stared. I would've squeezed Geoff 's hand if I'd felt comfortable holding it in public; but he didn't need the gesture of appreciation to know new that finding the places less traveled was the kind of thing I loved to do while traveling. Or did he?

The backlit menu sign behind the counter was in English, not for Westerner customers but because the laborers, no matter what country they were from, had to speak it. English was the lingua franca.

From what I could see, the local delights were variations on chicken and rice. I ordered a number three, chicken and rice.

"No chicken, madam," the order taker said. Totally serious. Hot chicken had no chicken. "Meat sandwich?" he offered.

Geoff and I looked at each other. "What kind of meat?" Geoff asked.

"Meat? Sandwich?" our counter helper replied. Or asked. Or insisted.

Geoff looked at me again. I smiled. I wasn't backing out now.

"Meat sandwiches for two."

The man behind the counter then informed us that our meat sandwiches would be ready, "after 20 minutes." Geoff misunderstood, thinking this meant we'd get our food *in* 20 minutes, but I could tell our server was promising nothing so precise. We could rest secure in knowing the food would not arrive any sooner than twenty minutes from that point in time, but beyond that he wasn't guaranteeing anything. It was a phenomenon I'd begun to notice everywhere, curiously nonspecific references to events in time. "Tomorrow, God willing," the dry cleaner hinted. "Call back after some time," went the prerecorded message. "Close," said the shopkeeper. Was this Zen heaven or just hell for a Type A personality? Would that be the same place?

"They don't have a past tense in Arabic," I told Geoff, having done a little Googling. "Or future. It can be constructed, but it's awkward. Maybe that's why."

"I guess that's life in the desert," Geoff said. "It's like, the future is too uncertain to even contemplate, and even five minutes ago is so horrendous it must never be spoken of again."

A half-hour later, our meat patties arrived. If this was what it looked like to get better at communicating, I wasn't sure I saw that point.

Geoff picked the thin, gray slice of a bed of lettuce and held it between his fingers. "No idea," he said.

"Everyone else is eating it," I said. "Besides, they say when you travel it's better to eat at places like this. Cheap places where the high turnover means the food is generally fresher."

"No, *you* say that," Geoff said, the corner of his mouth lifting as he poked at his patty on its bed of iceberg. "You never get sick."

I felt a pang of guilt as we clinked buns and dug in; Geoff's stomach was far more finicky than mine. Mercifully, the taste was unremarkable, making me hungry for more of the local scene.

It was 10:30 p.m. on a Thursday night, the end of our work week, our Friday. Typically, I'd be ready to head home, but for Geoff's sake I wanted to keep going. Nighttime was when Qatar came to life, a fact I'd discovered on my pre-employment trip with Kyle when one night I found myself at the Sheraton's gym at midnight. To be clear, I was not typically awake at midnight, let alone working out at a gym. But what made the workout memorable was the company. Beyond the window were people. Heretofore the only humans I'd ever seen spending any time outdoors in the ungodly heat were the blue-suited laborers, toiling away at Doha's nascent skyline. That night at the Sheraton, it was as if the entire country appeared from nowhere. They toted babes-in-arms, played catch, even picnicked while enjoying the night air. I got it, the thermometer's plunge to body temperature was a welcome respite, but for me I didn't see this altering a lifetime of circadian rhythms. I was a morning person in a night country.

But not tonight.

"Hey," I said to Geoff. "What do you say we go back to the apartment to pick up the scrabble board, then head back out for shisha?" I knew Geoff would be game. He'd always been a night person.

"I know just the place," he said.

He did? He was supposed to be finding and pitching stories during the day. A feeling of resentment spiked in my belly. *Is this why he hasn't placed a single story?* In a single month he'd become awfully adept at finding his way around. *Do not go down this rabbit hole now, Lisa.*

"There won't be any Westerners," Geoff added, helping me force myself to back toward the thrill of partaking in another "only with the husband" opportunity.

I t turned out the shisha place was also nearby, though, again, I'd never have found it. Scrabble board in hand, we walked past a patio of empty tables and chairs as we approached the glass storefront. Inside I saw upholstered couches lining the walls, with men perched atop, sandwiched side-by-side. A full-on Arab rainbow, some men in blistering white thobes with red and white checked headscarves, others all in blinding white, and still others in jeans and overly tight buttondowns. Jackpot!

The assembled sipped tea, watched TV, and languorously hit their shisha pipes. As if the air wasn't thick enough, many smoked cigarettes to boot. Like most of Doha's interiors, the room was just a notch above freezing. Much as I wanted to observe that all-male atmosphere up close, I couldn't handle the actual atmosphere.

"Can we sit out there?" I asked the man at the register. "We just want tea and shisha." He did not ask what flavor, this was not the kind of trendy place that offered "grape" or "cappuccino" blends. He simply smiled and waved toward the door.

It was late enough that the air was almost comfortable. Before we could finish setting up our Scrabble board our waiter appeared with our glasses of tea and shisha.

I looked at Geoff and laughed. "At least we can still hear the TV."

"Good," he said. "It'll distract you while I kick your ass."

Sweet. Though I viewed him as the intellectually superior one by far, Scrabble was one area where I regularly trounced him.

"I don't need more than that for distracting," I said, motioning to the glass wall with a side tilt of my head. In a reverse through-the-looking-glass, all eyes inside were on us. We both laughed.

We sat and played and hit our bong—hookah, really; tobacco only — while every now and again a man would come out swinging a bucket of cinders. Using a pair of tongs, he'd place one gingerly atop our shisha bowl, then head back to make his rounds inside. I was thinking I could get used to this, when all of a sudden I was seized by the uncontrollable urge to vomit.

Barring drunken episodes I cannot actually claim to recall, I could count on one hand the number of times in my life I'd thrown up. That night, however, I barely made it to the sidewalk before emptying the contents of my stomach. Repeatedly.

Geoff paid and gathered up our things while I headed back to the car. We never went back to Hot Chicken or the shisha parlor, though not entirely by design.

W e'd just settled the date for the university's Grand Opening celebration — March 2005. Though our students had already begun classes; the party was meant to launch the brand in a country rife with potential students and donors. Work spilled from six to seven days a week. Ultimately, this event would involve the university's trustees, His and Her Highness of Qatar and the Hooter's corporate jet.

In one of the many desperate phone calls I made to Mary Ellen, she assured me, "God won't give you more than you can handle." Apparently God, like the people who'd hired me, over-estimated my capabilities.

DOHA, QATAR
August 2004

T HE SITUATION BETWEEN FADHEL and I continued to deteriorate. Partly, because he never came out and said no to my requests.

"Fadhel," I began one day. He stopped and turned. He was carrying his prayer mat.

This had been the biggest shock of all. Based on his dress, I took Fadhel to be, I don't know, a Reform Muslim? Not so conservative. I did not realize when we met that the mark on his forehead was a permanent feature, the bruise of the devout, earned by hitting the prayer mat five times a day. Hard.

But I needed to focus. Be the boss.

"Fadhel, I was hoping you'd send me your list of media contacts so I can set up appointments," I continued. "I'd like to meet them sooner rather than later. Before Ramadan starts next month."

He smiled his big Fadhel smile. "Mafi mushkilla," he said, "No problem. I am going to *arghchtorahminalra* now."

Then he turned and disappeared. I didn't see him again that day.

Later that night Geoff quipped, "It's *not* a problem. "Not for him anyway."

Funny. And true. But I needed a strategy. The phone bills were racking up, but I needed some input from Mary Ellen.

"I'm sure some of what you say to him gets lost in translation, hon," Mary Ellen said. "But I don't think his English is the problem. You say he's never worked in PR or marketing before?"

"Exactly. His English is fine. I think he convinced them he had the wasta to get things done," I said.

"Now I don't know what the hell you're saying," she said. "What's a wasta?"

I explained that wasta was a form of influence, somewhere between graft and bribery. Because the other thing about Fadhel? He wasn't a job candidate when we met on my initial trip with Kyle, but a fellow employee. His job had been as university's "fixer." Shady though it sounds, all organizations had fixers. Whether you needed to turn on a utility, get a package delivered, or deal with a government official, the underlying premise seemed to be, Insha'Allah. Or, put another way, Ech, if God wills it things will work out no matter what I do, so there's no reason I shouldn't do as little as possible. So you got such things fixed. You went to Fadhel.

Fadhel would combat the indifference with cash, paying other expats to stand in lines and shuffle papers for you. A real bargain in the face of bureaucratic inefficiencies — just getting your car insured could take weeks, as I'd soon enough discover.

Getting these tasks accomplished was a delicate balance of spending and compiling wasta.

"You can bet wasta's a real currency here," I told Mary Ellen. "But neither Fadhel, nor I, nor any non-Qatari will ever have any real power. Vitamin Wa belongs to the good old boys. The only reason we have any at all is because we work for the Qatar Foundation and, by extension, the ruling family. Take us away from the job and our supposed wasta is gone, too. And that's not how the university works, anyway. Carnegie Mellon is totally in synch with the information age, the key to success isn't to hoard knowledge, but share it."

"Careful, you're starting to sound like a CMU robot there," joked Mary Ellen, a lifelong Pittsburgh resident.

"The worst part is, my co-workers love him. He's fixed everything for them. Me? They hate me."

"Oh, of course," Mary Ellen laughed, "it's all about you."

"Hear me out, really. Last week I was working on this RSVP list that was driving me batshit crazy because, you know, Arabic is transliterated. There is no conventional spelling. The name Fatimah might have an "h" at the end, or it might not. Or those *might* be two different people. So, you know me, I let out an 'oh Jesus fucking Christ,' and as my eyes roll I see the dean's assistant has got a Psalm taped to the side of her monitor."

"You've got a God squad out there," Mary Ellen said. "Of course you do. There's a lot of saving to do in the Persian Gulf."

"Right? And up to this point my most constant refrain has been, 'This is so nothing like when I worked on the start-up of The Andy Warhol Museum. That was all sex and drugs and rock and roll.'"

Now I was laughing. "I mean, *I* know I'm no longer prone to drug-addled sex to loud music, but my new co-workers don't."

"Have you forgotten that feelings aren't facts?" Mary Ellen

asked. "But getting back to Fadhel, cause I'm about to pull up to my office here in a minute. Can you un-hire him?"

Un-hire? Genius.

I hadn't yet signed Fadhel's offer letter. Technically, he was still the fixer. If I didn't hire him, he wouldn't be fired, he simply wouldn't be in my department. He'd move back to operations. Getting the un-hiring done was going to be the tricky part.

Fadhel's boss — Mohamed, the head of operations — was technically my colleague. To un-transfer Fadhel, I'd need buy-in from above. I'd have to go to the dean, Chuck.

Chuck was one of the most rational — if not the most socially adept — people I'd ever known. He agreed with my plan immediately. "Hiring Fadhel never made any sense to me in the first place. He doesn't have any experience in marketing." Right.

Now to face Mohamed. Despite our co-worker status, part of Mohamed's job was approving all university expenditures. Our encounters usually entailed me getting his approval, not telling him what to do.

Handsome in the way many Arab men are, Mohamed had large dark eyes, thick black lashes and hair. He was also enormous in girth. Originally from Yemen but raised in Seattle, Mohamed had returned to the region only recently for the job. While we worked together, he completed a master's in business from Thunderbird university and began work on a juris doctorate. He had a wife and four kids at home. There was a mischievous quality to his personality that I quite enjoyed, and in any other circumstance we might have become good friends.

I laid out the new staffing plan calmly and rationally. "He won't listen to you if you get the least bit emotional," Mary Ellen had advised. Thus I was unprepared for *him* to react emotionally.

"That's just mean," he said, scowling at me from behind his desk.

It was clear I'd just made a grave error, but the deed was done. It would take a year to replace Fadhel, and during that time Mohamed's refrain to me — as he denied one expense after another — was this: "We didn't have a budget for your job when this campus started."

SIX
TALAQ!

Talaq:
"I divorce you." When a man repeats this word three times, he has officially released his wife. Not an option for women.

DOHA, QATAR
July 2004

I NEEDED A MENTOR, someone who understood the peculiarities of university culture and the ways of the Arab world. I found just such a person in Rima, the school's head of admissions.

When we first arrived we were both at the Mövenpick, a hotel along the Persian Gulf, where date palms grew amid islands of carefully manicured, Astro Turf-like grass. Over breakfast one morning, I learned that Rima, after raising her sons in Florida, had just gotten her master's at Columbia. Lebanese by birth, she'd been raised in Cairo. This woman had knowledge that did not cross borders as easily as she had. She would be my exemplar of how to comport myself in this strange new world. The role came to her naturally.

"Don't," she cried one day, grabbing my arm in mid-air, as I reached for my bag at the airport. We were leaving Doha to go on a recruiting trip to Kuwait. "You must hire a porter. Otherwise it will reflect badly on the university."

With her I had explored Doha's mild side. We went to the malls. The Golf Club. The car dealership. All with a driver, of course. This was before either of us was driving anywhere. I took her cue on that, as well. Many of our co-workers had gone out and gotten fancy cars, but Rima was in no rush. So, neither was I. One night, this was before Geoff arrived and we were still at the Mövenpick, I stopped by her place to kill some time until the dinner buffet opened. She organized clothes while I flipped through the channels.

"Talaq!" cried a man on the TV, as the camera panned to a woman in extreme distress. I looked over at Rima.

"I divorce you," she translated.

"Talaq!" the man repeated, followed by another close-up of the woman, now rending her hair. A musical crescendo ensued.

I hit the mute button and raised my eyebrows. "What's with the drama?"

"He says it one more time and that's it," she said, "marriage over."

Rima was the perfect translator. Between her knowledge of Arab dialects and American customs, she could illuminate nuances that might be difficult for an American to grasp, let alone ask about.

She told me the film was a classic of Egyptian cinema. The scene was so intense, she explained, because talaq was not meant to be said all at once like that. According to the Quran, it should be uttered three times over the course of three months.

Though I had no personal experience — my parents are still married — that seemed almost reasonable. The first utterance marked the grave offense, while the month-long cooling off period allowed the chance to reassess. If repeated, there was yet another month to take corrective measures. By month three, neither party was likely to be taken by surprise.

"What if she says it back?" I asked. "Would that speed things up?"

"Oh, but talaq is an option only for men," she laughed. "Women must take their husbands to court."

As a Western woman with a poor track record in discretion, I knew to be careful around my Arab colleagues. But other than a slight accent, Rima came across as so... *American*. I dropped my guard.

"That is fucked up," I said. "And why bother getting divorced when you can have as many wives as you like?"

"Not really, Lisa. The Quran is very specific about these things," she said. "A new wife must be kept as well as the first. It's very costly. Better to just start over."

That was, in my opinion, even more fucked up. But I knew I'd crossed a line. Cursing is a massive affront in Arab culture; it shows you've lost your cool. Rima's response struck me, in that particularly civilized way of the Islamic world, as a means of letting me know I'd screwed up. Or maybe I was being overly sensitive to what I perceived as a dig.

Rima's mention of the Quran's dictates on how men should financially care for their wives felt like an affront because Geoff was the "trailing spouse." Though we'd decided to move in a single phone call, I'd agonized at the thought of bringing a non-working husband into one of the world's most patriarchal cultures. Imported white-collar expats like us lived in employee housing, which meant your address announced your employer for you. By virtue of the fact that we lived in university housing, our so-called nontraditional roles were more obvious than I would've been comfortable with back home. The arrangement was official too; I was Geoff 's "sponsor." Sponsorship meant, among other things, that I had to sign a permission slip for Geoff to leave the country.

But surely these thoughts were not preoccupying Rima's mind.

"Say the marriage is not producing children," she went on. "This is a perfectly acceptable reason for divorce."

That *had* to be a dig at my childless union. In the Arab world, marriage without children isn't marriage at all. Forget about Machiavelli. He was pre-dated by the Arab sultan Saladin, famed for charming you even as he conquered your land. As is my detrimental way, I wanted to prove I couldn't be cowed that easily.

"When is your husband coming?" I shot back.

Not so cunning as Rima, but at least I'd managed a subject change. Rima had come without her husband, who was an architect. Though just then it struck me as a clever way to avoid the whole dependent spouse issue altogether.

"We're not sure," Rima said, the very portrait of serenity. "He's very busy with his job in Lebanon. He's just gotten a commission to do a major building."

This absolutely blew my mind. Like me, this woman has just signed a contract binding her life to Qatar for three years. It's true, I hadn't been in the country terribly long yet, but it seemed abundantly clear there was damn little to do outside of work.

"You mean he might not come at all?" I blurted, overly familiar.

Not cool at all.

"But how can you stand the thought of it?"

"Well, I get to Lebanon all the time," she replied, neatly avoiding my question. Again.

Damn, she's good.

I had yet to learn how good. Two years would pass before

I'd learn that Rima and the man she referred to as "husband" hadn't lived in the same country for nearly twenty years.

After we ate, I went back to my room and looked up Muslim divorce customs. How had I never heard of this talaq thing when I was in Tunisia? But there it was, plain as day. According to my internet search, Malaysian courts had recently deemed a text message sufficient to instigate talaq. Sure, I was supposed to be learning, loving, Kumbayahing. But once again, I judged. That kind of thing would never go down in my culture. Or so I thought.

I had much to learn from Rima.

That summer, I was stunned to see Michael Moore's *Fahrenheit 911* playing at a theater in Doha. Much as I wanted to support something indie and something recent-ish, I didn't like the idea of watching a documentary about America's war on terror amidst a group of men clad in thobes. When Rima said she wanted to see it also, I figured nothing too bad could happen to us both in a public venue. I even offered to drive.

For a couple of weeks I'd rented a car with a driver. I'd have been happy to keep the driver, but the nausea wouldn't go away. Rima pooh-poohed my solution — riding in the front passenger seat — leaving me with no choice. Sitting up front cured the nausea, but did little to improve my sense of direction, a condition that plagued my tenure in Doha.

We were both to blame for the poor orientation. Maybe it was the roaming Bedouin past, but at the time Qatar had no street addresses. Even Fedex had to accept that all mail was delivered to post office boxes. Thus, all directions were given in landmarks. This presented a severe handicap for yours truly.

You say there's a bank on the corner I can't miss, I miss it.

Throughout my life I've relied on mile markers, street names, and a straightforward accounting of right and left turns to get me from point A to point B. Suddenly, all I had to go on were landmarks. And I was supposed to keep track of them while spinning through roundabouts? *Please.* As for the roundabouts, their names were more a matter of opinion than convention, maybe because the obvious attribute shifted depending on which way you entered. For instance, "Panasonic Roundabout." I called it that because of the giant Panasonic sign, and because that's what the dean's wife called it. As time went by I heard others refer to this intersection as "TV Roundabout." Not because of the sign, but because this was where — behind barricades and completely invisible from the road — Al Jazeera was located.

Once you added on the constant churn of construction, these so-called landmarks moved and/or disappeared with alarming frequency. I could get lost going into work; I often dawdled over breakfast, waiting and watching for a colleague to leave so I could follow them.

When Rima and I set out for the movies it was broad daylight. I could see the mall where the theater was housed from our hotel. Still, I was amazed when I actually made it in a fairly straight shot — not once did I have to double through around a roundabout. But I'd barely finished patting myself on the back before realizing another challenge the driver had absolved me from: parking. Who *wasn't* at the City Center mall?

After circling the floors for what seemed an eternity, I found a spot. We hacked through the dense air of the garage to the City Center's gleaming glass elevators and up to the third floor. The doors opened right at the theater. Things were loQataring up. For a moment. There was no marquis showing the films, no Plexiglass window. Just these two long, low counters flanking the entry. What were we supposed to do? As we stood pondering, a group of men in thobes cut in front of us. Then a group of women in abayas swirled past. I was struck by the realization that was akin to being the object of racism. Mild, to be sure, but there it was. To the residents, I was simply another of "the help." Maybe I could interview Qataris about what it was like to grow up as a significant minority in your own home country, and write about how this phenomenon manifested. Then Rima nudged me.

Following the lead of the groups that went before us, we stepped toward the unmanned desk where, as if attending a play, we selected our seats from an embedded screen that showed the seating chart. Despite that the theater was almost full, we were able to pick from the front row in the back half, my favorite seats for the legroom. "Too exposed," Rima told me, selecting seats further back.

To my surprise, once inside the room was barely half-full. "It's a two-hour window to rendezvous at the mall," Rima explained.

"Boys and girls sneaking around together?"

"Some of them, maybe," she said. "But mostly they hang out with their friends and text each other."

Weird. But I kept my mouth shut as the movie was starting. Not that this made up for the rest of the audience.

The ticket holders who did show up made no attempt to be quiet. Not only did they let their cell phones ring, they answered them. During the movie. Not wanting to call any undue attention, I didn't even try to shush them. Of course, my presence was ignored. As usual. I, on the other hand, was riveted by the nationals.

As shots were fired and bombs exploded the audience laughed. "This is horrific," I whispered to Rima. "People are dying and they're laughing?" She whispered back, "Osama's a Saud."

So that's why they could show this movie.

Armed clashes over border disputes had erupted between Qatar and Saudi Arabia for years; Osama bin Laden was thus a shared enemy. Despite that the war was being waged in Afghanistan, the war on terror was seen as a strike on Saudi Arabia — exactly the kind of reckoning behind so much of what goes on in that part of the world, and about which we are so ignorant. The light shed on issues in the Arab world is one reason that—despite what happened— I'm still glad I lived there.

"Your husband must have a very difficult time with you," chastised a Taliban leader to a female news reporter asking questions. The crowd went silent as I burst into laughter. Fearing some reaction I held my breath. Nothing. Not even a cold stare.

By the time we left it was dark out. Considering we were in the city center, I was surprised at how poorly lit the roads seemed. And how far we were traveling. Then I saw a sign in Arabic only, not even an English translation, and that's when I realized—we weren't in Doha anymore. In Doha, all signs there were either English or bi-lingual. And years later I'd meet resident Qataris who couldn't speak Arabic, though that's changing now. None of this was on my mind at the time, rather, in my emerging panic I wondered if we had any water in the car. Where the next gas station might be. Rima fussed with the map.

"What about Smelly Roundabout?" she asked. Like I'd know what that meant.

"The what?"

"I don't know, it's on the map."

We were both starting to panic. When I checked later it turned out there *was* a Smelly Roundabout labelled on the map.

At the time, all I could check was my anger. Though we'd only been lost about fifteen minutes, feelings of rage bubbled up inside me.

I called a co-worker I'd often followed into work, Keith. He very sweetly stayed on the phone, guiding me back to the hotel. This also kept me from losing it on Rima. Inexplicably I was angry that she wasn't driving. *What does she know that's keeping her from getting behind the wheel? And why won't she tell me?*

I'm not sure I hid my anger as well as I thought; this turned out to be the last time Rima and I would hang together for a long while; I'd have to observe my mentor from afar. It wasn't that I wouldn't have liked to find a new role model, there simply weren't that many people to choose from. I didn't overanalyze the disproportionate fury at the time; Geoff would be arriving soon, and I looked forward to exploring with him the "real" Doha, anyway. Until I discovered my most colossal miscalculation.

DOHA, QATAR
August 2004

I T WAS THE TAIL end of a long workday and I'd stopped by Mohamed's office to review another ad campaign. Though back on the main campus marketing had little truck with operations, in Doha his department approved all invoices over $1,000. I was spending a lot of time with Mohamed.

"This isn't clear enough," he said after scanning the ad. "You
have to come out and say it's the same degree they get in the States."

I thought including a line as awkward as "the same prestigious degree as in the States" raised doubts, but just then Rima stopped by. I was glad to see her; she'd temper things.

"Oh no, he's right," she agreed. "You have to remember, American universities have been marketed here for years. It doesn't mean they are part of an American school."

"And most of those schools are crap," Mohamed said, then cast a quick, apologetic look at Rima. "Not the American University in Beirut, of course. That's a great school."

AUB had a good reputation, but he'd mitigated his comment to appease Rima, who was from Beirut. No matter where they actually lived, Arabs remained fiercely loyal to home. Not that I ever met anyone who identified as Arab. Instead, I was regularly astounded at how quickly, consistently, and correctly they pegged others' nationalities — Jordanian, Iranian, Palestinian, etc. Maybe this stood out to me because, having moved so frequently, I'd always been stumped when asked, "Where ya from?"

"Most schools that call themselves American universities are just a sign on a doorfront," Mohamed went on. "People send their maids and drivers to those schools."

I found that hard to believe.

"Not to get an education, to take the tests for them," Rima said.

That I could believe.

"Our main selling point is that you don't have to leave home to get a premier education anymore," Mohamed said.

It was a lightning bolt moment. Finally. I got it.

The class we'd enrolled was mostly female, consistently the stronger applicants. Not a huge surprise. Come Friday night, the boys could fire up their Land Cruisers and hit the town, whereas the girls were obliged to stay in. Studying was something to do besides watch TV or hang out with the female relatives.

Putting a good university in their backyard, I now realized, eliminated the last good reason these women had to leave the country. Far from being a vehicle for liberation, I'd become a tool of the oppression. Leaving immediately, however, was out of the question.

Geoff had just arrived.

SEVEN

RAMADAN KAREEM

Ramadan:
The holiest holiday of the Muslim calendar, twenty-nine or thirty days that move around the calendar based on lunar cycles. For Muslims it's meant to be a time of reflection, when daytime deprivations are followed by nighttime feasting. For expats in Qatar, it's a time of panic, as there's nowhere to eat during the day and no booze is sold.

Ramadan Kareem:
Season's Greetings in the Muslim world; literally a wish for a "bountiful Ramadan."

DOHA, QATAR
September 2004

D OZENS OF US WERE assembled in the lobby of the Qatar Foundation, headquarters of the charitable organization run by Her Highness Sheikha Mozah bint Nasser Al Missned. We called the complex a multiversity because the campus was also home to undergraduate branches of Weill Cornell, Texas A&M, Virginia Commonwealth, Georgetown and Northwestern. The incredible expense of such an endeavor boggles the mind, but the spending didn't stop there. The Foundation's other pursuits included, but weren't limited to, a diabetic association (adult diabetes being a major ailment among the locals), a science and technology park (great for ultimately putting campus ideas into the marketplace) and the royal horse stables (uhh...). The whole endeavor was headed up by Mozah (as she was more familiarly known), a woman regularly referred to as the Emir's "consort." She was the only one of his three wives ever seen in public.

The entire press corps turned out, as had most of the university's PR teams, all to witness the unveiling of the Foundation's new website. No, this wasn't big news in 2004, but when Her Highness held a press conference, you went. The swag bag alone made it worth the trip — we each got a Mont Blanc pen and planner — but as we sat waiting for the proceedings to commence, the Foundation's head of PR (not the same as Her Highness' personal comms team) grew restless.

"I cannot believe they're unable to get the sound working," Robert snickered. "How on earth are these bumbleheads planning to put on the Doha Debates?"

I loved Robert's candor. At our first meeting he'd cited incompetence and inertia as two of the Qatar Foundation's guiding principles; I'd enjoyed his company ever since. An Irishman who'd spent much of his adult life in London, Robert had been a BBC-correspondent for many years. The Doha Debates were to be hosted by his former employer, broadcasting directly out of the room where we now stood watching people futz about with microphones. I knew the Foundation would throw whatever money was needed at resolving any problems, but I wondered more how well debates would go over in this culture. Our profs were having trouble convincing our students they could raise their hands in class to ask questions. Education in Qatar largely entailed rote memorization, not the dialectical model.

"I only hope we get out of here before lunch," Robert said. "What!" I demanded. "The cafeteria doesn't close for another hour and a half."

Even as I said it, I knew full well this could happen. Her Highness was famous for making people wait.

"Arrggh. Why did she call a press conference during lunch? I can't not eat."

"Well then, Ramadan shall be an exciting time for you," he said.

That hit a nerve. I winced, encouraging Robert who knew about my hypoglycemic tendencies.

"Did you hear that last year Maha from Texas A&M was pulled over by a policeman for eating a breakfast bar. In her car?" "What? She's Lebanese, right? I thought the expats would get a bit of a break."

"Oh no, they're most strict with other Arabs," Robert said.

"Particularly if they suspect they're Christian, like Maha."

No one would ever accuse me of looking like an Arab, yet I dreaded the upcoming holiday. Frankly, it boggled my mind that it was possible the prophet Mohamed, who lived in an age that pre-dated air conditioning, thought his people needed a better understanding of what it meant to suffer. Even the organization pained me. Rather than coming at set times, the holy month moved around the calendar according to lunar cycles. This meant that every year it started a little earlier than the year before, circling the calendar every twenty-three years or so. Calendars can show approximate dates, but only the imam can say exactly when Ramadan starts, and that only happens at the last minute.

"Why doesn't somebody get a Farmer's Almanac?" I

quipped, but Robert didn't even crack a smile. Maybe it wasn't that funny, or maybe he didn't know what a Farmer's Almanac was. I was having a hard enough time just being understood, forget about irony. Expats may have been the minority, but there were more Kiwis than Americans back then. The lack of shared cultural references was surprisingly isolating. Think about trying to go a day without using humor or anything idiomatic in your speech to convey meaning. Multiply by three years.

"Damn imam," Robert said. Goddamn Brits are always funny. "I can't schedule my holiday till they tell us if we're going to have Eid off."

Eid al Fitr was a three-day feasting period that followed Ramadan, a kind of re-acclimation period after the month of daytime fasting and nighttime feasting. Some years the emir decreed it could be taken as vacation, some years not. Since I worked for an American organization and the decree didn't impact my schedule, I could appreciate his tactic. This made it clear who was really running the show, and it wasn't the imam. That year His Highness would turn out to be in a very generous mood. Working hours would be from 8 a.m. to 1 p.m., and Eid would be three paid days off.

"And I've got to get to the booze souq," Robert added.

While I worried how to sneak food, my colleagues were becoming consumed with hoarding their alcohol. The country's restaurants, coffee shops and grocery stores only had to close during the day, but there would be no liquor for the duration of Ramadan, not at the five-star hotels, or even the booze souq. This souq, as the name suggests, was Qatar's marketplace of booze.

Open only to card-carrying members, even shoppers at the booze souq were regulated. Your license was nontransferable and only allowed holders to spend a percentage of their earnings. This amount was tracked each time the card holder swiped their little plastic card. This cut down on Qataris pressuring their staff to buy alcohol, since they were paid so poorly.

Though these stores shuttered for Ramadan, there was a workaround. For the month preceding the holiday, licensed shoppers were able to purchase double their standard allotment. This generosity assuaged exactly no one. In the face of all that abstinence, and with drivers and nannies omnipresent, the Westerners went at it hard every month. Adding on the hardship of the holiday only meant they went at it harder.

Legend had it that no matter how much people laid in, the booze often ran dry before the end of the month. In response to the widespread panic, even Geoff had gone out and gotten a license, though he rarely drank at home.

The generally accepted wisdom was that nothing got done during Ramadan. Because every night relatives got together to break the fast, I imagined the experience would be like working through a month of Christmas eves. Thus another task I wanted to accomplish before Rammers (as we called it) was to hire an assistant to replace Fadhel.

At the press event that afternoon it hadn't occurred to me to ask Robert if he knew of to fill the role. Back in the States such a plum job would be easy to fill. But back at my office, thumbing through resumes, I began to more fully appreciate the problem I'd created.

There was no real labor pool of people hoping to move up in Qatar. Career-minded types came over *with* jobs. Anyone with the language skills needed for a university's communications department could leverage a better title and salary elsewhere. It was difficult to find a resume free of errors. Thumbing through the stack, I resigned myself to the idea that *I* would be the department's copy editor.

"Your next appointment's here," became a sentence I

dreaded. One candidate interviewed with her father present, another brought her husband. Neither man shook my hand, but neither did the female candidates. Though this was not unusual — the cultural norm is to let a woman extend her hand to signal her openness to touch you — I was turned off. These women didn't seem like the types to put in the nights and weekends we were going to need in the weeks leading up to our opening celebration.

And then along came a British expat, close to willing. She wanted just a little more money than what we were offering. My dean, in his oh-so-rational way, told me to run the request past Mohamed.

"There wasn't even a budget for your job when we started this campus," were his last words on the subject.

DOHA, QATAR
October 2004

RAMADAN WAS ON. Though fall was an auspicious time for it —the shorter days meant less fasting —it made my life hell. My office, now Fadhel-free, was a place where I could shut the door, curse, and scarf down illicit snacks, but my troubles with Rammers extended beyond these pesky personal grievances.

No matter what the business, during Rammers the concept of "hours" disappeared. Shops opened and closed at mysterious, completely unpredictable timings. I couldn't even figure out how employees knew when to show up for work, let alone figure out if I'd be able to pick up dry cleaning on my lunch break. I pushed all errand-running to after work, which presented a whole new hell. Muslims break the fast with juice and dates, and then hit the mosque. After a quick prayer, the real partying begins. After the sun goes down, sugar-addled Muslims start clogging the streets, roaming from one party to the next. Traffic jams could last till sunrise, when the fasting would begin again.

That year Iftar, the meal that broke the fast, roughly coincided with the end of my workday, which—unlike Robert's and most everyone else's—had not been shortened. Thus my days began with a rush rush rush to get in meetings before 1 p.m., then an afternoon of trying to follow up on yesterday's meetings. A near impossible task since no one was around to do anything. Then day broke on the American work morning, and those colleagues would start emailing, setting in motion a new list of tasks that needed to be accomplished. I'd fight my way home through traffic, only to have reporters and vendors spring to life, their fast having ended so their workday could begin. If I wanted to get anything done it meant working into the wee hours. I was miserable, but Geoff kept me grounded. "Baby, we can do anything for a year," he'd say, whenever I made wistful comments about leaving.

———

One Ramadan bonus was getting to know Michelle a bit better. Having been in the country a couple of years already, she was able to take better advantage of the holiday.

"Careful," she said, one night, when she came to pick me up in her Porsche Cayenne for one of our weekly gatherings. "Don't throw your bag back there. The dog vomited when Dave took her to the vet, and our maid was out with the girls so it hasn't been properly cleaned up yet."

How did she manage to keep a dog in this country?

"It's no problem at all," she said.

Because of the maid?

"Oh, no. The maid's terrified of the dog," Michelle said.

"Which cracks the kids up since she's a Golden Retriever. The hub walks her round the compound a couple times a week, and we go out to the beaches on weekends."

God that sounded amazing.

I stared out into the traffic — a solid line of cars. I had every intention of learning my way around, but not now. Not during Ramadan. Maybe if we brought the dogs over it would feel more like home.

What to do with our dogs, Little Bear, 11, and Grandpa, 9, had been our biggest stumbling block in making the move to Qatar. Dogs are considered unclean in the Quran, and so it is haram, or forbidden, to enter a mosque if you've had any contact with one until you scrubbed clean. In general, Qataris wanted nothing to do with dogs.

Given that the five daily mosque visits required a wash anyway, I never was too sure why dogs got such a bad rap, but they did. There were Qataris who kept dogs for racing, but those could not be confused with family pets. Or even other racing animals. In Qatar, everything was a hierarchy.

On my first visit, on a tour of the royal stables, I found Arabian horses housed in air-conditioned stalls and exercised in temperature-controlled pools. Canines, on the other hand, were kept outdoors in makeshift kennels. If found wandering the streets, a dog in Qatar was as likely to be shot on sight as rounded up and taken to the pound. Our boys liked to run off; Little Bear especially, and he was Geoff's heart.

Then there was the trip alone, more than 14 hours in the cargo hold of a plane. It could kill them. If the dogs made it, there was still the problem of life on the ground to contend with. They were used to winters on the Northeastern seaboard.

I could barely stand to sport the requisite cover on my arms and legs, and both our boys were covered in thick, black, furry coats. When the friend renting our house expressed an interest in keeping our dogs, the plan fell into place. At the end of my contract, we'd move right back into our house with our dogs and pick up right where we left off. But home didn't feel right. More and more, I longed for their unconditional love and good will.

M ichelle's laughter interrupted my thoughts. "If only Dave wasn't so hopeless when it comes to basic mainte- nance," she said, shaking her head. "How hard is it to clean up?"

Such a relief to have a female friend whose spouse seemed so clueless. *This is just how it is*, I thought. *You can't expect to get all your needs met by your partner.*

Michelle would be divorcing within the year.

I n a smoking circle after our gathering, Paul — whom I'd met the same day I had Michelle — also told me he'd brought his dog from Canada. A German shepherd, no less.

"Nannette lets him out back when he needs to go," he said. "And I usually take him around the compound at night. You just have to stay with him. The guards are afraid of him." I never did understand why canines inspired such fear in all of Asia — compound guards always seemed to be Pakistanis — but it was clear that people were living successfully with dogs in Qatar. Maybe we could, too.

There was one last hurdle. Our housing.

Given the climate and lack of cultural amenities, employers lured prospective employees with perks beyond paychecks, including allowances for plane tickets, children's schooling, and housing. But these incentives varied wildly. For instance, whereas I got business class plane fare annually, many received coach tickets only once every three years. For live-in nannies, "fat pay" was two hundred dollars a month. Housing varied as well. The options ranged from the impressive — massive gated compounds with pools and tennis courts and grocery stores — to the improvised — the laborers who worked construction in our area lived in units they'd built from scrap materials.

Unaware of these disparities before arriving in Qatar, I had no interest in living in a compound. The fishbowl effect of a 7-day workweek was bad enough, surrounding myself with my co-workers in my downtime at home was repellent. Where would I smoke? Worse yet — like the Salmon Palace where we were temporarily housed — all these residences came furnished.

Now, however, the thought of living in a compound was starting to solidify. Michelle and I discussed some of the possibilities on the way home.

"They're all the same on the inside. Take a turd, dip it in gold and that's your décor," she laughed as we inched through the traffic.

"That's one reason we picked the Four Seasons residence tower to begin with," I said. "But they don't allow dogs."

The Four Seasons was building a hotel along the sea-fronting Corniche with two residence towers beside it. This stunning beachfront property, with its Miele kitchen appliances, sleek, contemporary furnishings and muted color scheme, was the only exception I'd seen to the phenomenally tacky villas. But no pets allowed.

Coupled with our concerns about bringing the boys over, and the synchronicity of finding a tenant who wanted to keep our dogs, we imagined morning coffee on our sea-facing terrace would ease the trauma of temporary dog-lessness. But construction had stalled and, even more ominously, it was no longer called a "Four Seasons" project. Who knew what else might change.

"God knows when they'll even be finished, and I can't live in the Salmon Palace until they figure it out, we may never leave," I said. "We couldn't even bring our dogs *there*."

"You're in the fishbowl no matter where you are here, so at the end of the day it doesn't matter if you're in a compound or not," Michelle said. "Besides, other people's opinion of you should be none of your business."

"D o we care if the villa has a gold-burnished, wrought iron stair rail as its most prominent indoor feature?" I asked Geoff when I got home that night.

"Being able to have dogs is one benefit of the way the compounds enforce segregation," Geoff said.

I'd never thought of it that way, but he had a point. My husband was so smart.

"That and I can wear short sleeves outside," I said. Because really, when it came to quality of life, this was a hot button issue for me. "When I'm on the compound anyway."

And so we agreed.

By the time that first Ramadan was over, it felt as if we'd lived in Qatar about a decade. Or at least that I'd aged that much. What got me through was the thought that soon we'd have our boys with us. Geoff and I vowed to never spend a whole Ramadan in Qatar ever again. *We* didn't.

DOHA, QATAR
NOVEMBER 2004

MY time and attention became further absorbed by work, and my patience wore thinner and thinner. To his credit, Geoff withstood my many tempests, but even that could piss me off. Like one night when he came to pick me up at work.

My mobile beeped and I looked at it. *Geoffy*.

I m here, read the text.

But I wasn't ready to leave. A jolt of anger stabbed at my gut. The thought of him just sitting out there with nothing to do made me insanely jealous. In theory, I wanted to be the woman who could support her mate while he advanced his career, but I was having a hard time with the reality. So he did most of the cooking, but he'd always done that. Otherwise, our household roles felt fairly similar.

When I finally made it out to the car and he was not even upset that his time had been wasted, I hit the roof. "What do you mean you've been waiting out here a half hour and you're not mad?" I lit into him. "Because I really should be in there doing more work."

"You need to eat something," he said, and not unkindly.

He was always the good guy. Why was I such a creep? It would be years before I'd see this actually was his part, this refusal to engage. If you're not willing to fight with someone, you're not willing to fight for them either.

At the time, it only made me more fearful of my feelings. I'd been in recovery long enough to know that anger was a cover-up emotion for something deeper, but it seemed like I was all anger, all the time. Some of it had to be legitimate, didn't it?

The lack of sleep was worrying as well. I began to wonder if I might be losing my mind, and not in some superficial, oh-that-shit-makes-me-so-crazy, kind of way. The move to Tunisia had brought on the trauma of a nervous breakdown. Though it had been a good decade since I'd had any kind of mood-altering

EIGHT

VALLEY OF THE ROSES

Zahrat Al Wadi:

The Arabic name of our compound: *Zahrat*, rose; *Wadi*, valley.

DOHA, QATAR
November 2004

ROBERT, THE QATAR Foundation's head of PR, lived on the compound we would be allowed to move into with our dogs. He invited us over to check it out.

"Turn left at TV roundabout, pass Landmark Mall, drive till the lights stop and it looks like civilization's come to an end. Turn right and you're at the compound."

Though I'd been to the compound, those directions meant nothing to me. Geoff got us right there. So much for freelance foreign correspondent. The reality is, *Driver*.

of course, I said nothing. At the time, I believed this was sufficient to cover my feelings, but in a land where English was not the native language, I would learn the hard way that what you say is less important than what you think. Thoughts are what transmit.

Zahrat al Wadi, or Valley Rose as it was more commonly called, was a compound we'd initially rejected for its sheer ridiculousness. There was not a rose in the place, or anything else in the way of foliage. Perhaps this was why it was our sole option for keeping dogs. What creeped me out the most, however, was that Robert's unit was identical to ours. All the units were identical to ours. Right down to the thin, leopard-print rugs.

The first floor featured a large room with a gold-burnished, metal stair-rail opposite the front door, the first thing your eyes landed on. To the left was a large, utterly unusable, low-ceilinged space carved out beneath the return staircase, and to the right were three brown velour couches, the aforementioned hideous rug, two ornate end-tables topped by equally over-wrought lamps, and behind that a formal dining table with a buffet and seating for twelve. The kitchen was enclosed to the left of the dining area, beyond the stairwell. It was as if a buyer for Walmart had been tasked with decorating for Donald Trump. In the years I spent there my decorating efforts largely went into tamping down the prevailing aesthetic as much as possible. But we hadn't taken the place for its looks, we'd taken it in spite of them. For the yard.

Out back was a 6' wide brick path that separated our house from the compound's exterior wall. This area also happened to be where our giant, white plastic water tank and pump were positioned, alongside six enormous air conditioning units, curi-ously all positioned to blast their sweltering exhaust right back at the house. By enclosing the pathway with gates on either side, we formed an outdoor space for the boys. We figured we could probably stand to have the a/c shut off about as long as the dogs could stay outside.

The compound itself was a large rectangle comprised of a hundred units: a pool, clubhouse, tennis courts, convenience store and a dry cleaner. That list sounds nice, but the pool and tennis courts sat mostly unused in that heat. The convenience store specialized in off-brand candy, Marlboro Reds, and nothing else anyone would ever need. No matter what I asked for — butter? Toilet bowl cleaner? Napkins? They never had it. OK. The dry cleaner was awesome. While it lasted. Prone to mysterious "timings" to begin with, one day the shop mysteriously closed. The handwritten explanation on the sign read only, "back after some time." That time turned out to be never, and I was down one bedspread. But all this was still to come.

That night Robert and Geoff and I sat on Robert's porch, Geoff and I smoking, Robert and Geoff drinking, and all of us gossiping. The participants would vary, but this would become a near nightly ritual for the duration of my stay in Qatar.

———

Our shipping container of household goods had yet to arrive from the States, so when Ramadan ended we were able to move in one car trip. This worked out well since the first order of business was to clear out as much of the furniture as we could live without — excess couches, animal-print anything, and any fixtures that weren't built in — and dump it in the maid's room out back since we never planned to have one.

"Look baby, a bidet," Geoff announced as he strode through our three bedrooms the afternoon we arrived. "In every bathroom!"

"Not down here," I called back from the first floor bathroom. Like every stall I ever visited in Qatar however, it did feature a hose. Toilet paper was not universal, but most often those hoses were employed in pre-mosque ablutions; this I surmised one day at the mall, as the call to prayer sounded over the speakers and water flew in every stall. It certainly explained why the stalls were often water logged.

"Why do you suppose there's a kitchen sink on the second floor?" Geoff called back, his voice echoing madly.

This reverb, I'd soon realize, was a tipoff to a person's whereabouts. Desert sands made for a town of marble floors and granite counters, an effect compounded by the bigger-is-better building mentality. The intent was to portray grandeur, but these façades failed to mask the poor construction, the sense that nothing was meant to last.

"I have no idea," I said. "But I'm planting some shrubs out front as soon as possible."

Geoff popped his head over the stair rail. "How're you gonna dig into the ground? I mean, besides the fact we didn't pack any gardening tools, the desert floor is essentially a thin coral shelf. That's why there aren't any basements. Why we have an electric stove instead of a gas one. It's pretty ironic when you think that natural gas is how they make their living."

"Ask one of your groundsmen to put it in," Michelle advised later on the phone.

And that's exactly what I did. It was a world apart from spending afternoons in my garden in Pittsburgh with Little Bear and Grandpa traipsing around, but the bougainvillea and hibiscus grew just the same.

DUBAI, UNITED ARAB EMIRATES
November, 2004

G EOFF and I decided to take advantage of a business trip I had in Dubai. To celebrate our move and the end of Ramadan, we booked a hotel for the weekend, eager to experience the Las Vegas of the Gulf. Minus the gambling. Though that would soon change. They were just building an artificial island off the coast, The World. Technically it wouldn't be Arab land, so gambling was mafi mushkilla.

Our weekend package included a car rental, and since Geoff was willing to drive it seemed like the smart thing to do. Unbelievably, the traffic was worse than in Doha. Their roundabouts came with red lights, yet this helped exactly nothing. As we inched through the city, snaking between the enormous buildings, Dubai struck me as an arena where families did battle, with blue-chip architects playing the gladiators in a show of one-upmanship for the most otherworldly construction. I was thrilled to hit the parking garage of our Jumeirah Beach hotel. We planned to spend the day on the beach, but the sand was too hot to walk on.

"How about we check out Wild Wadi next door?" I asked. Wild Wadi was a waterpark.

"What's the worst thing that could happen?" Geoff replied.

We burst out laughing but on we forged. It turned out to be the best thing we could've done. Yes, we'd just left a beach because it was too hot. But at Wild Wadi, they air conditioned the outdoor spaces. Forcing myself to ignore the environmental carnage, I gave in to the thrill of gliding down giant slides. We stayed till closing.

"Let's go to the souqs," I said.

Neither of us were big on shopping as recreation, but souqs were market areas that featured tourist kitsch fare that I much preferred to malls. We eschewed the gold souq in favor of the old souq, but soon found its plastic combs and stuffed camels depressing. We decided to walk the quay that ran along Ras Al Khor, the inland bay that divided north and south Dubai. Mercifully, it didn't seem terribly touristy — enormous ships were offloading flat screen TVs and cars and bottled water — until a man called out to us that he was about to start a dinner cruise. Very strange. We looked at his boat, then each other. There were other euro-expats on board, they must have had a sign-up elsewhere earlier but still had seats to fill. Or perhaps there had been cancellations? Again, what was the worst thing that could happen? Thinking of one possible worse thing I asked a question.

"Is there a belly dancer?"

It wasn't belly dancing that concerned me, it was bad belly dancing. Perish the thought of being trapped on a boat with uncomfortable entertainment.

"No madame," our captain replied, sounding wistful. I didn't know it then, but belly dancing was on the way out. Haram! At the time I was happy not to have it. "But we have shisha!"

That I could skip.

The meal was quite delicious: olives, grape leaves, hummus, tabouli, flat bread, rice and lamb kebabs. Afterward, floating along the water, I could observe Dubai from a more removed perspective. White fantasy constructs, one after another, lit up. Stunning.

"I'm glad we came," I said to Geoff.

"Yeah, the food wasn't half bad."

"No I mean here. Not to Dubai. To the Gulf."

Moments like this could keep me going.

DOHA, QATAR
November 2004

W ITH THANKSGIVING and the end of the semester right around the corner, I began to suspect I wouldn't be able to hire anyone until the new year. If I could even find someone then. The stress kept me exhausted, yet unable to sleep. I was thrilled that Geoff had Robert to hang out with at night; it gave me a bit of a break from the feeling I needed to entertain him after an exhausting day at work. I didn't have to, and he never asked, but I felt it was the thing I should be doing. One night Geoff came home from Robert's to find me staring at the television's blue screen. He pried the remote from my hand, laughing. "It's not that hard to use," he said, knowing that I'd not been able to figure out how to use it.

In fact, I hadn't noticed there was nothing on TV; I had been enjoying the time alone. Geoff sat next to me on the couch and put his hand on my knee. "I think I'm gonna start looking for a job." I remained transfixed by the TV, one of those times that there were advantages to exhaustion. Inside I reeled.

We moved here so you could advance your journalism career. How're you gonna do that if you can't place stories when you don't have a job? What about your dream, fuckwit? What about my dream?

My dream was to be able to step back and take some time off when my contract was over. I couldn't imagine what kind of job job he'd get in Qatar that would advance his career to the point where me taking time off to write and/or start our family would be possible. I could not articulate this in my stupor, which was just as well since I had conflicting thoughts anyway.

If my search for an admin had shown me anything, it was that there were some intriguing possibilities. People who could walk, chew gum and speak English could find good jobs. It wasn't even necessary to do all three at the same time. Or well. Or even really, all three. A native's grasp of English was a hot commodity. Besides, there was that English-language station Al Jazeera was developing. In truth, from the moment we'd begun talking about this move, and despite that my beloved worked in print journalism, I'd pictured my Geoffy, grainy and small, issuing televised reports on the state of world affairs. It could happen. *Something* had to. He'd gone from writing multiple think pieces in a week to zero output. Whereas I was a natural freelancer, Geoff seemed to do better in an office. I was hating being the sole breadwinner, and hating myself for hating it.

"I think that's great, honey," I said, smiling weakly. "Let's go to bed."

I didn't think it was so great when Geoff interviewed with Al Jazeera's web team, but I could get on board with that. All he needed was to get his foot in the door. But this was not the job he took.

"I'm going to take a PR associate's position with Robert," he said one night after coming home from Robert's porch. "The pay's not so good, but I'll be making some great contacts in this role."

his job search was a walk across the yard? And goddamn that Robert. He'd just gone and hired Geoff for exactly the position I'd created in my office and couldn't fill for the life of me? he hadn't even mentioned to me he was looking. Had Geoff forgotten why we'd moved here in the first place?

"Are you sure you want to do that? What about Al Jazeera?" I asked. Trying, and probably failing, to hide my dismay. I have never been described as having a poker face under the best of circumstances, and these weren't the best of circumstances.

"I'm sure I want to start working," he said. "And I haven't heard back from Al Jazeera."

Did you try calling them? I wanted to scream. Instead I tried to be supportive. What I didn't realize at the time was that the more I wanted him to take charge, the more passive-aggressive I became.

"Well, too bad Ramadan's over, there were so many sales," I said. "We'll have to go out and buy you a whole new wardrobe."
"Yeah, I guess you're right," he said. "everyone's always so
dressed up here. I'll have to get used to that."

This was really too much. I missed working from home in my pajamas. Didn't he care about that?

"I'm still not used to it," I said sarcastically. "But you should always dress for the job you want, not the job you have."

I wish I could say I meant that last part sarcastically, because I loathe corporate "wisdom" like that. Only I didn't. My feeling was, if you're about to ditch journalism for a PR job, you better turn it into a damn good job. Maybe he can become a politician.

Yes. I actually thought that. Because the shitty job itself was barely the half of it.

Not only would Geoff and I be driving in to work together, we'd be attending the same meetings. I'd be running them, and he'd be taking the notes. It was now official. I'd become the dick-wilting image of a "feminist" that I'd never wanted to be. But what could I say? Much as I wanted to think I had a husband who could support me should the need arise, I didn't believe I deserved it. I was 13 when my father cut me off financially and put me to work at less than minimum wage. I knew I had issues around money, and I didn't want to be that person anymore. But this post-Cinderella fantasy officially felt like a nightmare.

"Hi, could I have a coffee please?" I asked the man at the Coffee Beanery, before going back to my phone conversation with Michelle. I know, rude to be on the cell phone in line, but this was nothing compared to the phone etiquette that pervaded the region. I'll never forget the first business meeting I was in, where the ad rep's phone went off. "Ha-bi-ii-i-bi!" sounded the pop song ringtone, bad enough. Until he proceeded to take the call. In the meeting. I wasn't that bad. Though he also smoked at that meeting, despite the presence of my pregnant colleague. Maybe he wasn't the role model I should be resting my laurels on. But Michelle and her husband had just had a huge fight; I needed to be there for her.

"He supposedly has this job selling sailboats," she was saying. "But we spend more money than he earns to keep him working. Right now, I don't feel like paying for him to fly to Greece to not sell another boat, because I have to go to Hong Kong for a recruiting trip and he needs to stay with the girls."

Nightmare. Worse yet, I was handed a café au lait.

"Oh no, 'scuse me, Michelle." To the barista I said, "I asked for a coffee."

To get this straightened out involved getting a manager, who then seemed to brutally yell at the waitstaff in some mysterious language.

"Geez, Indians have some pretty bizarre management techniques," I said.

"I'm pretty sure that's Pakistani," Michelle said.

"Impressive," I said.

"I can't tell from what they're saying, silly," she laughed. "It's the fact you're at a coffee shop."

She was referring to the ethnic cartels that prevailed Qatar's various industries — Filipinas in hairdressing and nannying, Nepalis in construction, Pakistanis in food. I imagined this was convenience, as much as anything else. How else would anybody know when to show up? English may have been the lingua franca, but that wouldn't have worked. "Come later, maybe after one hour we open. Insha'Allah," was too vague for employment. They must've been coordinating actual hours in their native tongue.

But this got me thinking about Geoff 's job hunt. Going into my job, I'd imagined that Geoff's glamorous line of work would help make up for being a "trailing spouse," but it turned out that journalists in this part of the world were mere scribes.

Qatar — a country the size of Connecticut but with fewer people — supported five daily papers, though they were more like family newsletters than factual accounts. Above-the-fold, grip-and-grin shots of the emir and his cronies were front page features every day, and Indians pervaded this cartel anyway. Mention of my beloved's career invariably elicited a look of sympathy. Other than Al Jazeera English, where they were making headlines with their hires — real journalists! — there really wasn't anywhere for him to look for work. I had no idea why it might not be working out for Geoff, but maybe he would meet people at QF. People who could get him a real job at Al Jazeera.

"Getting back to your husband," I said to Michelle, "doesn't your maid watch the girls most of the time anyway?"

"But that's not the point," she said.

ouch. I felt like an idiot. Like when a single person asks someone who's coupled up for love advice.

"I'm sorry," I said. "I hear you. What are you going to do?"

"Well, he's going to Greece," she said. "Obviously. Has to feel

like he has some balls left. It's maddening."

DOHA, QATAR
December 2004

"YOU don't have to take this job," I said to Geoff as he drove us to Education City that first day, still waging my little campaign. I hated my job so much, and if all it was doing for Geoff's career was derailing it, why were we here?

"I know," he said, which annoyed me. I'd like not to have to take a job.

"You can always go back to trying to place articles," I went on. *Had* he been trying? I had so many doubts about everything at that point, but mostly I doubted myself and my tendency to find the black cloud in the silver lining.

"We can do anything for a year," he said.

Did he mean a year from now as in next December? A year from the time he'd arrived in August? Or were we on my clock? I'd been in Qatar since June. I was definitely thinking June. But I also knew, this was why I'd married this man. So that, after all that childhood moving, I could finally have a sense of constancy in my life. I looked at him just then; we'd replaced his jeans and T-shirts with custom suits and ties. Very sharp. And I could barely imagine how hard this must be on him. How I longed for him to tell me, but I didn't want to push.

This was the other benefit of marriage, this promise to let things lie. To wait out the tempests. To keep coming back.

Geoff was the best-dressed administrative assistant on campus. And he had his own office.

NINE

LA, LA, LA!

La, La, La:
"No, no, no." Repeated for emphasis; usually preceded with a tch and followed by a headshake.

Nam:
"Yes." The only language I know of in which the "no" sound means yes; usually, "n" means no.

PITTSBURGH, PA
December 2004

TENTS WENT UP around Doha every weekend, creating little oases for birthday parties and weddings. They didn't look like much from the outside, but they were fantasy
environments inside, with themed table settings, floral décor and air-conditioning. It occurred to me, one afternoon in the passenger seat, why not host our Grand Opening celebration on the plot of ground where our new building would be going up, in a tent!

As I told my friend Mary Ellen over the phone, this was my big idea for wowing my boss in the States, Kyle.

"Then I can ask about creating a consulting position for my office, which would solve my hiring dilemma of having to go through Mohamed. Maybe that British expat is still available... so long as the job is temporary, I'll have the budget for it."

During that same lengthy chat, I had to tell her we'd only see each other on this trip at her Christmas party. Probably for less time than we'd just spent on the phone.

"Yes it sucks, but there are so many people at the university I need to meet with in person if I want to get this party arranged. But I can't wait to see you and your place!" Mary Ellen always went all out at Christmas.

"You're working too much," was all Mary Ellen said.

Two weeks later, Geoff and I were pulling up to our old house in Pittsburgh. There was a light dusting of snow on the ground, postcard pretty. Kim, our dog's caretaker and tenant, answered the door and shocked me. The house looked amazing —her décor suited the place far better than ours ever had. But there was no time for moping. Little Bear and Grandpa bounded toward us, licking and prancing and barking. *Yes*, I thought. *This is absolutely the right thing to do.*

I was a little nervous about staying at my parents' house with the boys; our family had never had dogs. We had cats. Cats that I'd brought home. They still had two of them.

Lovable as they were, Little Bear and Grandpa were completely untrained. This had been immortalized in songs sung by Geoff and his friends around bonfires through the years. To wit:

> *Little Bear and Grandpa, they sit around all day.*
> *Little Bear and Grandpa, looking for a way*
> *to play. At a party, looking for food.*

Decide to pee on my seersucker suit.
Little Bear and Grandpa, they sit around all day.
*   Little Bear and Grandpa, looking for a way*
*   to play.*

It never occurred to me to try and remedy the training situation; they were Geoff's dogs and that's just how they came. The best love, I felt, was an "as-is" situation. I considered it nothing short of a miracle when over that Christmas they neither went to the bathroom in the house nor chewed anything beyond recognition. That we discovered, anyway.

L ater on, at my first of many meetings on campus in Pittsburgh, I pitched my "big idea" for the Grand Opening ceremony.

"We can combine the old-world charm and Arabic influence of a tent with a high-octane presentation about Carnegie Mellon," I told Kyle, giving it my corporate all.

But she barely seemed to notice.

"Sure," she said nonchalantly. "Hey, what's the deal with the newsletter you were going to start."

Tears stung at my eyes. The newsletter? I could barely get a press release out with all the approvals I had to run it through, how was I supposed to get a newsletter together? had she even noticed I was a one-person department? If I'd thought about it clearly, as Mary Ellen had been suggesting when she reminded me that feelings weren't facts, I would've known that Kyle was just going down her list of deliverables and trying to figure out what we did and did not have. But I was sleep-deprived and a little bit out of my mind. Despite being closer to friends and nearer to Geoff, I still felt lonely.

"I can't possibly," I started, and then broke down into tears. "What's the matter, Lisa?" another colleague in the meeting asked. I was mortified. I'd never been a big fan of crying, and at work?

"I'm sorry," I sniffled. "I'm really worried about this Grand Opening celebration because I can't find anyone to hire and there's so much work to be done."

I went on to try and explain the situation, what I got across was enough.

"That's easy," Kyle said. "Just write up the job description and the salary you need and I'll sign it. No problem."

Really?

I actually had found someone I wanted to hire — Michelle had suggested using all those after-hours work functions I attended as opportunities to interview — and already I knew she wanted more than Mohamed would ever agree to. Despite my bravado on the phone with Mary Ellen, I knew if I circumvented him again, he'd be hella pissed.

Then again, he already hated me. And I was seriously losing it. Much later I'd realize that Mohamed was only following QF policy on payroll, he didn't mind a bit that we hired someone as a contractor; it was actually less paperwork for him.

The night before Christmas eve, I left Geoff at my parents' house and broke away to Mary Ellen's. Strictly a hen's night, no men. We were pulled up to the coffee table in her living room, stolen moments before the rest of the girls arrived. Between Mary Ellen's large extended family and many friends, we rarely got time alone.

"Oh my God, I can't believe I almost forgot the gorgonzola dip," she said, jumping up to get it from her kitchen. I marveled at her fully decorated tree, the wrapped presents and the food spread she'd put out. The scented candles. "Hey hon," she called out from her bathroom a few moments later. "Have you got a tampon on you? I don't want to run upstairs."

"Nope," I called back. Then I stopped and thought. "I didn't even bring any with me. I haven't had a period since I've lived in Qatar."

Seconds later Mary Ellen flew from the bathroom. "What? Are you pregnant?" "No!"

"Are you sure?" "of course!"

"You don't seem too worried about not having a period!" "Well, I was on Depoprovera for years," I said. I'd been

so thrilled when that birth control came out — no periods ever!

"I'm used to not having a period."

I'd blithely attributed the lack of a period to stress. The first six months I "lived" in Qatar, I crossed time zones 10 times, including four trips to the U.S. — that's 8,000 miles each way. Then there was the job itself. I wasn't sleeping at all. Of course my body chemistry was jacked. But Mary Ellen was having none of it.

"I'd drive you to the doctor's right now if it wasn't the night before Christmas eve," she said. "You have to promise me you'll go as soon as you get back."

"Mary Ellen, do you have any idea how much time I don't have?" I asked.

"Lis, that's one of the dumbest things you've ever said," she said. "How much time won't you have if you find out there's something wrong with you that you didn't take care of?"

Please.

But she was so vehement I promised, and then promptly changed the subject back to work, of course. Soon we were howling.

"You know, I'm in the hall walking past a group of covered women, and they're talking and laughing and looking around, and I'm sure it's me they're talking about," I laughed, shaking my head. I really had felt this way, but since they were speaking in Arabic, I had no way of knowing, or any reason to suspect they'd be talking about me.

"Or maybe they are talking about you," she laughed. "But so what? We love you anyway."

———

The lack of training reared its head again when we were trying to leave the country. Coaxing the dogs into the crates was easier than keeping them inside; they'd never been in crates before. Little Bear kept turning circles in his, and Grandpa howled.

"God, what if they carry on like that on the plane?" I said to Geoff. "But I've heard mixed reviews about giving them doggie downers."

"I think it's better for them," Geoff said. "Bear ate four boxes of Thin Mints once."

"Can't chocolate kill a dog?"

"Exactly," Geoff said. "He'll be fine." "What about Grandpa?" I asked.

"Would we know the difference?" he joked. Grandpa's name was a clue to his haplessness.

We decided to tranquilize them.

since Geoff wasn't working when we'd begun this process, I'd left the pet transport details for him to arrange. It was quite complex. Vet visits and shots had to be organized months in advance — Kim had been incredible about helping us. There were the proper size crates to get, and, of course, we had to book with a dog-friendly airline. I would hate to see a dog-unfriendly carrier.

our triumphant return to Doha with the boys in tow didn't make it out of Pennsylvania before coming to a grinding halt. At the Philadelphia airport the baggage handler stopped and asked us casually, "These guys are chipped, right?"

I pulled out our papers. Per Qatari regulations:

Vaccines up to date and properly timed for travel. Check.

Demonstrable proof of "breed" (as mutts they neatly avoided Doha's list of disapproved specimens). Check.

Disease-free. Check.

There was no microchip on my checklist. What the hell was a microchip, anyway?

"A microchip is an ID tag that gets inserted beneath the skin," the baggage handler explained. "They have to be microchipped or they'll be destroyed in europe."

sounded disgusting that, but I breathed a sigh of relief. "We're not staying in europe. Just passing through."

"Doesn't matter," he told us. "They'll be destroyed if they don't have 'em."

Whose rule was that? The airlines? how were we supposed to know that?

I threw a fit.

The micro-chipping was an airline regulation and, as far as I was concerned, something that should have been listed on their web site. The university gave business class tickets home, but many traveled coach and pocketed the difference — it could mean a whole other trip. But for this trip we went all out with business class, assuming it would entitle us to better treatment. That meant our tickets had cost $6,000 a pop; frankly, I felt they owed us. Still, I was blown away when Geoff joined in my complaint. usually, he liked to play good cop, but on this occasion we were a team.

We had to retrieve our bags, find a hotel that allowed dogs, then a tax I large enough and willing to transport them, and finally find a vet and book an appointment for micro chipping. We booked that same cabbie to take us to the vet the next day, and from there straight back to the airport for re-boarding. Homecoming complete.

Check.

DOHA, QATAR
January 2005

T HANK God for Farah, the woman I was able to bring on board thanks to the paperwork shuffle with Kyle.

Of Indian descent, Farah had been raised in the U.K. She and her husband had moved to Qatar a dozen years earlier, where she'd raised her two children. She didn't have much in the way of office experience, but her English was flawless and she knew everyone in town. And apparently, this was how things got done. The difference between her and Fadhel? She had no problem taking charge. Need to create a 360° brand immersion environment? Try a wedding planner, they design client-specific environments every week! stumped on how to deliver a couple thousand invitations in a country without addresses? hire a driver! I cannot imagine how I could have pulled off that event without her. She taught me other tricks, as well.

One afternoon, I came back from a meeting to find my Qatar electricity and Water Co. bill waiting. You couldn't pay them over the phone or by mail, you had to take the bill in and pay in person. This had been one of Geoff 's tasks before he started his job at QF; most people had their maids or drivers do it. With all the travel, I'd missed paying the previous month's bill, but I didn't see how I was going to make it over to their offices in time to pay this month either.

"Oh God, I hope they don't shut off my electricity," I moaned. "I don't know how I'm going to get this bill paid."

"Don't be daft," Farah said. "Send the university's driver. He took mine yesterday."

Cheeky! I thought. But also a damn good idea.

ostensibly employed to run university errands, it had never occurred to me to ask the driver to take care of my personal tasks. I had no idea he was paying everyone else's utility bills, and picking up dry cleaning, and more. Usually the fixer sorted this out for folks, but Fadhel, my erstwhile assistant director, hadn't been forthcoming with any fixes for us. Couldn't I just get through the rest of my contract without having to deal with that situation? The answer would turn out to be a resounding la. Or, as the Qataris liked to trill, la la la. No no no.

TEN

HIS & HER HIGHNESS OF QATAR & THE HOOTER'S CORPORATE JET

Sheikha Mozah bint Nasser Al Missned:
The only one of the emir's three wives ever seen in public, officially known as his "consort." Gorgeous, feminine and powerful. Runs Qatar Foundation; Carnegie Mellon patron. (The Missneds: Sheikha Mozah's wealthy merchant family.)

Sheikh Hamad bin Khalifa Al Thani:
Emir of Qatar since 1995, during which time he's completely overhauled his country. Terrifically overweight, often sports a purple suit when traveling, oddly less royal looking than Barney. (Al Thanis: The family that has ruled Qatar since the late 1800s, when Qatari pirates defeated the ottoman empire in the Gulf.)

More liberal than their subjects, both these leaders walk a fine line between approval and taking action to bring the country into step with today's flat world.

DOHA, QATAR
January 2005

THE AIR IN the conference room was heavy with the scent of men's cologne, perfume being one of the locals' go-to strategies for dealing with the desert heat. Even as a smoker I'd always had an overly sensitive nose, so this was a regular trauma while I lived in Qatar. And since Qatar's only tent company apparently didn't have any English-speaking staff, there we were arranging the Grand Opening party: me, two guys from the tent company, and Fadhel.

Since there were no phone books in Qatar and the internet was but a fledgling — my banker had given me a card with a hotmail account listed on it — I had no idea how to set this thing up. None of my colleagues at the other universities had arranged anything like it, not even Farah. So I pretty much had to go with Mohamed's word on how to get this tent done. He had arranged the meeting with Fadhel as translator.

As we discussed guest entry and exit, a private area for the highnesses, subsurface, and lighting, I held back my doubts. Surely Fadhel wouldn't screw me on this, he'd look worse. Wouldn't he? everything seemed to be going so well. Until the very end of our meeting.

"You will have to find the portable toilets," Fadhel said to me, seemingly apropos of nothing.

"You mean to tell me we've been discussing how to handle 1,000 guests without bathrooms?" I asked. "They're bringing chandeliers, right? Are they planning on providing light bulbs?"

He smiled his big Fadhel smile.

I tried to smile back, but have no doubt my face conveyed a desire to tear his head off. He didn't answer. I broke first.

"Would you ask who they recommend supply the Portapotties?"

He turned and spoke to them. Much head shaking, smiles all around.

"Mafi mushkilla," he finally turned around and said. More smiles, goodbyes, well wishes, meeting adjourned and I was left wondering how to find portable toilets in the desert. I thought I might cry as I limped back to my office. At this point in Qatar, in addition to the sleepless nights, I'd developed a pinched nerve in my neck and a wicked case of tennis elbow.

"A wedding planner can sort toilets out for you," Farah said without looking up from her computer.

Of course.

I had yet to make good on that promise to Mary Ellen to see a gynecologist, and I doubt I would have, had Nathan not suddenly shown up in our little recovery community. Besides my inherent disdain for the medical establishment, I had good reason to be suspicious of doctors in the Asian world. Most places, you could simply rock up to the pharmacy, open a tray and take your pick from Xanax to Chlomid. In Tunisia, I'd seen a fellow volunteer spend four weeks in bed getting daily narcotics injections to resolve a muscle she'd pulled in a volley-ball game. Then there was my friend Paul, the guy who'd taken Kyle and me to that first sober gathering on my pre-employment trip. Paul also happened to be a teacher at Doha's largest medical training facility, and regularly regaled me with tales of his students' academic underachievements. The prevailing treatment modality seemed to be — medicate first, diagnose after some time. But this Nathan was a British citizen, trained in the U.K.

Hand-picked to run the fertility clinic at Qatar's main hospital, I knew he had to be good, because if there was one thing these people took seriously, it was procreating. Beyond their religious beliefs, the Qataris themselves were acutely aware of their tiny population. Thus he worked at Hamad Medical Center.

Most Westerners went to the American hospital, not because the doctors were American, or even that they were trained to Western standards. They went for the Westernized atmosphere. Hamad was halal, Islam-approved, meaning it was sex-segregated. Geoff could not be in the ladies areas with me unless Nathan helped sneak him in, which we did on a couple of occasions. I would have preferred the American hospital myself, but securing a competent doctor was my larger concern. Even the facility itself was off-putting.

Hamad was a sprawling, sooty white, single-story structure at the heart of Doha's worst traffic snarls. Its clientele was largely Qatari nationals, for whom healthcare was provided free of charge. The only expats I ever saw there swirled about in a massively disorganized fashion, looking to tick the chest X-ray requirement off their employment visa list. When I'd done the same I'd been ushered to the front of the swell, a service I'd not appreciated until my appointments with Nathan gave me the chance to watch people wait. His waiting room was organized like any other doctor's, which I took to be a good sign.

"You've got a cyst the size of an orange on your ovary," Nathan told me at my first appointment. "You need to have that removed right away. We need to schedule surgery."

Nathan knew from my shares at our meetings how tight my schedule was. Is no one capable of maintaining a Western work ethic in this country? I thought.

"I'm in the final stretch of this huge event, I could barely make this appointment," I said. "Anything requiring anesthesia is going to have to wait."

"I'd think most would view that the other way 'round, Lisa," he said.

But I'd known plenty of people with cysts on their ovaries, it didn't seem like such a big deal. Words like rupture and cancer did not occur to me. I scheduled the procedure for mid-March, just after the opening. Mafi mushkilla!

"That way we can still have sex on our anniversary," was how I billed it to Geoff later over dinner.

Not that he needed any convincing. Had Geoff tried to protest— at the waiting or at going to Hamad — I would've proceeded just the same. It was only much later that I even thought about these possibilities, when other people seemed shocked by Geoff's reaction. Or lack thereof.

Also, I really meant what I said about wanting to have sex on our actual anniversary. I was nervous about undergoing surgery in Qatar, but it just so happened that the Grand Opening fell on the same weekend as our third anniversary. We'd already spent our second annual celebration apart, and this was not a tradition I wanted to continue.

At the start of the second semester, Mohamed threw a big party. I thought he was hosting of staff appreciation thing in consideration of all the hard work we'd done to make the Grand Opening happen, so I was shocked when Geoff and I were asked to separate at the porch. Apparently Mohamed kept a halal house.

At the side door I was shown to I was greeted by his wife. At least I think it was her. I'd only "seen" her at Hamad Hospital when we went for chest X-rays as part of our visa requirements. She was then, as now, fully covered. And by "fully" I don't mean just the head scarf and matching black robe, she also sported the niqab, or full-on face mask, and gloves. Wasn't one of the benefits of being at home that you didn't have to cover? She didn't really greet me either, merely opened the door and stepped aside. As I watched her retreat, I remembered she'd worn glasses at Hamad; she wasn't wearing them now. Were they meant as another layer of concealment? *Is anyone that dangerously sexy?*

I buckled in for the night, taking a seat in the squished chair-arm to chair-arm seating arrangement that prevailed in the Arab world, a setup I found counterproductive to relationship building. Trapped in a straight line between the wives of two of my co-workers, I was unable to talk to Rima who was only a few chairs away. They were nattering on in Arabic anyway. I tried not to look too helpless, and felt a pang of jealousy that Cindy, the office manager, had skipped out. She was a hard worker, she just didn't give a flip about kissing up; for her this job was pocket money. I wanted a job for mad money. The only other colleague in the ladies section was Roxanne, the HR director, sitting way on the other side, working Mohamed's wife. What on earth are they talking about? Probably kids. More jealousy.

Dinner was announced when a thin plastic tablecloth was thrown onto the floor in the foyer. A slab of rice was placed in its center, then an entire baby lamb went down on top, head, tail and all. Forget about silverware, we had no chairs. The idea seemed to be that we should squat and dig into the carcass with our fingers. While this was exactly the kind of "local" activity I'd supposedly been craving after hours, I didn't feel so good about digging into the side of a sheep while I was on the clock. I sidled over to Rima and mouthed, *What the hell?*

"It's machbous," she whispered.

"No wonder there are no Qatari restaurants," I said.

"Just be glad they put dinner out early," Rima said. "It'll be an early night. After the food these things wrap up quickly."

Rima went and had a few words with Mohamed's wife. A set of plastic knives and forks and plates did appear, but the spectacle continued to defy my appetite. I put a few scraps on my plate and pushed them around before I could decently throw the whole thing away. Machbous wasn't going to be joining our meal repertoire anytime soon.

We retired back to the chair-lined room for dessert, but now people were standing and mingling. A mountain of what looked like baklava had been placed on a sideboard. Not my kind of dessert. The family's maid came around with a giant urn of coffee. That I could go for. I took a shot glass from her tray, and held out my cup as she poured me a pus-colored concoction. I looked around the room, this seemed normal to everyone. I sidled back over to Rima.

"It smells like Turkish coffee, but what is it?" I asked. "It's Arabic coffee," she said. "Try it."

"All righty, bottoms up," I said before taking my swig, which I immediately wanted to spit out.

"It's not my favorite either," Rima laughed. "I prefer Turkish."

Suddenly the maid was back refilling my glass.

"Shake your cup three times," Rima said. "That means no more. Helas. And next time just take a sip."

Or pretend to take a sip.

Suddenly, just as Rima had predicted, it was time to go. No milling. Just, go. On the way out I saw Mohamed standing at the entrance to a tent I hadn't noticed before on his side lawn. Back in the car Geoff told me the men had retired to the tent after supper for shisha. Then he dropped the bomb. "Did you know your trustee was going to be there?"

What?

Apparently this was not team appreciation, but an event called to honor one of our visiting dignitaries and present him with a souvenir dagger. I wasn't sure what pissed me off more, that someone thought it was a good idea to send an old Jewish guy to the airport with a knife, or that my husband — the nonuniversity employee — had been the one to watch the presentation go down. I vowed to rush development of executive gifts emblazoned with the university's logo. The following week, I would put together an email for the school's head attorney, mentioning the segregated event the university had just paid for. It would be the last halal event the university sponsored.

"I don't know if I can last here for three years," I said to my husband when we got home. "I'm so sick of his *there wasn't even a job for you when this campus started* bullshit. Dick."

"There wasn't a job for him at a certain point in the planning either, I'm sure," Geoff said. God he was good at knowing exactly the right thing to say. "We're just giving it a year before we make any decisions. We can do anything for a year."

By this point the conversation was a placeholder with well-worn grooves. In truth, I was far too busy at work to even think about abandoning ship. What I needed was the confirmation that we were in this together. This was one of the things I loved about being married, this tempering. I was more prone to action, but being with Geoff made it easier to stay still without being afraid I was missing something. I would have said this right up to the moment he ended our marriage via transcontinental phone call.

ELEVEN

(MY) CHANGE IN THE MIDDLE EAST

Bint, Bin:
Daughter of, son of. used to connect family names.

Umm, Abu:
Mother of, father of. Family is so important in this culture that often, after having children, a person is only referred to as *Umm* (insert the kid's name here) or *Abu* (same).

DOHA, QATAR
February 2005

L ITTLE BEAR WAS LISTLESS.
Gone was the frolicking, scampering boy from Christmas. It was almost as if he was having a bad case of jet lag. Maybe we shouldn't have given him sedatives for the plane trip. Had I made a huge mistake insisting we bring the boys over? Then I discovered the lump under his left shoulder. The problem wasn't the trip, it was the lump! Which put me right back to worrying. The lump? I dreaded Geoff 's response. He'd rescued Bear as a pup, and loved to tell a story about how

at one time he'd been so poor that the only thing he could afford to buy was a pumpkin, and how the two of them lived off of that for three days.

"Take him to Dr. Troy," Michelle advised.

As it turned out, Dr. Troy lived at the same compound, though his area of Valley Rose had a separate entrance, an even less fashionable section of our already unfashionable compound. Troy was able to see Bear that afternoon; I skipped out of work to take him over. I hadn't yet said a word to Geoff, so I was glad I could find him myself; I just four-wheeled it over the strip of desert between our lots.

"It's probably nothing," he said. "He's 12? older dogs get tumors all the time."

Tumors?

"I can do the surgery Sunday morning and you'll have him back that afternoon."

Deal.

Only when I sat to write this story did I realize I made my dog's health a priority over mine; at the time I didn't think about it. On the way home I called Geoff, which seemed easier than facing him in person.

"Bear needs to have a procedure on Sunday," I said. "There's some kind of cyst under his front leg. I'm thinking he'll perk up after that. Be back to normal."

"That's great, honey," he said. "I'm going to be here late tonight. Are you going to be home for dinner or should we just do our own thing?"

My emotions were a mix of anger and relief that he wasn't more upset about Bear. I was angry that he had no trouble with me organizing the whole thing at one of the busiest points of my professional career. But once more, his job was taking prece-dence over mine. Plus, how could he not be concerned about Bear's cyst? Not that I thought, *or mine*. No. My guilt over insisting we bring the dogs was top of mind. Mercifully, Bear's tumor turned out to be benign, and I put the whole thing behind me.

———

"I want to show you something," Geoff said one Friday morning, as he brought a second cup of coffee to me, still in bed. "Get your bathing suit on."

Friday morning was my one reliably work-free time slot every week, and it confounded me every single time it came along. Because of religious observances on Friday, the work week ran Sunday to Thursday. But Friday mornings in Qatar were no substitute for Saturday. Nothing was open on Friday mornings. Not even grocery stores. The week's *rush rush rush* came to a grinding halt. You couldn't run errands. Nothing. Businesses began to open by the evening, at which point the traffic jams limited what was physically possible to accomplish. By the time Saturday rolled around, I always had this impossibly long list of things to do, which was never done before work began again on Sunday morning. The puddle of anxiety never dissipated; it was the opposite of restful.

After I changed, Geoff called me out to the driveway, where he was loading up the boys and a picnic— stuffed grape leaves, fizzy water, hummus, some lamb kebabs and a little grill and charcoal. Wow.

"We're going to the beach," he announced proudly.

With Geoff working full-time we'd finally caved and gotten a second vehicle, a used Jeep. Exactly what we needed for excursions like this.

Doha's five-star hotels (and the five-star beaches attached) dotted the Corniche, but that left plenty of empty coast. On weekends, residents would head for the remaining unrestricted shoreline, toting kids, dogs and yes, even beer. Very subtly, of course. Even Qataris could be found here, generally ripping along the sand in their Land Cruisers. It was another world. I loved it. Even if we didn't have a picnic, we started making a point of taking the boys to the beach at least once a week to run around.

In my mind's eye I pictured us — once the Grand Opening was over — inviting friends and having picnics. Back home in Pittsburgh, our dining room was rounded by a bay window, making it perfect for our enormous round table. On weekends we'd spend the day cooking together, then enjoy dinner parties late into the nights. This wouldn't be that exactly, but it would be something. Bringing the dogs had made everything better.

DOHA, QATAR
March 2005

The big boss, Robbie (another woman I worked for with a man's name), was flying in from Pittsburgh to help me with the final stages of preparation for the event. Robbie was in charge of development for the university, which made her Kyle's boss. Except that Kyle had been mysteriously fired. This, and the fact that marketing people were often unceremoniously dumped in the wake of Grand Opening events on campus, had my already frayed nerves a-jangle. Then the unthinkable happened.

In the hours before Robbie's arrival I went to Mega Mart to stock up; I'd be way too busy to grocery shop in the coming days. I was unloading the car as Little Bear and Grandpa pranced around me in the kitchen. Bear's recovery had been dramatic. I shut the door behind me after bringing in the second load, but as I finished filling the refrigerator I noticed Bear was gone.

"Geoff," I called upstairs, where we'd made a little office area. "Do you have Bear up there?"

"No," he called back.

Oh my God.

I looked out back, no Bear. Then rushed to the front door. "Little Bear!" I cried. "Geoff, get down here. I can't find Little Bear."

We split the compound, walking to opposite ends of the rectangle. It took only a few minutes to realize Little Bear was no longer on it.

I lost the dog.

We got in the Jeep and began to drive in widening circles around Valley Rose, crossing roads at perpendicular angles, four-wheeling it through the desert, and nosing through construction sites. All the while I kept thinking Little Bear would be waiting for us when we got back home, that maybe one of us should be there since it had likely been the guards who shooed him away in the first place. They certainly steered clear whenever we walked the boys around the grounds, staring wide-eyed from afar.

"I have to go to work," I finally said. Geoff drove me back to the compound so I could meet Robbie while he continued the search.

I didn't mention to Robbie that Little Bear had gone missing. I was certain he'd be home with Geoff when I got back. He was not.

We drove on, late into the evening, silently looking. Getting out and stopping when we'd see a pair of silver eyes reflected in our headlights. I was amazed at the number of stray dogs that did seem to live in Qatar. There was no natural source of food or water. For a house pet like Little Bear, accustomed as he was to gentle hands offering scraps of cheese, finding sustenance would be a near insurmountable challenge. Then there was thirst, and last, but not least, the threat of Qataris on a tear. Finally we called it quits for the night, but I wasn't done looking.

Of course I had to work the next day, but I remained hopeful. Though the kind of animal cruelty that had kept us from bringing the dogs over in the first place was still widespread, the sheer numbers of incoming expats had begun to change the game. An animal shelter had gone up, and there were two vets in town. I'd seen "missing dog" posters at the grocery store, and even heard success stories. So I was incredibly frustrated when I got home the next day to learn that Geoff had failed to produce such a flier. At a time when speed counted, he slowed down.

That night we drove around again, also in silence. When we got home I made a bulletin with Little Bear's picture, sending it via email to the Education City community. Hope stirred the following day when Geoff took the flier to guards at nearby compounds before the nightly drive, less so for finding the dog than for Geoff. He was lost to me in his grief. I tried to remain hopeful, but it was getting harder. Any dog-friendly expat would know about Bear by this point, so his only chance was if a less-than-dog-friendly expat had kept him for bait in a dog fight. This was another sad reality for dogs in Qatar. I hoped the reward we offered — a thousand Riyals — would be enough to get him back but not incentivize dognapping. I was crazed with guilt and afraid that Geoff couldn't handle taking the calls, so, despite the fact that my big event was now mere days away I used my cell number. This was not my smartest moment. The calls flooded in.

One call: "Good dog. Very skinny, no?" No. But maybe he'd lost a lot of weight. It had been a week.

And another: "Short hair? Brown?" Not how I'd describe

him, but then, I couldn't even begin to describe him in whatever this guy's native language was.

And: "Yes. Dog. Come now."

The urgency behind these calls was, of course, that the compound guards ringing me up — it was always guards, not once did I hear from a fellow expat — wouldn't touch a dog. So off I'd race, in between trying to pull off the Grand Opening.

The night before the big shindig, a group of us sat stuffing gift bags — me, the HR Director, the Associate Dean, Robbie and several other high-ranking members of the Pittsburgh team who'd flown in a few days ahead of the event.

"Where's Farah?" Cindy the office manager asked pointedly. That I didn't have an answer made it feel painfully obvious that I couldn't manage the one person I had working for me. I was embarrassed that my higher ups were helping, but not my assistant. When Farah harrumphed in, an hour or so later, she looked around the room without taking a seat.

"I'm just not, I just can't..." she began, shaking her head and then leaving.

"You have to get rid of her," Cindy leaned in and said. She'd switched out of the general admin pool and into a job in HR, suddenly making her an expert on all things related to personnel. Not that she was wrong.

Farah had broadly hinted she wasn't interested in staying on after the event. "I couldn't afford to work here," were her actual words. Since her free-lancer's salary was higher than that of the existing position, her stance didn't leave much room to negotiate. Nor did I bother asking Mohamed. Her delegation skills, genius though they were, meant she was the wrong person for the job. Long after the gala, the menial tasks of stuffing press kits, offering tours, and filing would continue, but the helping hands would be gone.

My mobile rang.

"She is tall dog?" he said.

Not again.

I was going to blow this one off but Robbie wouldn't hear of it. By now I'd told her about the dog, and so discovered she was an avid dog-lover herself.

"Maybe it is him," she said, pushing her bag aside and slamming the table for emphasis. "You have to go!"

Leaving the gift bag assembly behind compounded the guilt I was mired in, but I felt I had no choice. I sped toward yet another compound, this time to find a terrified, skin and bones creature, tattered by sores and scars and wearing a "collar" made of duct tape. She was a short-haired, sand-colored thing, with long legs, a crooked snout, and a tail that curled around on itself. She looked absolutely nothing like Little Bear, pictured in all his Rottweiler-esque glory on that poster.

She wasn't the most unlike Bear of all the dogs I'd been called to see, but she was by far the most pathetic. I didn't know what to do, only that I had to get back to work. But she would die if I left her.

Despite her terror, she was not aggressive. Surely her owner was desperately looking for her just like we were looking for Little Bear. So I did what I hoped someone would do for Bear, scooped her into the back of my car and prayed she would neither pee nor vomit. When I dropped her at Valley Rose #50, I put out food and water but left her in the yard with the a/c. It felt cruel to leave her outside but who knew what disease she might be carrying? I was damn sure going to keep her separate from Grandpa. God forbid something should happen to him, too.

And then I hurried back to the office. I'd arrange a vet visit later.

The event spilled over three days. We held a symposium. Meetings with corporate and government leaders. And, of course, the gathering in the tent.

The highly scripted affair included students from the main campus, speeches from our president and Her Highness, a 3-dimensional hologram of the new building, and the pièce de resistance, a narrative film about the achievements of Carnegie Mellon graduates and professors. It went off without a hitch. Kyle's fingerprint, if not her presence, was all over the evening, and I looked forward to giving her credit when the kudos started coming my way.

The following day I ran into a colleague from Weill Cornell at the mall, and she congratulated me. "All of Doha is talking about it," she said. This woman was Syrian, in other words part of Qatar's Arab community, and this was exactly what we'd hoped to achieve. I felt a moment of personal and professional triumph, one I would hold onto in the face of the criticisms that were about to fly at me.

But that was yet to come. Just then I had a spare dog to deal with.

No one came forward to claim the dog. I couldn't just leave her outside in the heat, but if she was going to go near Grandpa she needed a thorough exam.

"Aw, yeah, she's a beaut," Troy said. "A racer for sure. Saluki.

Can you believe they turn these marvelous animals out?"

That's when I knew. There was no family looking for this dog. This was our dog. I wasn't sure how Geoff, still tormented by the loss of Little Bear, was going to take the news.

"She's a lady dog," he said. He liked his boys.

But another dog was good for Grandpa. Without the anchor of Little Bear, he'd chewed up our wedding pictures and was making a good dent on the couch.

And maybe another dog would be good for us, too, making less evident the missing presence of our Bear. I missed him terribly, but there was no room for me to grieve. I needed to be strong for Geoff. I feared the depths to which he might sink; depression ran in his family. Both his father and maternal grandfather had committed suicide. I refused to lose him to sorrow. Particularly sorrow I'd caused.

———

Once we got the green light from the vet, we introduced the kids — our dogs weren't "the boys" anymore. Those first days our new addition mostly stayed glued to the corner and moaned, long high wails that managed not to sound sad. I feared she might be dumb as a box of rocks, her head was quite small after all. Then I realized what she was trying to tell me — she'd never been inside a house before. She had no idea what to make of the lack of sky overhead. Even in a kennel she would have seen the sun.

To acclimate her to being indoors I started moving her bed and food from the kitchen, foot by foot, into the center of the house. She caught on quickly, and in no time we had her setup back to normal. Maybe she wasn't so stupid after all. Then, one day at the beach, another expat confirmed it; she was walking with her own saluki.

"These dogs are incredibly smart. And loyal," she told us. "Every one is a gift from God." A dental hygienist, she encouraged us to visit her at work. "I'll give you a discount on a cleaning!"

She warned that salukis needed to be the top dog. So far, as the four-legged creatures went, that was not a problem. Grandpa, bow-legged and compromised from the start of his life, was the perennial underdog. Geoff was the one who had to relent. When at last he named her — Ms. Sophie "Ma Barker" Masloff, after the Jewish former mayor of Pittsburgh, and in deference to her early barking, though it had subsided almost entirely — I exhaled. Even if nothing would ever be the same again, order of a sort was restored. We never saw Little Bear again.

My date with Nathan arrived.

On the big day I was afraid, and not — people had operations at Hamad every day. They had all the latest equipment. At least it wasn't Ramadan. (How did they handle that, doctors and anesthesiologists and nurses unable to eat or drink all day? Was there a special provision for these occupations? I knew there was for pilots.)

Other than the abundance of covered women— clientele and staff, no men were allowed — it was pretty much like any hospital. A place I never wanted to be.

Cindy took me. She'd had her daughter at Hamad and knew the ropes. She stayed beside me while I waited for surgery and made me laugh.

"When Farah was leaving she made the driver carry her boxes out," she giggled. "And then she went to HR and complained that you were firing her."

Cindy's lack of confidentiality was appalling and appealing, like a second dessert. But when it came to being at the hospital, she was a godsend. She even offered to stay and help me out of post-op, but that seemed unnecessary. Nathan had assured me the operation was minor. I'd miss work Thursday but could go back at it by Sunday. Luckily, Cindy ignored me.

She was back at Hamad before I came out of anesthesia, and helped me out to Geoff and our waiting car. I don't know how I would've made it without her. Geoff took me home and I fell back asleep, and everybody went back to work.

When I woke up, I suspected the good doc had been more than a tad optimistic in sending me home with only aspirin. Had he thought I'd want to regain a sober state as quickly as possible on leaving the hospital? The pain intensified over the next few hours. It was nearing midnight when Geoff took me back to Hamad, driving right up to the automatic ER door. Inside was deserted.

While my husband propped me upright, I begged in as many languages as I could and that might apply — Arabic, French, English — but the gatekeepers at Hamad wouldn't budge. Geoff was not allowed to accompany me. I limped alone into their deserted emergency room while he watched from the other side.

Despite knowing Hamad was sex-segregated, I was stunned they barred my husband from helping me across the threshold for crisis care. I lay writhing on a gurney in an empty cubby, waiting for the doctor-on-call to show up, thinking I'd reached the lowest, loneliest point yet in Doha. Then, for the second time in less than a year, I began to vomit uncontrollably.

I have no recollection of what the doctor finally gave me, only that I had to make my way solo back out of the ER. For the next week I plopped myself on the couch. A bright spot was a visit from Cindy, who came by one day with lunch.

"Where's Geoff?" she asked.

At work, I told her, without admitting to my resentment. I wasn't sure why Geoff wasn't coming home or checking up on me, but I felt very alone. Had he been shaken to see me so physically wrecked? Was he a shitty caregiver? Was I a shitty patient? Maybe we shouldn't have kids, after all. If this was the pain of having a cyst removed, I could hardly imagine expulsing a small life form.

In the end, I missed ten days of work.

DOHA, QATAR
April 2005

When I went to Nathan's office for the follow-up, he snuck Geoff in.

"I've some good news and some bad news for you," he began.

By all means, the good news.

"We've figured out what's wrong with you."

This is the good news? I didn't know something was wrong with me.

"The bad news is, you won't be getting your period anymore."

That's the bad news?

"These symptoms you've been having..."

I've been having symptoms?

"The sweating, the inability to sleep, the mood swings, the cessation of your menstrual cycle... you're in menopause."

I'm what? But... how is that possible? I'm thirty-eight years old.

"Many factors can contribute," he started. "Genetics and stress and blah, blah-blah blah, blah blah blah blah blah..."

But I wasn't hearing a word he was saying. I was overwhelmed. With relief!

I wasn't losing my mind after all. There were actions I could take to feel better.

A few years earlier I'd done an interview with fitness guru Kathy Smith, who'd just written a book about peri-menopause, the years prior to menopause. She'd recommended acupuncture and yoga and various supplements. Maybe I'd start sleeping through the night; I could sense my life was about to improve.

Which isn't to say the news didn't bring its own stress. Geoff and I shuffled out of Nathan's office to the car, where I was lost in thought the whole way home.

"The change of life is not seen so much as a change but an end," Smith had also said. "The end of femininity, the end of being a woman."

Absolutely, I'd agreed when I read that line. Jesus. I had to be in perimenopause at the time.

So, I wasn't a woman anymore? I didn't feel any different. It's like, when someone asks you how old you are and you have to really think about it. The outside may be changing, but the inside doesn't so much.

Nonetheless, on that ride home, I was certain I'd become less attractive to my husband. Who would want a non-woman? As soon as we walked in the door, I screwed up all my courage.

"Geoff, if you even think you're gonna want to have children, that you're just gonna leave me at some point, then just do it now," I said. "Because the longer you wait, the worse it will be for me."

he pulled me close and said, "Baby, I didn't marry you for your ability to reproduce."

I never wanted anything more than to be loved like that.

TWELVE
AIM LOW

Insha'Allah:
"God willing." Used at least once in every sentence: e.g.,
"Lunch is at noon, *Insha'Allah*," or "Yes, I can meet your dead-
line, *Insha'Allah*."

Aim Low:
My version of *Insha' Allah;* a life-saving stance I discovered
through Owen Wilson and Ben Stiller. Thanks, guys.

DOHA, QATAR
March 2005

"DID YOU HEAR THAT noise?" came Michelle
over the phone. Not even a hello. Plus it was after
10 p.m. on a school night. Not the standard
behavior of my workaholic friend.

"What noise?"

"Maybe not a noise exactly," she said. "My windows shook."

"It's nothing," I said. "Go to bed. That's where I'm headed."

I'd just returned from seeing a colleague perform in

Mozart's Ave Verum with Doha's all-Western expatriate chorus. Big night of culture in Doha, and my first venture out since my surgery. Geoff had stayed home to hang out with Robert. Choral music wouldn't have been my pick either, but since the Grand Opening I'd begun to rearrange my priorities, per the erstwhile Kyle.

After the big event I'd tracked her down at home to let her know how well the event had gone and thank her.

"Well congratulations," she'd said. "But you better watch yourself. You've got some damage control to do."

Huh?

She wouldn't say how she had this information, but I was well of the tenuous relationship I had with my colleagues. I am horrible at office politics. I don't care about your weekend, and please do not explain the plot of your favorite half-hour sitcom to me over 45 highjacked minutes at my desk side. And I never need to hear about your dream. On top of that, this was Qatar. Language and irony barriers were in full effect making these interactions even more dull. Add to that the hormonal war that had been raging inside (and unbeknownst) to me. In general I had to suppress my churlish way, but the menopause made staying on top of that another full-time job I didn't have the time for. I figured that doing a good job would win the day.

"I used to make the same mistake," Kyle said. "Take it from me, if you have to choose between getting the job done and building the relationship, pick the relationship every time."

At the time it had been a huge blow, so I was lucky when, during my post-operative recuperation period on the couch, HBO was screening Dodgeball. I got to watch it about a hundred times. This is the way the God of my understanding works in my life, pretty much putting the clues right under my nose. There it was, their team motto, my solution: "Aim low!"

And so it had been that on that particular day, rather than

work until I had to go home and rest, I cut out early to support my co-worker who was performing in the show, and hang out with another colleague while I was at it. A long day any way you looked at it, now all I wanted was to call it a night. Fortunately, Michelle was better connected to the Doha grapevine than I.

Not ten minutes later she called back to tell me that, according to her source at CENTCOM — the U.S.'s largest offshore military base, right there in Doha — a man had driven his dynamite-laden car into the lobby of the Doha Players Theatre, one roundabout away from where I'd been. At that theater, another all-Western expatriate group had been performing Shakespeare's "Twelfth Night." Besides himself, the bomber killed the theater director, who'd run to the lobby on hearing the impact. The people attending the play were a safe-ish distance from the bomb.

Learning the details I wondered if the bomber had ever been to a play and so didn't grasp the concept of intermission. Or layout.

"Turn on your TV," Michelle said. "The Minister of the Interior is on. You won't believe what he's saying."

"I won't understand what he's saying," I said. "And since when do you understand Arabic?"

"I don't, I'm just looking for signs he's lying," she said. "My friend at CENTCOM tells me he's spreading the story that the explosion came from a gas leak."

Lying couldn't be good.

I called Geoff and asked him to come home immediately. Did we need to pack? Were there going to be riots in the streets? Should we go to the embassy? What about work?

Mohamed called, activating the crisis communications plan we'd set up to get a handle on everyone's whereabouts, staff and students alike. Senior staff was to report to work the following day, but no one else. And no students.

Despite that I'd written the crisis communication plan, I didn't want to go in the following day. What if there was more violence? If these terrorists were protesting the Westernization of Qatar, wouldn't campus be the perfect target? or would they start coming for compounds like they had in Saudi Arabia?

Meanwhile, Geoff and I flew to the internet, where I quickly realized how out of touch I'd become with the outside world. This was disturbing on many levels, not the least of which was the fact that I looked at Qatar's five daily newspapers as part of my job. Light as they were on content, it was all I could do to keep up. Swept up in reports of visiting dignitaries and Qatari bigwigs, I'd neglected to keep track of our "peace-keeping" activities in Iraq.

It was March, our wedding anniversary month and once again, Al Qaida remembered Bush's declaration that we'd won. On this year's call to arms, Qatar — because of its friendly relations with the U.S. — topped the list. Of course none of this had made the family newsletters that passed as Doha's dailies, but the information wasn't exactly hard to find. Except for one thing. In different parts of the world the news is reported so differently, you can barely tell it's the same news. Take for instance, news of the bombing itself.

Local press described the bomber as a lone operative using a "crudely fashioned" weapon. They even characterized the play-going audience — which I knew to be entirely Western— as "mostly Asian." Because violence against Westerners was bad for business?

The BBC, reporting from Qatar, noted that of the 12 people sent to the hospital, six were nationals. This may have been the case, but not because they were at the play. They would have been locals who'd rushed to the scene to help, then found themselves overcome by smoke.

As for the so-called mouthpiece of terrorism — Al Jazeera —

they said little, a treatment I'd come to expect. On my first tour of the station I'd asked my guide about the possibility of covering Education City. She looked at me over her niqab, the scarf that covers the face, and said in a distinctly British accent, "We've a fairly strict policy of not reporting on Qatar."

Outside the country reports were more damning, indicating the attack showed signs of sophisticated activity by a terrorist cell. The truth was probably somewhere more in the middle.

Al Qaida is no CIA; in fact, the CIA isn't really the CIA, either. Not the way it's portrayed in film, but that's another rant. Al Qaida mostly functions like a social network, sparking activity with pronouncements that tap into existing rage. That year's fatwah comprised a laundry list of countries. Whoever issued it did not have authority over the people in the various countries who carried out attacks; that guy was probably as surprised as we were when it happened. They didn't even claim the incident for weeks.

Though the bombing rocked Doha, it barely registered beyond a single news cycle worldwide. Far more emphasis was placed on other strikes of the day, specifically bombings in Kirkuk (which left four police dead) and Beirut (eight wounded). When I called my parents to tell them we were OK, it was the first they'd heard of it.

"That's good, honey," Mom said. "You're father's finally having that hernia operation."

This, from a woman who'd been hysterical at the thought of my moving to the Middle East and its hotbed of terrorism? Part of me wanted her to beg me to come home, but why would she? I'd also become good at sanitizing news. I hadn't mentioned the cyst till after the surgery. And like that I saw my own hypocrisy.

Prior to the bombing, I'd looked down on the Qatari way of doing things, what I viewed to be a poor work ethic. Though I couldn't help but wonder what would the country look like if it was my family, flooded with untold wealth and trying to run the show. Beyond mere secret keeping, I could imagine pettiness aplenty. "Dad, I am so not opening the airport till you take cousin Steve off the Ministry of Culture. That man has no taste!" In fact, the Qataris were masters at diplomacy, which is a fancy word for always getting their way.

Then there were the actual people I knew, like my colleague Jameel.

Her look of stoic disbelief was one I saw in many nationals' faces in the days and weeks following the attack. A stunning young woman, Jameel had married into the ruling family, which made her a sheikha by marriage. Prior to the bombing, Jameel's attendance at work was sporadic. Thanks to generous government-supplied allowances (amounts that varied according to the importance of your family), Qataris were better described as holding posts rather than having jobs.

After the bombing, however, Jameel became a regular fixture, though I didn't realize this actually had anything to do with the bombing until we got to talking after a meeting one day. I asked about her family, pretty much the only polite topic you could broach with a Qatari female.

"Hamdulilah," she said. Praise God. Or, we're all good.

She returned the family question volley, which was weird since she'd just been in the meeting with my whole family, but I stayed with it a moment— "Geoff's great. He's just gotten certified to scuba dive and I'm really looking forward to going on a trip." — before moving in for the kill. "It's so nice to be seeing so much more of you lately. Did you change jobs?"

She smiled. "Oh no, I am here for my family." Which threw me for a second. Jameel certainly didn't need the money, and with five children, I don't know how she managed to even hold a post. Then there were so many weddings and babies and cousins... even the extended family needed constant attention.

"My husband, he doesn't like it," Jameel said. "But it is for my father to decide. We still cannot believe what has happened. It is hard, my youngest has not started school yet. But this is our home. We want everyone to know it is safe to be here."

And then I understood; work was simply one of many family obligations. Side note, it was her father who'd decided. All children take their father's names and never change them; you could follow a family tree right on down the line through the bins (son of) and ibns (daughter of). Thus a father can have more sway than a husband; the eldest male guardian is in charge.

I was struck by her effort. The Qatari notion of home was as much about blood relatives as it was about place. Always courteous and generous to a fault, there was nonetheless a wall. *It must be so strange to grow up as a significant minority in your own country*, I thought. No wonder they were so private.

───────

About a week after the bombing, I was driving home from work when I got a call from Geoff.

"I won't be home till later, I have to work," he said. "You should go to that schwarma place you love and get a sandwich."

I did love that shwarma place. You drove up, honked, ordered, and then waited interminably. After some time, however, they brought out a salad and a carved chicken sandwich, all for like two bucks. I ordered two. So decadent.

Miles Davis' "Some Kind of Blue" interrupted my thoughts. Michelle's ring tone.

"Great news!" she said. "I got a bonus equal to two months' pay. For the bombing. We're going to Bali!"

All I'd gotten in the wake of the bombing was more trouble. A reporter from Pittsburgh had called wanting to know if everyone was OK. I said yes, though we'd not yet accounted for all our students. The locals were not the targets nor whom he was asking about, and I knew none of them would have been on our commuter campus at that time. Thankfully, everyone was OK. I got a deserved scolding anyway, but then the conversation turned into a larger discussion about me.

"We're concerned with how you're getting along at work," Chuck had said in a surprise performance review.

I replied with a spiritual axiom I do deeply believe — "other people's opinion of me is none of my business." But this was a terrible response. Though I wasn't fired that moment, I felt it could happen at any time.

"I hate my job," I told Michelle as I drove home.

"You need to call that therapist you told me about," she said. "Then call me back."

A few months earlier a woman had come to the school and given a presentation on culture shock. "Aw, yeah," she'd said, in all her Kiwi glory, "it's awful hee-yah."

I'd found her no-nonsense style compelling, but didn't make an appointment. No time, and furthermore, I couldn't have my neighbors and colleagues see my car in front of a therapist's villa. As if that would be their first clue I needed therapy.

But now that I was all "aim low!" I figured, *Why the hell not?* I was wondering where I might've stashed her number when I realized I'd passed a roundabout I'd needed to turn on. Where had it gone?

When I doubled back I realized my so-called "pile of rubble" roundabout had been transformed, planted over with palm trees. I actually pulled over. How am I supposed to maintain anything like serenity when everything around me is in the effervescent frenzy to become something else? Little did I know, this was Zen boot camp.

Fuck dinner, I needed a saloon. I turned and headed toward my old apartment on Al Saad. Time to take the plunge.

DOHA, QATAR
July 2004

S ome people like to be opinion leaders on restaurants, the latest music or maybe films. Me? I like to know the ins and outs of all spas within a 20-mile radius of my house. It's my dream to live somewhere that I can't cover more than five miles with any kind of authority. In Doha? This whole scheme had fallen apart. No phone books, no Yelp! But after a month in the country, I needed some maintenance. There was only one place I knew to call for the gentle transformation of a spa, and that was the Ritz Carlton just down the Corniche.

"Ahh-LOOW," the woman on the other end purred. "Thank you for calling the Ritz-Carlton. How may I help you today?"

I asked for the salon expecting the next line in their script, "My pleasure to connect you."

Instead I got, "Excuse me?"

I tried a few times before another approach came to me. "Where they give massages. Manicures? Pedicures?"

"Oh," she said. "You mean the saloon."

Yes, neither of us was able to make that linguistic leap. But that's when I realized, the reason I'd not seen salons anywhere was because they'd been hiding in the *saloons* I'd seen on every corner — Saloon of Hearts, Al Diyar, Modern Unisex (really?). The Ritz could take me; I could always check out the other options later.

It's true, going into this mani/pedi, my expectations were unusually high — I'd never paid so much for a service I considered upkeep. Right away, the chair I was supposed to sit in put me off — a massaging fingers special, the seat felt like a bed of cement rocks pummeling my backside, even when the "fingers" weren't in motion. Once I was seated, the nail technician slurped into the room toting a plastic tub of soapy water into which she dunked my feet without speaking a word. The water was tepid.

Pulling out another plastic basket, she proffered seven or eight shades of brownish red nail color straight from 1989. I looked at her in disbelief, but by this time I'd gleaned that her English wasn't so good. I pointed at clear. Out came the cuticle scissors. I tried to ask her not to cut my cuticles. She smiled and nodded and began to snip away at my nail beds. Maybe if I didn't fight it, things would start to pick up. I laid back and closed my eyes until I felt her struggling to smear the polish on my nails. The polish had coagulated in the bottle.

Sitting up, I scanned the implements. Nothing looked clean. This was not long after singer/dancer/reality TV star Paula Abdul had made headlines with her personal story of fungal nail tragedy. Though I'd never before stopped a manicure in process, I feared an imminent and wicked case of nail funk.

"Stop, please." I said. "Stop."

I shifted in my chair, attempting to rise. She pushed me down.

"No, ma'am, please, no!" she cried.

Thinking she feared losing out, I fished for a tip but that did not appease her. I managed to stand but she'd taken my shoes. Finally, I left the room barefoot in search of the manager.

Breaking up with him probably took more time than it would have to endure the service, drive home, remove the polish and start over. We discussed the pros and cons of the visit. I told him they needed more variety and disinfectant. He assured me of the quality of their other offerings. "Madame, please come back for a complimentary hair styling." Was he kidding? This was a country where hands and feet were visible; hair was totally hidden. Who knew what might happen? I got my shoes and vowed to find something local, a task I wrongly presumed would come with ease, given the large numbers of saloons I'd seen.

Closer inspection revealed the corner saloons catered to Arab men. We'd drive by and I'd peek in, only to see Pakistani or Filipino gentlemen flourishing vinyl capes, lathering necks, and dousing clients with cologne. To enter one would have been an unspeakable breach.

There were a few places I noticed that specified "ladies," but these were off the main drag and, beyond the signage, hidden from view. A few times I'd tried to locate one — because again, with no phone books and no web presence for these businesses, the only way to get in was to physically get in — but I invariably lost track of where the actual business was in the maze of shops behind the strip mall.

Until now. *Aim low!*

DOHA, QATAR
April 2005

The Thai Lady saloon was right behind the apartment we'd lived in those first weeks in Qatar (long before I knew what a saloon really was). Considering the large community of expat Thais, I figured the joint was at least authentic. The décor was promising; the harsh white cement of the porch was muted by a profusion of cacti and bougainvillea. Brown and burgundy cushions lined contemporary, minimalist-style couches. Wood and glass and clean lines completed the picture. They even sold Buddha heads and incense burners, a kind of brand extension merchandising I hadn't seen in Doha.

Following that phone call with Michelle, I nosed my way over to the Thai Lady. There was, as was often the case, no wait. Immediately, I was led to a small, warm room with a straw mat on the floor and instructed, without much in the way of actual words, to undress and then re-dress in a set of vaguely Asian-looking, cotton jammies. Seemed odd to get dressed up to get a massage, but I was game. My treatment began with some heart-felt beating, a technique I've never been a fan of — I feel less like knots have been worked out, more like I've been worked over.

As our session wore on, I suspected the pounding was a way of numbing me for what was to come, a good forty minutes of getting twisted and pulled and bent into submission. I have since learned that this was, in fact, a traditional Thai massage, but at the time it felt like a massage to simply recover. As I sipped my post-treatment glass of water, the nail area caught my eye. I needed a pedicure desperately. *Maybe...*

Suddenly an employee came screeching out of the back, a band of angry Thai coming out of her mouth. She was carrying a small paper sack which held everything she'd ever get from the Thai Lady saloon. A minute later, the woman who'd checked me in returned to the counter. I had to ask what happened.

"She was a problem," the counter woman told me. "It's nothing, she's gone."

A few moments later, a Western expat emerged. Apparently she'd been getting an unsatisfactory facial and was refusing to pay. The manager promised her a better experience the next time she returned. She snorted something about never coming back because there were too many other places. *Where?* I desperately wanted to ask, but she was gone, taking her tempest with her.

Then I recalled the Ritz, and realized why my nail tech had been so upset. She'd probably lost her job. Getting fired could ruin her chances of finding work in any GCC country, crushing the dreams of the family back home she was most likely supporting on her $200 monthly allowance. No doubt that family had worked for years to afford to take on the debt to send her overseas and wait on overprivileged expats like me.

I wanted to talk about the fact that I couldn't have children. All the time. But since our first conversation, we'd found nothing more to say. If I brought it up Geoff changed the subject.

"I saw you playing with the neighbor's son out by the pool," I'd start. "It made me nervous about thinking you'd want kids."

"I don't even remember talking to him," he'd say. "Should we have Brussels sprouts or asparagus with dinner?"

My sense was that he didn't want me dragging on the issue indefinitely, so I better get over it. Why complain endlessly about a problem for which there was no solution? It would be years before I'd see Meryl Streep play the childless Julia Child in *Julie & Julia*, and the gentle way her husband, without over-much ado, would hold her hand or pat her back when the sight of children made her sad. *Could I have found a way to ask for that? Should I have?*

I'd even broken code and asked my mother about her experience with menopause. Would I ever sleep through the night again? How long would the hot flashes go on? What about other health issues? Bone loss?

"I was too busy to notice," she said. "I don't remember."

Then there were the things I wanted to discuss with friends, namely sex. Would my interest plummet? Would I dry up?

Sadly "my We" was of little help. We (minus me) were a good decade away from even thinking about perimenopause. I'd try to talk to them about how I felt physically and emotionally, but there was a reluctance to engage. They'd listen over the phone, but no one ever took the conversation further. They certainly never brought the topic up. I got the feeling that menopause was such a horror show, nobody wanted to talk about it. Even the word needed to be whispered. Perhaps my friends had the same fears I did, and none of us had any answers. I wanted to tell them that menopause wasn't a disease they were going to catch from me, though if we were lucky, it was something we'd all experience. Insha'Allah. But nobody wanted to hear that.

Victoria and I were the same age. I doubted she'd be much more helpful than my friends, but as a therapist, she was being paid to listen to me vent. When my trusted comfort fall-back — the saloon — failed to fix me, I'd found her number and made an appointment. It turned out that Victoria was also the vet's wife. I could pretend I was there for the dogs, I thought as she answered the door, two tow-headed children running around behind her.

"Office is at the side," she said, pointing to my left, where the "maid's room" was in my identical villa. "Be there in a sec."

She didn't have live-in help? This would have made her the only person I knew in town who had children but didn't have live-in help. I warmed to her instantly. *Oh please, oh please, let this be a help.*

Victoria leaned forward as I briefed her on the basics. That I'd taken a job I hated to give my husband the kind of opportunity I would've loved to have. I also told her I was a recovered alcoholic. This might seem like a normal admission to make to your doctor, but it was a fact I'd often been inclined to omit. By rights, alcoholism is not a sympathetic illness, and experiences like I'd had with Nathan, where you're treated differently because of it, weren't experiences I was eager to repeat. But I felt the need to tell on myself, to be accountable to someone. Not only to hedge my bets, but because I imagined Victoria might have clients who might be having trouble with drinking. I had met zero people who were new to recovery in Doha, and previously this had been a big part of my own path. I told her she could give out my number.

"I don't drink either," Victoria said. "Never liked it. I prefer to remember everything."

My natural tendency is to disregard anything a non-alcoholic says about alcoholism, but her remark didn't sound judgmental, thus it didn't spark my judgment in return. At last we ventured to The Change.

"God I hate that phrase," I said.

"Me too," Victoria laughed. "But you'll want to get on Vitamin E right away. It's the same thing as evening primrose oil, only less expensive."

She even told me where to get it.

"Here," she said, pushing a number at me. "This guy will get you sorted."

It was an acupuncturist. How was she such a fount of information? These two had been in the country for less time than I had.

"Most of my clientele are the housewives of men who can't quite bring themselves to retire," she said, sitting back and adjusting her sleeves. I admired her pulled together business casual look. "They're *all* in various stages of menopause."

I told her about Kathy Smith. How I feared losing interest in sex. Drying up.

"Well have you?" she asked.

In fact, quite the opposite.

"Enjoy that then," she said. "How do you feel about not having kids? Did you want them?"

Her matter of fact style made it easier for me to examine my thoughts without drama. "I've never been very interested in having my own children," I said. "But I've wanted to have my husband's children almost since we met. I look at him and think, the world should have more people in it just like him."

"But you didn't have kids and you've been married now, what, three years?"

"We didn't want to rush."

"At 22 that's a rush. At 35 you're kind of postponing."

"My marriage has always been more important to me than kids."

"Perfect," she smiled, sitting back in her chair. "Now, I want you to think of the absolute worst thing that could happen. Global devastation, floods, plague, famine world-wide."

"Mmmkay."

"Now think of the absolute best day possible. World peace reigns, everyone's fed, all diseases cured. Etcetera."

"Uh-huh."

"Where does not having children lie on that scale?" she asked. In that light I gave it about a one.

"I'm not trying to get you to ignore the very complex feelings we have around womanhood and fertility. If you try to avoid feelings, they just fester," she said. "But the perspective helps, and it's a technique you can use on other crises. For now we're out of time. We'll talk about it more next week."

I liked this Victoria.

THIRTEEN
MUSCAT LOVE

Muscat:
Capital of Oman; I was fortunate to tour the Middle East with
my colleagues as part of our student-recruiting efforts.

Muscat Love:
Play on "Muskrat Love," the title of a wildly popular 1976 song
by Captain and Tennille about furry critters doing it.

KUWAIT CITY, KUWAIT
September 2004

DESPITE THAT THE universities at Education City
were entirely separate entities — each had its own
building, curricula, and even individual school
nurses — before our school's big Grand Opening event, we all
banded together for a two-week promotional tour of the Middle
East. This was not effective for recruiting students in the least,
but it was a crash course on the region for me.

Our first trip was to Kuwait. I asked Fawzi, the admissions
counselor, to translate a survey someone had filled out in

Arabic. It didn't bode well for the prospect, since our campus delivered education exclusively in English, but I was curious to know what the survey said.

Fawzi looked at the paper, nodded and smiled. "He writes he would not come to Education City if we paid him. Kuwaitis and Qataris are like the Aggies and the Longhorns."

Fawzi, a graduate of Texas A&M in actual Texas, must've been speaking of some college rivalry.

Why, then, had we gone to Kuwait? Surely the ruling family knew of this enmity before greenlighting a student recruitment fair in Kuwait. Sending a large group to travel in style would have zero return on investment. Was it a way of bragging to their distant relatives about what they were doing with all their money?

Genius. And at least I did learn not to spend ad dollars in Kuwait. Not yet anyway.

CAIRO, Egypt
September 2004

When we hit Cairo I finally asked Fawzi, who I knew to be Yemeni, why he dressed as he did. In his bright white thobe — Mont Blanc pen tucked into the front pocket, white gold watch (yellow gold being haram for men), and Tamima-brand sandals— Fawzi looked more Qatari than most Qataris. Yemenis, on the other hand, usually (though not in *every* region of Yemen) wore a white calf-length shirt with a Western-style coat and jambiyya, a ceremonial dagger. Yes, they sported swords in public.

Fawzi smiled and adjusted his ghuttra, the headscarf, and proudly relayed, "I am a Qatari citizen."

This confused me. I understood he was from Yemen. Naturalized citizens were practically unheard of in Qatar.

"My family is from Yemen, yes," he said. "In fact, I am related to Mohamed."

Jesus God, I thought. *Better not piss this one off on top of Fadhel.*

"But my parents were born in Qatar."

Plenty of people's parents were born in Qatar, that didn't make them citizens. I knew of two people who'd been given citizenship: one a longtime employee of Sheikha Mozah, the other a famous soccer player.

"Oh, but we were," Fawzi said. "I am not anymore. When I was young, in college, I said some things. My citizenship was revoked."

Things? What things?

"Things the ruling family did not like."

I pressed further, dying to know, LIKE WHAT?

"I don't say such things anymore," he smiled. Helas, subject. Closed. (Or close.)

"And now," he said, growing quite animated, "I work every day to regain it. Do you know?" he went on, grabbing a calculator that was on the table. "I should be getting free housing, free utilities, a social allowance?"

As he spoke his fingers stabbed at the keys. By his estimation he was out millions of Riyals in allowance and other perks, like paid-for electricity bills. No wonder they're so choosy about who can become a citizen.

MUSCAT, OMAN
April 2005

After the suicide bomber struck Doha, we had another recruiting trip scheduled to Oman. We considered cancelling, but in the end we forged ahead. We couldn't let the terrorists win. Well, I could've. But off I went, terrified of losing my job.

I'd loved the previous trips. No matter where we went, someone in our group was a local. That meant I got to experience local culture. In Syria we'd gone to an underground (literally under the earth) restaurant; in Cairo it had been an uber trendy shisha parlor; and in Jordan we'd traipsed around a massive Christian area I'd never heard of before called Mt. Nebo. I wasn't sure what might be in store in Oman, but my fear of attack was mitigated by my joy at getting out of Qatar.

It occurred to me, and not for the first time, there was something wrong with living in a country where my main recreational activity was planning to leave. Though I'd grown more ambivalent about actually moving. Between the supplements, the acupuncture and the yoga, I was finally sleeping through the night again. With the Grand Opening over and done, my general mental state had dramatically improved. Geoff and I had decided to table discussion of whether we should bail on my employment contract till June, which would be my one year anniversary.

On the short flight between Qatar and Oman, I was delighted when Joe, the head of admissions for Texas A&M, changed seats to sit beside me. He was a superb traveling companion.

Perpetually clad in a well-cut suit, he'd been everywhere and always had a tip.

"Alice and I stayed at the Chedi the last time we were in Muscat," he said, throwing back his tie before digging into his freshly prepared eggs. (Oh, how I miss the flying living room that was Qatar Airways business class.) "When the place first opened, did you know the locals thought it wasn't finished? That's how clean and modern the lines are. Just spectacular."

He told me that he and his wife had visited the wadis, Oman's river valleys.

"They're dry now," he said. "Which means the visibility is perfect for scuba diving. Alice is coming on Thursday and we're going diving."

Wait a minute. Geoff had just gotten PADI certified.

"What if we join you and make it a foursome?" I asked. "It's Geoff's birthday in a couple of weeks."

And so it was decided.

As soon as I got into my room, I was going to call Cindy back at the university and see if she'd to book a ticket to surprise Geoff with when we spoke that night. In the meantime, I had a few hours to kill before the recruitment fair kicked off, and I wanted to enjoy some down time in Muscat's Grand Hyatt. Maybe I could grab a massage before the evening ceremony kicked off the event. I was poring over their services leaflet when I realized I was the only one of our group still at the front desk. I looked around. Like all the upscale hotels I'd been to in the Gulf, the lobby featured an elephantine glass chandelier, heavy wood paneling, gold accents, and heaps of wasted space. Not a colleague to be seen.

"I'm terribly sorry ma'am," the concierge said. "We have no reservation under your name and we are fully booked. So I've arranged a room for you at Al Bustan."

Joe had filled me in on that hotel as well. Renowned for its views, Al Bustan was an old palace built into the hills of Muscat, on the other side of town. I'd be marooned.

"Didn't I see another hotel across the parking lot?" I asked.

From the look of horror on the man's face, it was clear the place was not up to the standard of the Grand Hyatt, but anything seemed better than being trapped across town. I was in the Peace Corps, buddy. I can handle a cheap hotel for a couple of nights.

"Really, it's fine," I said. "Please just book me there."

He did as I asked, then arranged a car to whisk me across the parking lot. This seemed excessive, but he was trying to be helpful and I figured it was best to let him. Plus I didn't want to sweat in my suit. As I entered the adjacent Coral Boutique hotel, just a parking lot away, it dawned on me how long it had been since my days of low-rent accommodation. The lobby featured wood and brass accents all right, only here they were shaped into a registration desk that looked like a sailing ship. There was no massive chandelier — a giant spiral staircase took up most of the lobby. To the left was a grimy-looking restaurant that emitted no smell, never a good sign. And the elevator was not working. Possibly a worse sign.

I circled the staircase to the first floor (what we Americans would call the second floor) to find my dimly lit chamber. My room offered a bed, a TV on a rickety stand and a small refrigerator. I flipped on the AC and out came a stink of stale smoke and rotten eggs. I looked around for the remote for a bit before realizing the set had knobs. When I did manage to get it turned on, the stations were all Arabic, all the time. No cable. Or internet. Except on the one computer terminal in the lobby. There was only one way to deal with this. Head over to the Hyatt for a massage. I called to book, but they didn't have any openings.

Finally, I called Joe.

"Guess where I am," I said, kind of hoping he'd offer to switch rooms when I relayed my plight. I was happy enough to take him up on his offer to come over and enjoy his room's amenities.

"Come watch a movie," he said. "I have room service..."

I laughed. He had me at movie, though I was never opposed

to a snack. I crossed the lot on my own this time, which took less time than traversing the Hyatt's enormous interior. The hallways stretched on forever before I found his room. This, too, was huge, complete with a living area, settee and dressing room. The giant TV, however, faced the bed. Only one place to watch. I hesitated a moment, but this was Joe. Everybody loved Joe. I hopped in. That's when Joe decided he wanted to take a nap. Wasn't this at odds with my movie watching?

"Go ahead, watch TV," he said. "I can sleep through anything."

Alrighty then.

I started surfing his gazillion channels — the wonder of a simple remote control! — but Joe was struggling under the sheets. He asked me to get under the covers so he could be more comfortable. That seemed a bit much, but still, I wasn't about to head back to my room; there were *hours* to go before the group met for dinner. I thought about stealing a pillow.

Duly settled, I went back to channel surfing. Then Joe yawned and stretched and rolled over and reached out. Suddenly his left arm was draped across my lap.

What the hell? Was it an eternity or five seconds later that he shifted and the hand was gone? But wait. That move so high school, I couldn't be sure it was a move. Was that a move? I froze in my seat wondering what to make of it. Maybe it was best not to make anything of it. Why isn't there anything on the TV?

I looked down at the side table to my right. *Reading Lolita in*
Tehran.

"My wife says that's good," Joe said, getting out of bed and going into the bathroom.

So now he's awake and invoking the wife. Of course that wasn't a move. How could I be so juvenile?

I turned off the TV and started to read, scooting down a bit, turning onto my side. I was barely onto the second page and the hand was back, only this time he took the side of my ass and gave it a squeeze like it was a roll of Charmin toilet paper.

I practically fell out of the bed.

"Uh, I have to go," I muttered. Up and at the door in seconds, grabbing my shoes from I don't know where but they're in my hand. Joe was right behind me but I didn't turn, didn't look, I just kept walking. Marching down those infinite corridors, my anger at Joe turning onto myself. How could I have gotten into such a stupid situation? What was I thinking? I felt dirty and disgusting and slutty. I wanted to go right home.

"There's just the one flight a day, love," Cindy told me. "What happened? Why the rush to come home."

Telling Cindy anything was a bit like handing out a press release, and I was pretty sure I wanted to keep this quiet. My plan was to tell her I'd come down with food poisoning, when the hotel room phone interrupted us. It was the concierge saying there was a man downstairs who wanted to see me. Has to be Joe. I told him I did not want to be disturbed and hung up. Then I realized where I was.

"Cindy, I have to call you back."

I got the concierge back on the phone. Yes, he had given the man my room number. I insisted on changing rooms.

No sooner had I bolted the door on an identical room down the hall than my mobile started going off. It was Joe.

I sat at the table ignoring multiple calls, smoking and wondering what to tell Cindy, when another colleague called; it was getting to be time to meet so I assumed she wanted to make arrangements.

"Things got pretty intense there." It was Joe.

Did that mean he thought I liked that. That I was complicit?

And what in the hell had he said to borrow this phone? "Mmm," is what I said.

He asked if I'd meet him for coffee.

Absolutely, I said, 15 minutes from now, your lobby bar.

Twenty minutes later I sent him a text: "I am a happily married woman. If you want to stay a happily married man, you will stay away from me." I never heard back from Joe.

By now it was time for the recruiting fair to get started, so I snuck off to an early dinner at one of the restaurants along the sea-fronting promenade. I feared seeing one of my colleagues and having to come up with an excuse for my absence, but there was no way I was eating at Coral Boutique. That restaurant looked sticky. Getting in a cab to go somewhere further away felt like asking to get in another situation where I had no control. I wolfed down my meal and rushed back to my room, took a seat at the table and resumed smoking.

I wanted to call Geoff and talk it over with him, but I was afraid of the consequences. For the first time in our married life, I decided not to tell him about something that felt monumental. *Or should I?*

That's when I called Cindy. Ostensibly it was to tell her to forget the tickets, but there was no way I could play coy. I needed someone to talk to, and despite whom she might tell, there was no denying she'd managed to find a way to live within this dichotomous society. This had not always been the case.

Cindy, the brassy Australian office manager I suspected might have a drinking problem, also happened to be married to a Muslim man. She'd told me that not long after she'd moved to Qatar, she'd been sent to jail. Her offense was swearing at a Qatari after he hit her car. On purpose. Three times. He'd backed into her because her car was in his way. Thus she'd learned the hard way how offensive these folks found cursing. Yet, mere months earlier, this same woman had refused a ride from Geoff, saying she couldn't get in the car with him because it was Ramadan, and she shouldn't be seen in a car with a man who was not her husband.

As for me, regardless of whether I was going to say anything at work, I still wasn't sure if I should say anything to Geoff. I had to talk this out with someone, gossip be damned.

"No, you can't tell him, love," she said, making me feel sane for understanding my conflicting feelings. "You don't want your husband to be suspicious of you, and he probably won't be able to help himself."

This wasn't why I didn't want to tell Geoff. Later I'd wonder if this was where I made one of a million small mistakes. Just then I added to my personal list of failings the idea that I didn't know how to "handle" my husband. I believed I should be the kind of woman who could make my husband do things, like spend our anniversary together or feel compelled to be more of a partner financially. It would be a while before I'd understand the only way to handle any partner was with my genuine self, and if that didn't work, nothing would. I was mostly concerned about potential trouble at work. Geoff had to work with Joe, too.

Joe was a larger-than-life figure on campus, well loved by the folks at his university and at the Qatar Foundation. Much as I wanted to bust his ass for sexual harassment — I didn't think he should not be traveling with young, impressionable women — I didn't have his kind of wasta at Education City. I dreaded how things might turn out, anyway. It's bad enough the way victims are blamed in such situations in the West, but in the Persian Gulf? After all, I *had* gone to his room. I feared Geoff might insist that I rat him out. In his shoes, I'd want to claw the perp's eyes out.

I fell into a fitful sleep, hoping I'd know what to do when I woke up.

·   ·   ·

Morning came and still I had no desire to wander around an unfamiliar, Middle Eastern city. But the flight wasn't until the afternoon. There was only one thing to do. I lugged my bags over to the Hyatt and hit that spa. This idea started working its magic as soon as I stepped inside. Mary Ellen had recently sent some cds from home, and I recognized the music playing — Gwen Stefani's "Rich Girl." At last I was in the right place. I hit the circuit — sweating in the sauna, jumping into a cold pool, then sitting in a steam room, emptying my pores of anything Joe.

When I finally made it home that evening Geoff was already in bed. I told him I'd cut short my business trip but didn't want to talk about it. He rolled over in bed, perfectly fine with that.

I was upset, I reminded him. Nothing.

I felt compelled to hint. "I don't want to upset you."

But he was not upset. Or guessing. He was falling asleep. So I told him.

"Can you blame him?" he asked, before rolling over and dropping off to sleep.

Yes I could.

Was this the same man who encouraged me to apply to get into the Breadloaf Writers' summer conference a couple of years earlier? He believed I'd get in, and thanks to his belief I'd been accepted at something that, on my own, I'd never have tried.

I was deeply hurt. So much for trying to protect Geoff from feeling compelled to act on my behalf. Or was he genuinely trying to make me feel better?

Much as I was finally recognizing my emotions for the hormonal freak show that they were, I was still feeling them. I thought back to that interview with Kathy Smith; she'd described menopause as a combination of pregnancy and PMS.

"So you have that to look forward to," I'd said to Geoff at the time.

"Nothing would surprise me," he'd replied. "I was maybe 16 when my mom went through the change of life. One day I was coming in from a soccer game, wiping my feet off outside so I wouldn't track the dirt in. She must've been looking out her window at just the right time. 'Stop that!' she yelled, 'you're making a mess on the lawn!'"

Silly old bat, I'd thought at the time. Now I could relate. Except for the part about having a teenager to catch me behaving badly. And cue the self-pity while Geoff snored on.

Luckily I had Victoria.

"Intellectually I know that my feelings about this have more to do with me than him," I told Victoria in our next session. "That my feelings aren't facts."

"Well, yes and no," she replied. "It's certainly a fact that you felt bad when Geoff said what he said, it's actually your thoughts around those feelings that cause the problem. Your thoughts aren't facts."

This kinda blew my mind. It was opposite to how I'd viewed things, but I could see the wisdom in it immediately. That night I'd felt hurt, then angry. Then I'd thought about thrashing Geoff with a pillow. But in fact I did nothing. Hmmm.

"The other aspect of this is, what to do?" I said. "In my idealized version of life here, I pictured myself as a role model for women."

"It's not your job to be the face of Western feminism in the Middle East, Lisa," she said.

"Then I've lost the thread. What am I doing here?"

"Right now you're paying your mortgage," Victoria said. "You could try not figuring out what to do next for a little while. Just focus on healing."

"Heal what?" I said. "I'm supposed to baby myself because of the menopause? No way."

"Well ya could," she said. "But I meant the surgery. Your doctor said the tough recuperation was a direct result of stress." she pointed at me. "So's that."

I'd been awkwardly trying to adjust the pillows on Victoria's couch but couldn't quite lift my arm.

"You need to get that sorted," she said, digging into the address book that sat on the table next to her chair. We had the same table at our place. And chair. And couch. Different pillows; actually, I hadn't gone out and bought decorative pillows.

"I tried," I said. "The doc was a total quack. He gave me a neck brace to fix my arm and of course the arm still hurts."

"Looks like tennis elbow to me. Call this guy," she insisted, pushing the phone number at me. "He's in town working with the Asian Games athletes. You can trust him."

Good God, I was turning into a regular hypochondriac. At least this made my problem sound vaguely athletic, even if it was probably mostly masturbation-related. Geoff and I had sex maybe three times a week, but my drive was higher than that. Our love life at that point was serviceable, if lackluster, but I wasn't about to bring that up with him. What could be worse for depression than being told you're not enough in the sack? And what if mentioning my vague dissatisfaction ended up making us stop altogether? I didn't mention any of this to Victoria either, and so remained blithely unaware of how hard I was working to try and manage Geoff.

———

I never did press harassment charges. I just couldn't bear the thought of being pitted against Joe. What if I lost? easier to give up than stand up. So much for showing the way of Western feminism. I was exactly like the student who'd come to my office in search of her shayla, her headscarf.

"You're always losing that thing, I know you hate it," I said. "Why do you wear it at all?"

"Yeah, I could stop wearing my abaya and shayla, but I'd be disowned," she said. "I'd have no support from my family, nowhere to live, but still I'd be stuck in this country. So, yeah. That's my choice."

For all my bluster, apparently I lacked the courage to choose differently too. What had I thought I'd be showing these women anyway? Qatari females could be found at the highest levels of management; I didn't have to look further than my own employer, Education City. It had even stopped bothering me that Sheikha Mozah bint Nasser Al Missned was but one of the emir's three wives. Marrying a person you wanted to have sex with outside your marriage showed more accountability than we required in the West. I certainly couldn't view too harshly the fact that women weren't at the top of corporate or government sectors, my own culture set little standard there.

At a recruiting event in Jordan, grabby-hands Joe had once said to me, "They don't see covering as oppression!" I replied that starving people didn't ask for steak, as if ignorance were the cause. But it was all far more complex than that.

"It is not for me," said another student, who chose to cover during a trip to Carnegie Mellon's U.S. campus, despite that none of the other students did. "It is for God. I have the same God in Pittsburgh." But perhaps my rudest awakening of all came during this recruiting trip. At an airport in Germany, a woman in a mini-skirt and a sleeveless top marched past me.

Cover yourself, were the first words that came to mind. Cover yourself? If this was what a few months living in Qatar did, I could hardly imagine the affront I'd feel if I'd spent my life there. I thought again about Linda Babcock's *Women Don't Ask*. Sometimes we are our own worst enemies.

———

"There's another possibility, Lisa," Victoria said. "Maybe everyone's just doing the best they can."

FOURTEEN
HARAM

Haram:

"Forbidden," according to the Quran. Can feel like an *invective against women*, but there's stuff for men, too: like, *they're only supposed to wear white gold.*

DOHA, QATAR
June 2005

VICTORIA'S DOC RECOMMENDED A cortisone shot, physical therapy and yoga. I got the shot and started PT, but almost bailed on the yoga.

I hadn't worked out since moving to Qatar and discovering that the gyms held "ladies" hours during the day, when this lady was at work. Even the area at our compound that held four Stairmasters assigned separate hours to men and women. But there was this one yoga class on Friday mornings, when even the grocery stores were closed in deference to religious observances, making it a class I could actually get to on a regular basis. But. It's yoga.

My parents own a fitness center. In our household, yoga

wasn't considered a workout, so much as something to do "between sports" if you were injured or needed a good stretch. But I needed to do something. In the nine months since we'd moved, I'd found the gumption to work out on my own exactly twice. And I was injured. At least I should check it out. At the door, I almost turned heel immediately.

The class was on Friday mornings because it was being taught by a colleague, the dean of admissions at VCU. We'd met at a student recruitment meeting when she breezed in late, instantly charging the room with her shiny red hair, electric blue eyes and wide smile. She'd worn a suit that accentuated her extremely fit self, the embodiment of confidence and poise. In other words, she intimidated the hell out of me. This was not someone I wanted to watch me huff and puff my way back into shape.

"Lisa!" she cried. "There's a space for you right here."

Considering my options, well, this *was* my option. In one of those decisions you have no idea is huge, I stayed.

"Less effort," Valerie purred throughout the class. "Just keep breathing. As long as you're breathing, you're doing yoga." I had no idea what she was talking about for most of the hour and a half we spent together. Surely my brain was frozen because of the intensity of that workout. What just happened?

When class was over, I had to say something.

"Hi Valerie," I panted. "That was an amazing workout."

"It's great to see you here," she smiled, instantly going in for a hug.

Okay.

"No one comes to a yoga mat by accident. Especially not here. Why don't you pop over for a tea?"

I couldn't quite place her accent.

"Oh, I'm an Aussie, but my husband was American. We

lived in the States for many years," she smiled. "Just follow me, it's easier than giving directions."

Had she picked up on my awkwardness? My loneliness? I didn't know; I didn't care. I just wanted this woman to like me. "Sure," I said, thinking about the work I'd been planning to do that afternoon at the office. It would keep.

Val's villa took my breath away. In a world dominated by ecru, the interior of her home exploded with emeralds and burgundies and violets, from tapestries on the wall, to tribal rugs on the floor, to children's toys all around. Tears stung at my eyes to see the obvious richness of her existence in comparison to my own. I'd not yet managed to buy so much as a rug for our place at Valley Rose; I felt like I was barely surviving. How did she manage her big job, the yoga, the kids, *and* all this?

She picked up a photo from her dresser. "That's Jaya, my oldest. And that's my husband. Ex-husband. We had to split. He was alcoholic, and that just wasn't good for the girls."

Much to my surprise, I heard myself say I was a recovered alcoholic. My whole life I'd never discussed this with colleagues or doctors or anyone, unless I knew that they, too, were former alkies. I felt it put too much responsibility on the person you told. Compared with the previous 20 years I'd put into my recovery, I was becoming positively blabbermouthed.

"You made the right choice," I added. "We're hard to love, even when we're sober."

I decided to put off going into the office for the rest of the day. Then again the next day. I took a whole weekend off and became a regular at Val's weekly class.

"I have someone perfect for your admin," Roxanne, the HR director, enthused.

I looked up from my desk to see she was sporting her favorite, ill-fitting emerald ensemble which, on its debut, had gone around the office's mobile grapevine as "the turquoise turd." (Okay, maybe I'd started that moniker.) The point being, I didn't trust her judgment. For one, the outfit. For another, between the Fadhel un-hiring debacle, the ongoing admin search, and the fight we'd had over fast food restaurants in the staff recruiting brochure, I was pretty sure I was her idea of a nightmare. This was the first candidate she'd brought to me since the previous fall.

"Great, can I see her resume?"

"Well," she said, "She doesn't have one."

Mmmkaay.

"She hasn't worked in an office before, but she's a designer, which would be great with all the branding stuff you do. She's very intelligent. Very well put together. Her English is great."

Go on.

"She's new to town, and I think we should snatch her up. She's interested in working here."

Sold.

"And she made me this outfit," Roxanne finally finished.

In no other circumstance would I have continued this conversation beyond "doesn't have a resume," but this was Doha. And Roxanne— in a feat I could not help but admire — had negotiated a one-year contract for herself. I respected her business savvy, and the fact that she'd soon be leaving. For her replacement, finding my admin would hardly be a top priority.

"Let's bring her in."

"I say, if you're even considering artificial insemination, we should do it now," Nathan said at a follow-up appointment.

That was possible for a menopausal lady?

Yes.

We hadn't been but now I was. Yes, those pronouns are intended.

My main concern was the effect that hormone injections could have on my already overwrought emotions.

"I know it seems like a lot to take on board," Nathan said. "But there's a chance we might be successful if we try now. And that window's closing."

I had mixed feelings, but I wanted to experience parenting with Geoff, and it was now or never time. Then it hit me.

We'd moved to this part of the world thinking it would boost his career. Clearly, that wasn't happening. Undeniably, however, I had the best health insurance I was ever going to have. Where else can you get IVF treatment fully covered? Plus there was an enormous amount of support available after giving birth as well — the maternity leave was generous, live-in help was affordable, and one of the school's benefits was covering private school tuition for any kids. If ever there was a time or place to start a family, it was Doha in the early aughts. Maybe this move hadn't been about career after all. Maybe it was about family.

But did Geoff want to have kids at all? He was so remarkably unfazed by what had just transpired, I wondered. "Nathan suggested something at my follow-up appointment today that sounded totally crazy," I told him later that night. "You know how some women get pregnant late in life? he thinks I may have one last gasp of fertility left, that we should try artificial insemination. And my insurance covers it!"

I added that last bit because we *had* talked about this possibility before, as in, *We'd never take extreme measures, there are too many unwanted kids in the world!*

But that was then. In Qatar, artificial insemination was easier than adoption, which I had some serious concerns about. What if I got buyer's remorse and didn't bond with the kid? That I was even thinking this convinced me I was a poor candidate for adoption, and — in blacker moments — parenthood. But we didn't talk about any of those thoughts.

"Sure," Geoff said. "Let's give it a try."

Following suit, I kept my concerns to myself. See? I told myself. He loves you that much.

A few days later, I went to Hamad Hospital to pick up the vials of hormones from Nathan, and he and I got to talking. At first he'd found it difficult to work with patients whose faces were covered. He was accustomed to reading what went unsaid, as much as what he was told, but he'd learned to compensate by developing his investigative skills.

"It's a good thing too," he said. "I never would have guessed how much sex these people were having."

The people in the dresses were having sex? A lot? "Least four times a day."

Shut *up*.

"Why wouldn't they? What have they got to worry about?" he asked. "They have guaranteed jobs, housing, income, cars... it all leaves a great deal of time for the mind to wander."

Like most everyone, I dig sex. Even through the busy-ness, Geoff and I managed at least three or four encounters a week. But three or four times per day? Every day?

"I guess that's why they have more than one wife at a time," I said.

"It's not just the men," Nathan insisted. "Behind those compound walls it's a regular 'Coronation Street.'"

Must be some kind of British soap opera, I thought, loathe to interrupt his momentum.

"An extra visit to wife number one sends wife number two straight to the driver."

I reconsidered the shell-shocked look I'd seen on the faces of so many drivers.

"They like it that Hamad is sex segregated, wouldn't have it any other way," Nathan said. "My patients don't want their husbands along on these appointments."

———

That night Robert — my colleague, neighbor, and now Geoff 's boss — was throwing a party where I ran into Donna, another colleague from Virginia Commonwealth university's marketing department. Donna was the type of person you'd want on your side in a prank, the type of person who filled in work phone logs with names like, "Ima Twat." she was my favorite work colleague, and I couldn't wait to tell her what I'd learned from Nathan, as we poured over the magazines on Robert's coffee table, while the boys smoked cigars on the back patio.

"Wait, check out the look on Al Bakker's face," I said to Donna, pointing out the head of the airport featured in a profile. "Do you think he just did it with the photographer's assistant?"

"Of course. That's the look that says, 'Who's next?'" We entertained ourselves like that for the rest of the night; I felt like I was fifteen. Then the next day got even better. Donna texted me at a meeting.

Quick! she wrote. Check under the table! Someone's probably having sex there rt now!

It's 3.11. I replied. Do you know where your driver is?

I'm embarrassed to admit it, but we amused ourselves with messages like this for weeks. In an odd way it gave me hope for becoming a parent, because Donna and her husband had two young children. It was reassuring to think I might not have to abandon my own juvenile sense of humor. Nonetheless, I didn't talk to her about the fact that I was about to undergo artificial insemination either. In fact, I didn't talk to anyone about it, it was something I just did.

FIFTEEN

ASEXUAL HEALING

Asexual healing:
Play on Marvin Gaye's, "Sexual Healing," of which there was none involved in the making of my post-surgery recovery.

Ladies hours:
Appointed times where only women and children may patronize a business.

DOHA, QATAR
June 2005

O
UR PATH TO parenthood began with a trek down the school's long, white corridors to my department's storage archives. There, amid boxes of invitations, branded banners and the giant smiling faces of my dean and Mohamed mounted on foam core, I peeled back my jacket and pushed down my skirt so Geoff could inject me.

Looking back, I'm not sure why we did it at lunch instead of in the morning, especially since the medication was meant to be refrigerated. Of course, everything about Qatar seems poorly planned now, but I've wondered since if this in particular was deceit. Did Geoff keep the vials in a hot window half the morning? I wanted him to give me the shots because I believed that actions spoke louder than words, and if he was showing up and administering the shots, he was with me. But the shots affected neither my mood nor my ovaries — halfway through the treatments a sonogram revealed that nothing was happening — and we stopped.

"The next step for to take would be to find a donor egg to implant," Nathan said at that appointment.

"That could work despite the menopause?" I asked, looking for a sign from Geoff (we'd snuck him in for this appointment).

"You'd need to continue hormone treatment," he said. This was definitely ratcheting up the high tech factor. "And you'll have to leave the country for the implant. It's illegal here. Like adoption."

"Adoption's *illegal?*"

Geoff looked at me. "Dilutes the family lineage, Lisa." Oh.

"Where does somebody find a donor egg?" I asked, feeling Geoff's stare of disbelief but refusing to look. *I was just asking!*

"You can contact hospitals," Nathan said, "or search online. Some of the women here use their maids."

"What do you mean, use their maids?" I asked.

"They take them through the treatment you just did," he said. "Then they take them to London to have the eggs removed and get implanted with them."

God help me, my next thought was not for these indentured servants, who might not even have been informed of what was happening. No. I rued the fact that we didn't have a live-in maid. *Get hold of yourself.* We could find another option. For once in my life, money did not need to be a stumbling block. Could it be mere coincidence that I'd met a woman in Pittsburgh who'd used a donor egg? "The child you carry does take on some of your DNA," she'd told me. OK, we were definitely getting into extreme measure territory, but if Geoff had given any sign, I would've done it in a heartbeat.

"I've heard of people using donor eggs back home, and always thought that was about as crazy as you could get for babies," Geoff said as we got in the car. "But that maid story? That's insane."

I wish I'd said, *Well that's easy for you to say, you can still procreate.* Or, *I think I'm losing my mind, I miss my friends, I need someone to talk to, I miss you.*

But no. What I said was. "You're right. That would be nuts," I said. Adding, "Though I do have great insurance now."

And that was that.

Was this where we crossed the line between not discussing every emotional trauma and into total dysfunction? It was a slim line I wanted to stay on the right side of, even though I'd long related to the Dianne Weist character from *Bullets Over Broadway.* "Don't speak!" she often exhorted her young lover. Not everything needed to be dissected.

The last night I spent with my first boyfriend, Jeffrey, the night before he drowned, we'd been having a disagreement. It was some disagreement we'd regularly replayed, the type of thing that often comes between a couple in a long-term relationship. Though I don't recall what exactly, something like why did we have to visit *his* father, or about the laundry, or something. I was tired and had to go to work the next day, and so rather than talk it through we agreed to disagree. No matter the outcome it didn't change the fact I loved him even if he a) left the seat up, b) didn't take out the garbage, or c) failed to send that thank-you card. "Can we just not do this one tonight?" he'd said.

Of course. Instead we spooned together in a loving embrace. Not once have I looked back and failed to be grateful that this was how we spent our last night together. Being right or making your point was rarely that important in an intimate relationship. Except when it was.

Despite that Mohamed had just called me, I tapped his door as I poked my head into his office. "Is now good?"

He waved me in. "Shut it, would you?"

Oh Christ. That's never good.

"I've been looking over the budget you submitted."

Great. Thanks for not mentioning it when you asked me to come to your office. Why be prepared?

"I just want to be sure you have enough resources for next year."

I *what?* I sat.

Mohamed and I proceeded to talk about the hires I'd requested and the plans I'd made. In addition to the admin, I was asking for three more people to organize events, oversee design and work with the media. He was into it.

"I just started working on my MBA at Thunderbird," he said with a grin.

I kept to myself that all the word "Thunderbird" made me think of was malt liquor — Googling would show the school was a fairly prestigious, part-time MBA program for working professionals — and made to leave. My work was done here; I felt a little high.

"Oh, hey," he said. "About that brochure? The one you didn't let us put the school logo on?"

That brochure. Again? Crikey.

"I was in a meeting at QF this morning. They're pulling all copies. Apparently there's a section on dating in there?"

I put on a blankish stare and a half-smile, unsure where this was going.

"Dating's not legal in Qatar," he laughed. "Yeah, so those have to go. Good call."

"Wait, what do you mean it's not legal?" I asked. "I get that it's like, *haram*, but what do you mean not legal?"

"You can't date in Qatar," Mohamed said. "No matter who you are. End of story. I'm just glad we didn't have our logo on it."

I was dazed as I left the office. What just happened? I was getting my budget and an atta boy from Mohamed?

"That's great," Geoff said, when I called him five seconds later. "I'm going to be late tonight though. I have drinks with a journalist who's coming in."

The meant I could look forward to a lengthy soak in the bathtub. Alone. Could the day get any better?

And I pretty much stayed that happy till around 9:30pm. Where was Geoff?

I rang his mobile.

"Hello," came a voice I did not know. A woman's voice I did not know.

"Wait, hello? I was calling Geoff."

"Oh hang on. Geoff?"

Who the fuck just answered my husband's phone?

"Hello?"

"Who the fuck just answered your phone?"

"Oh that? That was Corinne. The journalist I told you I was meeting."

"Why is she answering *your* phone?"

"Why are you making such a big deal out of it?"

"Why aren't you is what I'd like to know! Who answers someone's phone?"

"You answer my phone."

"I'm your wife!"

"You're making a big deal out of nothing. I'll see you when I get home."

Which turned about to be about two and a half hours later.

And he was drunk.

"Oh baby, you're mad," he cooed. He was always a sweet drunk.

"We'll talk about this later," I said.

"Don't be mad," he said.

"Are you kidding me? Another woman answered your cell phone. Of course I'm mad. Do you know how proprietary that behavior is? I'm..."

But there was no need to go on. He was asleep.

The next time I tried to bring it up, he brushed me off with the same line about how I was making a big deal out of nothing. I took it to Victoria.

"Do you think he's cheating on you?" Victoria asked.

"No!" I said.

"Then what's the problem?"

"I'm not wrong here. It's not right to answer someone else's phone. And I can't believe he's acting like it's nothing. I feel like Ingrid Bergman in *Gaslight*."

"Like he's trying to make you feel crazy?"

"Yeah, like he wants to keep playing up this whole menopause thing as long as possible. But really, since I started the yoga and the supplements and the acupuncture, I'm sleeping through the night. That alone has done wonders for me. I'm actually, well, kind of happy."

"What about Geoff?"

"He's miserable," I said. "He never wants to go out or do anything but sit around and watch TV or hang out drinking and smoking with Robert. I'd send him here but that would be weird to have the same therapist."

"Why don't you bring him in for a couples' session?"

"Like couples counseling?" I asked in disbelief. "But we don't need therapy. We're just having a rough patch. Qatar's the problem. Not us."

"Might help."

"I don't think he'd do it. He doesn't believe in therapy."

"You'll never get what you don't ask for."

———

Finally came the weekend that Geoff spent practically immobile. He did not shave, shower, change clothes or leave the house all weekend.

"Hey sweetie, what would you think about coming to a session with me and Victoria?"

"What, like couples counseling?" he asked in disbelief.

In fact, I knew he didn't believe in therapy. In a weird way this was something I admired about him. Obviously, he was the good one, the one of us better equipped to deal with life's bumps. His life still included the privilege of drinking, after all. But couples counseling felt like coming at it from a different tack and I'd have done anything to help him.

"You know I'm not really one for therapy," he said. "I don't think people really can change."

That was just plain insulting. "Really? you're really gonna

say that to me? In the 20 years I've been in recovery from alcoholism, I've seen nothing but people changing," I said.

It pissed me off that he didn't seem to notice how I'd changed since therapy started either, but I was fully aware that he was noticing me (and everything else) less and less. Yet it felt wrong to push. The ever-present but unspoken threat of his familial suicides left me fearing I might topple him into deeper depression. Besides, you could force a person to therapy, but you couldn't force healing. Perhaps more than anything I wanted to believe. *He doesn't think we need therapy either!* And so another topic was concluded.

DOHA, QATAR
July 2005

Narita, the candidate for the assistant's position in my office, arrived in a taupe, raw silk suit. Very smart, thank God.

She'd moved to Qatar from India with her new husband, a bit muckety muck at Education City. He was American and I wondered how they'd met. Had he ordered a bride online? Not that Narita was some young chippy; she was older than me. No matter. I was terribly encouraged by the fact that we'd coordinated this meeting over email. Email! This put her head and shoulders above anyone else I'd interviewed.

"I don't have office experience but I learn quickly," she said when we met.

"You'd be a key team member," I said, "basically helping me manage the work flow. It might mean meeting with Her Highness one day, stuffing envelopes the next."

She was fine with that.

"It also requires some long days and nights."

Her husband also worked long hours.

Done.

Except she wouldn't be able to start till August. Like most of the rest of Doha, she'd be out of town for July. All of July. This maybe should've been my first clue that her dedication was not to the job; instead I decided to follow her lead. After hiring her, I scheduled a holiday. Two weeks in Turkey, the longest vacation I'd ever taken.

SIXTEEN

TURKISH DELIGHTS

Turkish Delight:
In fact, a disgustingly sweet, jelly-like sugar candy. *I always thought it meant hashish.*

MEDITERRANEAN COAST, TURKEY
August 2005

K AS IS A CITY in the south of Turkey, built into a hillside. By day, it offers stunning views of a bright blue bay, but it was the nighttime scene that really surprised.

Vehicles were banned from the town's center in the evening, when crowds moved from cafés to bars to art galleries. Its curving streets absolutely bustled with people, an urban planner's wet dream. And, apparently, mine.

"We're not even gone and I can't wait to come back," I smiled as I nuzzled into Geoff 's shoulder.

We'd rented a car in Istanbul, driven west to Assos, then dropped down the Mediterranean coast to hit Oludeniz and

Ephesus. By the time we got to Kas, steady access to a non-life-threatening climate had done its magic.

"I think we should leave Qatar," Geoff finally said.

Lord have mercy on my soul, at long last!

Sort of.

I'd responded so well to my various treatments — sleeping, yoga, vitamins and acupuncture — that I no longer felt quite the same urgency around leaving. I was even a little excited by the plans I'd made at work for the coming year. Not that I wasn't fine with leaving; I wasn't suddenly loving Qatar.

And Geoff's family history of suicide was never far from my mind. Returning to the States would be good for him, I believed. Get him back to happiness sooner. And wasn't this the stuff of marriage? You don't agree on everything. You take the highs, you get the lows, too. We didn't need to bottom out just so I could fulfill my employment contract.

Over fresh tomatoes and eggs at an outdoor café— just that we were eating fresh food was mindblowing enough, but outside, too? — we decided he'd start looking for work.

"Maybe I'll take the foreign service test," Geoff said.

Whatever.

"But if I can't find anything I can always quit QF at the end of the year and move back home to look for work."

Whoa. I couldn't leave that soon, could I? I was supposed to start hiring in my new team in the fall, I...oh who was I kidding? I'd have gone home on a plane out of Turkey if Geoff asked.

"I know that's not really ideal for you," he added quickly. Responding to some look on my face? I hadn't said a word. "But if I don't have a job by the end of the year, I'll have to go back to find something. It's too hard to organize from here."

Considering the trouble he'd had finding freelance assignments from Qatar, I agreed. In fact, it struck me as surprisingly pragmatic from him.

"You should stay in Qatar. Just till the end of the school year," he said.

Suddenly I was not liking this plan. But one of us had to pay the mortgage.

"That way you have plenty of time to leave everything in order," he said. "And I can worry about re-establishing our life back home."

And that's where he got me. The whole point to moving had been to get him to be able to take the reins financially so the power dynamic in our relationship could stay balanced.

That hadn't worked out how I'd wanted it to, but this "re-establishing our life" thing sounded a lot to me like him taking charge. If that was ever going to happen, I was going to have to step back and let him make the decisions.

"Well, I don't love the part about us being away from each other for six months," I said. "But I would feel better about not leaving another mess behind in the Middle East. That wouldn't exactly be reversing the karma I left the last time."

"And I'm not totally sold that we have to return to the U.S.," he said. "But it's easier to work from home base."

Naturally, my mind began to imagine the possibilities again. The embassy in south Africa. A journalism job in Moscow. Hell, even something in Buffalo. As long as we were together we could make anything work.

What we didn't spend a lot of time on was what exactly "re-establishing our life" would entail. I couldn't get the man to pay an online bill without some serious prompting, now he was going to find a job, a place to live, and voila! All our things and us would magically appear? Was it a bad sign that he didn't think I was necessary to "re-establishing our life"? And what had happened to the idea that when my contract was up I was supposed to take some time off? I hadn't finished my contract, one. And given the work experience Geoff had gained in Qatar,

I didn't see him poised to take on the full financial burden of our life. Just because Geoff had given up his dream, did I have to give up mine, too? Did Geoff even remember we'd made that deal?

Not that I thought this all through in the course of that conversation. Something felt wrong, but before I could fully formulate what it might be he sealed the deal.

"You'll keep the dogs in Qatar, of course."

This was a sure sign of his fidelity. He'd done the same thing before he moved to Pittsburgh, when he'd kept his job but given up his apartment. He sent the dogs to live with me, working at the paper and couch-surfing in Buffalo during the week, then spending the weekends with me. Even then I knew he'd never leave his dogs behind.

Anyway, this dislocation was temporary. I could easily come up with reasons to travel to the U.S. "on business," then take a couple extra days to see him. Sheikha Mozah was slated to be our commencement speaker in 2006, there was one trip already guaranteed to mitigate our six months apart.

I brought none of this up; I just wanted everything to work and thought if I held it together just a little longer everything just might be ok.

L ater that night we walked through the streets, perusing bookstores and galleries. It was Geoff who stopped at the paragliding booth.

"Let's do it," he said, to my shock.

On our honeymoon I'd begged him to go parasailing; I'd wanted to fly since I was a little girl and seen people hang-gliding off Florida's beaches. I knew Geoff was afraid of heights, but I couldn't think of a better way to start our lifelong adventure together than flight. He conceded, but on the boat we learned that because he was 6'3" and weighed close to 200 pounds, we'd have to fly separately. He went first and loved it. I, on the other hand, spent my experience certain the rope would snap and I'd hurl toward the water and my imminent demise. I hated every second. I tried not to think about those fears as we signed up to paraglide the next day . I wanted to prove I was equally ready to start our new adventure. This time I knew from the start our journeys would be in tandem; each craft held a pilot and a student. What could go wrong?

The next morning we went to a nearby cliff and strapped into harnesses. I was nervous, but eager to prove myself. The stone walls and green forests calmed me some, it was all so beautiful. Again, Geoff went first. Then it was my turn. From

T he moment we stepped off the ground, I realized the problem with parasailing. It was the tie. untethered, we rode the winds as opposed to creating an artificial current, floating above the treetops and rocks and waves. I looked down and saw the effort in a Cormorant's back as he flapped his wings. I was seeing a bird from a bird's eye view! Back on the ground we were both high from the excitement; we'd both loved it. Another auspicious sign!

DOHA, QATAR
September 2005

Y ear two for Carnegie Mellon's Qatar campus began, only this time our freshmen matriculated just as Ramadan was getting underway. I say getting underway because Ramadan, like Christmas, is a highly anticipated event. Everyone knows it's coming, and everyone's trying to hustle to get things done. When I say I decided to view this as perfect timing for my new assistant to start, know that I mean it was horrible timing.

But what choice did I have? I, too, was in a hustle to get things done. First up, a party at the dean's residence.

We'd finally finished decorating— er, branding — his house in time for the Grand Opening, but we ended up hosting only internal events there. It was time to show Doha a 360 degree Carnegie Mellon brand experience. The first real task I gave Narita was to organize RsVPs. The timing was critical. The school's driver had hand-delivered invitations around Education City; we had to have that event before Ramadan started, which gave us about a week.

Right away, I noticed that she never seemed to have the list when I asked about it, but I assumed this was a procrastination problem. I responded by putting off asking about it. I don't take well to being micromanaged, and I'm not organized enough to micromanage someone else. I figured she was handling it, and

I had enough other things to do.

Two nights before the event, Chuck marched into my office personally to get his hands on the RsVPs.

I told him I'd bring it right over and when he left I went to Narita's desk (part of my new budget included new space with offices for the whole team).

"I don't have it," she said. "I didn't know how to make the file."

Not knowing Excel was the problem?

"Narita, you could've let me know," I said. "No big deal.

Just put it in Word. And we can get you training in excel."

Was she staring blankly or just thinking? I went back to my office, only to hear her leave minutes later. I went back to her desk, her purse and keys were gone. She'd left for the day. It's true it was after five, but I was shocked at her blatant disregard for completing the task.

I cobbled together the RsVPs I could glean from the emails I'd been cc'd on (not all of them, not most of them), and took them to Chuck explaining I'd have more the next day. He didn't like that much, understandably. Had the job been done as poorly by Narita, I still would have taken the heat for it, but with my Aim low! Attitude, I was more disheartened about putting in another late night at work.

When Narita arrived the next day, I asked her to add the other names to the list I'd begun.

"I understand it was technically after hours last night," I said. "But if we're in the middle of doing something you need to tell me you're leaving."

An hour went by.

"Hey, are there that many other names?" I asked, laughing as I walked into her office. The tone quickly changed to panic. "Narita, have you even opened your email?"

Did she even know how to use a computer? Was it her husband who'd corresponded with me?

"Look, I have a meeting in 15, can you forward me all the emails you got so I can finish the RsVP list? I can show you what I'm doing."

When I got back to the office after my meeting a few emails had been forwarded, but Narita was nowhere to be found. The list never was fully finished. The party came and went.

This put me in a bind. Narita showed up. She sat in the

chair. She answered the phone. But it was clear she did not know how to use a computer. On my checklist, however, filling this job was done. I needed to go on and hire the rest of my team. Worse yet, losing another assistant? And what about pissing off her husband, the bigwig over at the Rand Corporation? I could probably come up with plenty of tasks that did not involve the computer, like creating files, sorting newspaper clippings and calling hospitality vendors.

I carried on with this solution, trying to be as specific as possible in my requests, annotating files and documents with Post-It notes and detailed instructions. As the days turned into weeks these papers began piling up in around her desk, on top of the files and — maddeningly — the printer. Thinking she might prefer a creative task, I asked her to decorate the door to our office suite for a contest the students had organized. The contest came and went and our door stood unadorned.

her appearance went downhill as well. At first she'd taken care with her clothes, but she began showing up in increasingly rumpled and mismatched attire. I decided Narita was depressed. It was my guess she'd only taken the job to please her husband, or at least relieve him the burden of her moping presence. Children did not seem to be in the offing and I wondered if she, like me, might have recently discovered there would be none. I tried to encourage her along the lines of designing clothes, but stopped short of telling her to quit. I hoped instead she'd get the hint.

DOHA, QATAR
September 2005

MICHELLE AND I stole a lunch hour together at the Landmark Mall for one last public, daytime meal before

Ramadan started.

"I think I'm really getting the hang of this Insha'Allah," I said. "I'm really ok with whatever happens with Geoff 's job hunt. And this new assistant. I'd rather let her do what she's going to do than try and get her to do what I want."

Yes, I was in that much denial and yes, the situations felt remarkably similar.

"Lisa please, you're a total control freak," she said. "You've just finally figured out no one's paying that much attention to what you're doing."

I burst out laughing. She was absolutely right. "My god, I might actually miss this job!"

"Course you will," she said. "But don't you ever just wish, for once, maybe your husband could take the whole load? Sometimes I wonder, what if I get sick? Could he even pay the mortgage?"

"Well I guess we'll see," I said. "So much depends on where we end up."

"You do seem calm."

"It's weird, right? We had to take my car into the shop," I said. "And I'm quite certain we won't get it back till after Ramadan. But so what? We made do with one car before, we can do it again. And Geoff'll be gone soon anyway!" Aim low. We both laughed. Then Michelle stopped laughing.

"Oh my God it's him," she said, squinting across the way. We were on the mostly empty second floor, across from one of the Starbucks. "I wonder if that's where he's been all this time."

"Who?" I asked.

"That guy over there in the thobe," she deadpanned.

. . .

Starbucks was chock-full of dudes in thobes. "He's my assistant director. I haven't even seen him in the office in two months. Least I know he's still alive."

"Don't make me nervous," I said, referring to the Qatari designer I'd just hired.

"You'll be fine. She just graduated from VCU you said?

They're a whole different crop."

But were they? I'd sized her up while she was still in school during a presentation I made at VCU. Even if I hadn't written the job description with her in mind (just like Victoria had suggested), I knew Mohamed would've been happy to approve the hire. A Qatari! It was such a coup, I was ignoring the fact that she was taking almost four months before she could start. First there was Ramadan, then she was visiting relatives in europe during what would be our Christmas holidays. Why not just wait till the new school year started? Mafi mushkilla! I could focus on the other hires I needed to make. I changed the subject. "I'm gonna miss Geoff, he'll be gone for two weeks," I said.

"But he needs the time to look for work."

"I wish mine would leave town," Michelle grinned. "Permanently."

Thank God I don't have her marriage.

"I'm just glad I've got Paris to look forward to, seeing some of 'my We' from back home," I said, referring to a trip I'd recently planned. As part of our vow never to spend another entire Ramadan in Qatar, Geoff had put together some interviews in the

U.S. and would be home for a couple of weeks, and I was going to meet some friends in Paris. "Though it's only a long weekend." "That's one of the advantages of not having kids," Michelle

said.

Easy for you to say, you have kids.

"I guess I'll never know," I said.

"Oh I'm sorry," she said. "It's just, your life looks so nice from here."

"Compare and despair," is what I said, despite that it was what I'd just been doing. "Don't do it!"

T he minute I got to my car, I went apeshit on comparing my insides to everyone else's outsides. I was worried about having to carry the financial burden of our family forever. It seemed as if every car going past me contained a woman, or several women, sporting their Prada shades, being chauffeured to and from the malls. Or even the expat women driving themselves. Clearly not at work. Where did I go wrong? Was there some flaw in my makeup that made it seem as if I didn't need to be cared for?

You are watching women shop and it's making you jealous?

What is this, your inner housewife? Snap out of it!

I cracked open the window on Geoff 's Jeep and lit a cigarette.

I didn't see it at the time, but little by little I'd fallen back into my childhood game of changing myself to suit my environment. In retrospect, it was no wonder my husband stopped loving me; I'd stopped being me. Was it because we'd stopped making our relationship a safe place? I knew that long term relationships were where you had the capacity to argue and express your ugly side, but I also believed the ugly side should be avoided at all costs. I suppose

I spent so much time repressing my feelings, I stopped being clear about them, so when they came out they were more of a mess than they should have been. I've since learned that the trick to intimacy is knowing there will be pain instead thinking unpleasant sensations are a bad sign. Something is wrong when I'm trying to figure out how I should behave to get the desired result out of another person.

Between work and Geoff, that's all I was doing.

SEVENTEEN
RAMMERS

Rammers:
Informal for *Ramadan*, used by me and my friend Paul and no
one else, but I love the onomatopoeia of it, for those of us who
weren't celebrants of the holiday.

DOHA, QATAR
October 2005

SOMEHOW WITHOUT GEOFF around — he'd gone
job scouting in the U.S.— Ramadan was surprisingly
easier the second time around. Between the holiday
coming earlier in the year meant the days were slightly longer.
With my new *Aim low!* attitude, I could get out of the office
before the traffic started up. This made hitting some of those
parties a possibility I hadn't even considered the first year.

"We're going to hit the Ritz for dinner then shisha at the
Intercon," Cindy said. Her own husband had gone home to
Nigeria for Ramadan. "The maid's got Layla covered. I can't
stay in every night or I'll be a terrible mother." *Interesting.*

The Ritz Carlton had created a fantasy of old Arabia, semi-private tents surrounded tables heaped with lamb and chicken and grape leaves and moussaka and cous cous.

"Try this," Cindy said. "You'll love it."

She thrust a spoon of something that looked like rice pudding at me.

"What is it?" I asked.

"Umm Ali," Rima said. "Can you taste the rosewater?" I hadn't spent time with Rima in months.

"Yum Ali, I can," I said. "But do we have to go to the Intercon? I want to stay here to watch the whirling dervishes."

"But they have the best shisha," Cindy insisted.

And this was the night Rima pulled out a pack of cigarettes. "Ooh, one for me," Cindy said. I looked more closely; they were cigarillos. Blech. But I went for it, too, pulling out my pack of Dunhills.

"And I'll be having one of those, too," Cindy said.

"I didn't know you smoked!" Rima said.

"I didn't know you did either!" I smiled.

Rima smiled back. Maybe we were going to be ok again. And in truth I didn't really care if we were at the Intercon or the Ritz. I'd seen so many of these so-called cultural displays that I knew the presentation would feel more awkward than enriching. I was just enjoying being out with the girls, though the Intercon did turn out to be the best part of the night. They had their own whirling dervishes, men sporting fezzes, red balloon pants and long jackets, all of whom spun in a frenzy on a stage they'd built at the center of the festivities. There was no faking that.

I passed on the shisha.

"Let's do this again tomorrow," I joked as we headed toward our cars later.

"Next week," Cindy said in all seriousness. "But night after tomorrow there's a belly dancer at the Ramada."

We went to that, too.

———

Geoff returned from the States without even a lead on a job, and so the rest of our scheme fell into place. At the end of the year he'd give notice, and we'd tell everyone he'd taken a consulting gig but that he'd be back, which was why I would be staying, because he'd be coming back.

Not wanting to be a lame duck, I thought this loophole was critical. If anyone knew Geoff was looking for work, I was sure they'd guess I was on my way out too. Especially since Geoff was going back to Buffalo — a choice that seemed odd even to me considering that our tenant had just vacated our house in Pittsburgh. But we didn't really delve into those details together. "So we'll get a new tenant," Geoff said. "All our stuff 's in storage, this is just easier."

Of course. It made as much sense as me staying behind.

DOHA, QATAR
November 2005

Before Ramadan hit, I actually manage to hire my whole team. Before it was over, I had to un-hire another one.

The new HR guy had just begun; a man who made me long for Roxanne.

The offer letter David generated for my events hire included benefits she was not eligible for by a significant margin. In our joint defense, these packages were byzantine and based on personal information, the likes of which would get you sued for asking about in the U.S. Were you married? How many kids? etc. The un-hiring came when I wrote to withdraw the offer and then had to ask if she'd still consider the job.

"Why don't you write the letter, David?" I asked.

"Well the offer didn't come from me," he replied.

Fuckhead. When she threatened to sue, I wondered if it would be me or the school she'd go after, but I couldn't undertake looking for a candidate to hire instead just then, because it had become obvious I was going to have to fire Narita. Fire, fire. As opposed to un-hire.

Pushing a pile of papers off the printer one day, I found a stack of my expense reports. After a few overseas business trips, this represented thousands of my own dollars. A review of my paystubs revealed that she hadn't processed a single expense of mine in the nearly three months she'd been on board. I dug further into the piles and found the office budget I'd asked her to organize. It had devolved into a burgeoning stack. I could not deny what was going on any longer. Narita wasn't doing any work at all. I went right to David's office, stopping to marvel at his door art, a giant, light-filled illustration that read "Jesus is my Lord and savior." This was around the time that Danish cartoons depicting the prophet Mohamed were resulting in riots and violent deaths. A grand religious pronouncement like this struck me as a poor choice at that time and in that culture, and almost certainly one that ran afoul of university policy.

Deep yogic breath. This was not why I was there. I tried to quietly lay out my case. Narita was still (but not for much longer) a "probationary" employee. Shouldn't we be able to get rid of her more easily?

"Have you tried smiling when you talk to her?" he asked, his ripe cheeks bursting like the seams of his bright pink shirt. "It changes the whole tenor of a conversation."

And constant sunshine makes a barren desert, I thought.

David suggested I thank and praise Narita often. That I should find solutions for her.

Yes! Exactly! "The problem with our existing solutions," I

said, "is that the online trainings offered through the university is no use. She can't use a computer."

"I refuse to try and show her how to do invoices again. She's untrainable," Cindy offered through the flimsy partition separating their offices. I'd never felt less discretely dealt with than when I visited HR. "Just bring your receipts to me, I'll do 'em."

Still not why I was there. But I'd take Cindy up on that.

David barreled on, thanking and praising me with sentiments like, "Of course you're more valuable to the university than Narita, we've invested more money in you."

That's when I got it. Narita had beat me to HR.

David suggested we keep Narita in my office until she could be transferred to a role opening up in Rima's office in six months.

"Thanks!" I said, smiling brightly and getting up to leave. "I really appreciate your help."

Fuck Insha'Allah. Having finally figured out that hiring people was a matter of lining up the candidates through your social network, I knew I'd be able to find someone else. Now it was me or her time. If Narita thought I'd been a bitch before, she had no idea what was about to hit her.

———

B efore that meeting with David I'd held back on assigning tasks to Narita, seeing that she was easily overwhelmed. Now I let her have it, rattling off colloquial to-do lists every time I saw her. "Narita, I need you to firm up tomorrow's senior staff meeting."

"Can you circle back with me on that press release?"

"I need the tear sheets from MEED asap."

Our every encounter was followed with a treacly email, cryptically summarizing tasks, employing multiple exclamation points, emoticons and, my personal favorite, offers to help in any way possible.

"You mentioned Oracle training. Great idea!!! LMK what I can do to push this through for you! Tx! :)"

The minute the holy month was over I scheduled an "end of probationary period" performance review with Narita. Using the university's system, there was a one to five scale — from below expectations to exceeds expectations — across a number of categories. Item one was the tipping point— "Customer service. Goes above and beyond ordinary duties to find solutions for clients and stakeholders."

I marked her below expectations, the lowest possible ranking. She gave herself exceeds expectations, the highest possible score. I tried not to roll my eyes. I tried to say it evenly.

"Narita," I said, unable now to address her without using idiomatic English. "We have a serious disconnect."

She grabbed her self-evaluation from my hands, looked me in the eye and said, "I quit."

Hallelujah! I thought. Then, *Wait, has she understood me all along?*

Oh, whatever. Deep breath. Respond, don't react, as Val would say. Or Victoria. Or both.

"Would you like to discuss this more? Get some closure?" I asked.

She stared blankly, her silence increasing my confidence. "I'd be happy to give you a reference, if you need it."

Again with the stare, only this time she added, "I don't need anything from you."

I smiled. It was Thursday, the Friday of the Muslim world. "How about we make Sunday your last day? You can come in this weekend and clear out your stuff."

She looked startled. "What about what I'm working on right now?"

My turn. "I don't really need anything more from you, either."

Also, what was she working on?

———

Sunday came and went without anything remarkable transpiring between Narita and I. She left her area a mess but that was nothing new. I was practically giddy as I climbed the steps Monday morning, until I turned the corner and saw the door was already open.

"What are you doing here?" I said to Narita. Unfriendly? Sure. But at this point in our relationship it was nothing.

"I'm working," she said, clearly ready.

"But Narita," I objected. "You quit."

A string of words flew from her mouth to the effect that, what she meant was not that she quit working for the university, but that she quit working for me.

"Narita, you're sitting in my office, in my assistant's chair. Exactly who do you think you're going to be working for?" I asked.

Haven't you had enough? I wondered.

"You may have hired me," she began. "But you're an employee of the university, just like me. And you don't make up the policy."

There was not time to ponder the meaning behind her garbled thoughts. I had to be across campus at a meeting that was starting in 10 minutes.

When I returned, I had to squeeze past Narita and David to get to my desk and put down my bag. The meeting and its attendees were marked clearly on my online calendar. No idea when Narita had scheduled this, or when she had learned to schedule meetings.

"Looks like I'm late," I quipped. Remembering too late, once again, that me and irony and Qatar didn't do so well together.

I joined them at the table and promptly felt like I was going to be sick. David had already been colluding with Narita; I had no idea what was about to come down, except that he had good reason to want to make me look bad.

Then from nowhere, the conversation I'd had with Mary Ellen at Christmas popped into my head. I knew I'd been difficult to deal with, and this firing scuffle could be my undoing. I also knew, it didn't matter. Not just because Geoff was leaving, if anything that made the situation more dire. But I could see clearly, their opinions of me did not matter. I was in the right place, at the right time, doing exactly the right thing. Even if that thing was fucking up royally. I was the judge and jury. There would be no winners or losers. All I needed to do was hold my dignity and that of those around me. Maybe this was what Mary Ellen was talking about. Humility. Peace settled over me as David began the meeting by asking Narita to explain.

Having spent the morning gathering evidence of my wrongdoings, she'd amassed a small forest of paper. She read aloud from the pages, trying to demonstrate I was intolerable. *Please have CS look at the scanner.* Or, *Make sure the dean gets this so we're on the same page.* And of course, *If you need anything LMK!* As she went on she grew increasingly agitated. On the verge of tears she finally said, "I can't take the constant criticism. I don't know what she wants."

"But Narita, those aren't criticisms, that's just your supervisor telling you what to do. That is what she's supposed to do." I was shocked. Had David just defended me?

She went on, talking about how she worked for the university, not for me. She had not quit. She did not like me and did not want to work for me, but she would still like to work for the university. Much as I'd wanted to force her out, this felt awful.

"Narita, you've had plenty of opportunity to dispute this," I said. "I sent an email to you and David right after our performance review. You never said a word."

"I didn't get any email," she said, looking at David.

"Lisa's right," David said, defending me in his own way. "You did talk about hating her all the time. What was different last Thursday was that you said you'd quit."

I didn't know it yet, but Narita had done me a huge favor.

"I already have a lead on some new people," I told Geoff on the phone.

"How?" he asked.

"Victoria put me in touch with some Kiwi group she knows, and I've already gotten responses," I said. "How's your job hunt going?"

"I'm in touch with a lot of people. There's something promising in DC and Chicago," he said.

Chicago would be great! Both my parents are from there.

"I miss you, honey."

"I miss you, too."

DOHA, QATAR / TRIVANDRUM, INDIA / THE MALDIVES
December 2005 — January 2006

By the end of the semester I'd hired three people, all set to start in the New Year. Val, the yoga teacher, asked if I'd teach a yoga class for her starting in January, and I actually said yes thinking I'd need some way to fill my impending empty nights. In a move both practical and fanciful, I'd signed up for a yoga course over the Christmas holiday in India.

Afterward, Geoff and I would take an early anniversary celebration trip to the Maldives. Geoff was not into yoga and so I suffered those deprivations alone — early mornings, hard physical work, spartan eating— while he lay on the beach. Then we were off to our resort island, where together we did nothing but eat and sleep and make love in heavy rotation. Our biggest decisions were what to eat next or whether it was time to nap.

In the email I sent to friends and family immediately following our return, I described our trip as the "perfect second honeymoon." The trip felt like a preview of my life to come — I could suffer the deprivations of the coming months in anticipation of fat times ahead. Did we even talk about what our life might look like once it was "re-established"? I just wasn't worried. I was living in the moment. Come summer I'd join Geoff whether he'd found a job or not. No one would blame me for not wanting to live apart from my husband, it was the perfect excuse to renege on my contract. I was flabbergasted when, on my return our lovely associate dean, Bob Kail, suggested otherwise.

"Is everything OK with you two?" he asked one day, not long after Geoff left.

I tried to brush him off with a joke. "Bob, I would've expected that kind of question from my family, but you? you see us together all the time. Does it look like our marriage is not OK?"

Certainly Bob couldn't have known about the dreams I'd been having, dreams I myself had been busily ignoring.

In the months leading up to Geoff 's departure, I'd dreamt again and again I was searching for him, only to discover he was not missing, that he had, in fact, left me. Knowing my tendency to find the black cloud in a silver lining, I did my best to accept his reassurances at face value.

"Oh, sweetpea," he'd say on those occasions I wondered aloud just why I wasn't needed to re-establish our life back in the States. "I'll just be busy, that's all. You'd be miserable, and I couldn't bear that."

Then there were the visions I had while wide awake, the ones I'd been having for years. The ones I never told him or anybody else about. We'd lose track of one other at an airport or even just running an errand at a store and I'd think, Is this how he's leaving me? Is it now?

I brushed this off with the knowledge it would never happen. Just like I'd believed that no one would ever get a divorce just by saying, I divorce you.

And then, talaq.

PART II

EIGHTEEN
HELAS

Helas:
Also *khalas*. "Finished." Malleable enough to indicate you're done with a meal (*"I'm finished"*) or it's time to go (*"We're outta here"*) or to declare the end of an engagement. (*"You may go; I'm done with you."*)

DOHA, QATAR
February 2006

WHEN I GET HOME from meeting Paul at the mall it doesn't take long before his "reassurances" ring hollow. I liked the sound of things turning out fine, but what did he mean by the end?

Later that night I hunch over my laptop in bed, composing letters to my beloved. "You ass," begins one. "How are we fighting when we're not even talking?" goes another. "Do you even miss me?"

Since my spouse left in January I've spent quite a bit of time putting together such drafts I do not send, in part because it keeps me online, monitoring for incoming messages. At least I'm not working, I think, knowing full well it's not better.

At 12:11 a.m. a missive from Geoff arrives.

We need to talk.

This is exactly what I want, just not exactly how I want it. Men never need to talk. Not only that, Geoff knows full well that I'm a morning person. Was he hoping I wouldn't see this note till morning? That would've been his afternoon. Deadline time. When there would be no talking. My best bet is to ring him at work immediately. Except I hate calling him at work.

12:12 a.m. I lay down and dial. The receptionist answers.

It's her job to screen calls, but my chest tightens when she asks for my name. "Lisa." Still a pause. "His wife." Does she even know he has a wife? Is she cute? She puts me through.

There must have been some kind of hello but all I remember is this, "I want a divorce." And then my stomach begins dropping out of my body.

I would've fallen down, but I was horizontal on the bed already. We'd had our difficulties in Qatar, but I'd never seen our relationship as the source. It's Qatar we're quitting, not us.

"Couldn't we try counseling?" I ask. "At least fighting?" But he gives me nothing. Says nothing.

"I don't want a divorce," I finally say.

His reply leaves no room for interpretation. "This is not negotiable."

I'm not sure how long the call lasted. Ten minutes? Five? Two? It's not like we can actually "talk," he's at work. His new old work.

OK, the fact that his "temporary" job had turned out to be editing the paper in Buffalo, the very same job he'd had when we first met, had been disquieting. But I'd only barely begun sorting out the difference between my intuition versus my negative thinking. And only at work had I acted that out, with

Narita. Now, despite the years of predicting this moment, I'm not ready for it.

I want to jump out of my skin, at least hop the next plane out of Qatar, but it's all I can do to run downstairs and grab the carton of Dunhills I'd just bought. I am immobilized, ruminating and smoking until 6 a.m. when I pick up the phone.

I don't know why we're over, but I know we are over. I dial Victoria.

NINETEEN

DOG DAYS

Dog Days:
Colloquial expression meaning "the hottest time of the year." In this case, a literal expression meaning days spent dealing almost exclusively with my beloved companions.

Hamdulilah:
"Thanks be to God!"

Bismillah!:
"God is great!"

Shukran:
"Thank you!"

DOHA, QATAR
February 2006

"GO TO WHURK," Victoria says in her Kiwi accent, softening the word if not the idea. "Now. Today. Don't think. Just go."

Is she kidding?

So she'd agreed to see me immediately. We're both morning people.

We're also both primary breadwinners with spouses whose careers are looked down upon in the Arab world, though I believe journalist is worse than veterinarian.

And she doesn't drink either, though not for the same reasons.

Usually, I will listen to Victoria like no one else; but seriously, has she not just heard me blaming *whurk* for all my problems?

If I hadn't taken this job, if I hadn't left our nice little life, if I hadn't been so busy... Geoff and I would still be together, surely. We'd still have Little Bear.

"When I was still just a consultant, I used to joke that I didn't hate myself enough to work at the university," I tell her.

Before taking the job, I'd been put off by the attitudes that prevailed in academia, where everything was a hierarchy. This wasn't a personal fear, the university separate faculty and staff by break rooms, paneled with leather armchairs for the profs, formica tabled and cadged together for the rest of us.

"Naturally I took a full-time job with them and uprooted my life to do it? For a man who would leave me over the phone? *Fuck* them."

But even as I'm protesting, I know she's right. Today we have a film shoot scheduled. For the promotional video I'm to create, we must convey a robust and lively campus despite that we have fewer than eighty students, and fewer still who are willing to be photographed. And the lack of resources is still in effect, so once again I've had to fly in the talent — photographers, cameramen and models — from Dubai and Bahrain. I've written the scripts and shot lists. I'm the only member of my team who's done this kind of work before. And it's a one-day shoot. Blowing it off really is out of the question. But how am I going to keep it together?

"Don't say a word," Victoria says. "You never know, this whole situation could change with another phone call."

I agree this is the right thing to do, but not because Geoff 's going to change his mind. No. My silence is part cowardice, part pragmatist. I'd spent the past six hours smoking and mulling over the scenarios.

Already I'd been looking into our departure. There are Ministry visits (to clear the dogs) and paperwork waits of up to 45 days (the bank account) before I'm free to leave. Then there is the mortgage back home. We'd just cashed in Geoff 's $6,000 home allowance for plane fare. Will I have to pay that back if I announce I'm getting a divorce?

I can't bear the look of pity-slash-certainty from Mohamed (any Mohamed) that says, *See that? Your Western brand of feminism doesn't work.* Or the same from Western colleagues thinking, *Wow, that's pretty extreme. Must be something really wrong with that one.* Did I sacrifice my marriage for a job I could lose at any minute? I am worthless at career and home.

But mostly I have no idea how I might possibly explain a thing that I myself do not understand.

The idea that I didn't actually have to explain anything? That I just might get some support? Didn't occur to me. If the man I loved with all my heart had discovered something so awful about me that I wasn't worth talking to about, it's just a matter of time before everyone else sees it. All my life I'd thought that being a feminist was at odds with having a happy domestic life; that you had to pick one or the other. Here I'd managed to accomplish neither. I feel wholly contemptible.

Besides, in not ten days' time I have a trip home scheduled.

Do I know Geoff 's not going to change his mind? Do I know Geoff at all?

B ack at the villa after Victoria's, I gear up. Got to move quickly if I'm going to beat the production crew to the office. I grab a yogurt out of the fridge. Cigarettes — fuck it. I'm smoking everywhere now. To-go coffee. Keys. Go.

After shutting the engine I move through the underground garage's stifling air, running through the list of the day's scheduled interviewees. First up is Chuck, the dean. Then David from HR. Then Mohamed, our COO. It's a veritable *who's who* of every person I want to hide from. Now I need to get them spouting our key messages, all designed to bring potential viewers to the conclusion: "I'm fulfilled here! Join us and you will want for nothing!" Awesome.

Dead as irony may be here, it's certainly not lost on me that I'm relying on models now. Whereas I used to be a stickler for using actual students, there were brochures and ad campaigns I had to trash to appease parents who revoked photography release permission after seeing their children's pictures appear. Pictures that often showed only a set of eyes. This is all fake. Fake I can do.

I steel myself as I reach for the office door. Keep it together.

"Here's your coffee," Noha says with a bright smile, placing a paper Starbucks cup in front of me. "The video people are setting up in Classroom A."

Already I want to cry. We've only been together for a month but I'm so grateful for this team. Though the university (and every office in Doha) had a "tea lady" or (their term, not mine) "tea boy" — an employee who brought drinks and snacks around — ours had become woefully unreliable. "I think 'coffee, please' must mean 'go away and don't come back' in Sudanese," Noha had joked. Then she sussed it out; our tea lady had just gotten engaged. She was busy planning her wedding.

What a joy to have an Arabic speaker on the team who would *talk* to me.

In addition to Noha — a young Egyptian woman who's handled media relations — I now have an admin from New Zealand, Emma (Victoria's Kiwi expat network was a success), and Aya, the graphic designer who'd just graduated from VCU (thank you, Val). Aya's attendance had proven spotty, but she got things done in whole new ways. Interestingly, she didn't cover at work. She'd show up in her abaya and shayla, then unwrap for the day. My delight at this discovery was almost undone by Fawzi, our admissions counselor and most conservative colleague. "Each of us, even this woman whose name I do not need to tell you, has opinions," he once said in a roundabout way of disagreeing with something Aya had produced. After that I'd realized, he never said her name. No matter. When Aya needs some piece of equipment, or if she designs an ad... poof! Mohamed approves it. Period.

"Fadhel just called," Emma says as she walks in. "Mohamed's running late."

I fold my arms and put my forehead to the desk. Why even pretend to check email? I try but fail to stop myself from wondering if Fadhel might have actually double-booked Mohamed to foil the shoot. When I lift my head I see Geoff's picture facing me, it shows him with Little Bear. I move the frame to the credenza behind me. Let them look at it. That's when I realize, they'd all started in January. No one on my team has ever met my spouse. I put the picture in the bureau's top drawer and shut it.

The dean is droning on, and I'm wondering if I should cancel my trip home. *That would look suspicious.*

Ding ding! Ding ding!

A text!

"Sorry," I say as I bolt from the room. "Noha, just get him to do that last take again and I think we're done. Then we can set up for David. Has anyone heard from Mohamed?"

I don't wait for the answer, but I can feel a collective exhale as I exit. I have been nothing if not bossy about getting this set up, ordering around the lights, plants and people. But what else to do? If I'm not actively working I'm thinking, and if I'm thinking I'm about to lose it.

I've pulled my mobile from the depths of my bag.

Do you know how fuckeen beezee I am?

It's Donna. We'd recently watched a black market copy of "Team America" purchased at what we liked to call (because everything they sold was black market) support-your-local-terrorists souq. This is our new thing, texting lines from the movie.

This has been one of my favorite activities of late, but a stab of bittersweet hits my heart. It's not Geoff. I have sent two emails and left voice mail. How fucking busy is he?

Why's everyone so fuckeen stupid? I text back. I'm about to ask if she'll meet me later, but I stop. She is one of many I won't be telling what just happened. She doesn't even know that Geoff 's "freelance gig" is a lie, that I'm planning to leave come summer.

Was planning. Whatthefuckever.

I go to the deck for a smoke. Also fuck it. The smoking I'm just not willing to hide anymore.

B y the end of the day I've gotten "students" in classrooms, faked a lecture, and interviewed a professor. The only person left to tape is Mohamed.

He comes to the conference room we've set up with my script in hand. *Oh God, what's he going to complain about now.*

He waves the pages at me as he takes his seat. "This is pretty good."

Generally I'm eager for praise of any sort on this job, but I'm too numb to care if he likes it or not.

"I know." No reason to suck up, I'm on my way out the door anyway. Little do I know, I'll be here on my own for the better part of another year.

DOHA, QATAR
February 2006

"What do you mean you're not going to see Geoff when you come home?" Mary Ellen yells into her cell phone. At some point I'm going to have to tell her that her loudness actually cuts off the mic and makes her more garbled, but now is not the time to remind her about the indoor voice, or even to discuss the relative merits of seeing my husband. Ex-husband. Whatever. I need to know if she'll keep the kids until I can extricate from Doha.

In the hours following Geoff 's wakeup call I'd thought through possible escape scenarios. But if there's one thing I'd learned from preparing to get out of Doha, it's that getting the dogs out of Qataris every bit if not more complicated than getting them in had been. Besides all the hoops with the vet, repatriating our animals requires approval from, get this, the Minister of Agriculture.

I'd heard horror stories of expats having to leave their pets behind for failing to get sanction. It just so happens that Sophie and Grandpa are in a perfect sweet spot, immunizations-wise. If I can get that Minister's stamp, I can take them with me. Only, I'm not ready to leave Qatar. Not just yet; leaving would screw the delightful women I'd just hired. I have no interest in adding to the karmic trainwreck I left behind when I was medically evacuated from the Peace Corps in Tunisia.

Then again, maybe I will just stay in Pittsburgh and not get on the return flight. Either way, I need a home for the dogs while I'm in the States since I won't be able to keep them at the hotel in D.C., which is where Mary Ellen comes in. Why is she bringing up Geoff?

"You have to find out what's going on," she says. "You can't say he doesn't want to see you, you haven't talked to him since that one phone call."

Which is kind of my point. Of course we should be seeing each other. He knows damn well I'm coming home soon, the whole reason I'd planned the trip was to rendezvous with him when the conference I'll be attending ends. I've called. I've written. He hasn't responded.

"He might want his dogs back," she adds.

"Let him try. On the one call he did deign to have with me, he didn't even *ask* about the dogs. So fuck him, I'm keeping them. I don't even know if it's going to work, but I can't bring them at all if they don't have a place to stay."

"Good thing you two didn't have kids," Mary Ellen says. She then proceeds to tell me about an acquaintance whose husband had spent the family fortune setting up a business for his lover, the person for whom he'd just up and decided to leave his wife and their two children for. That person turned out to be a man. She may have been trying to lighten the mood, but knowing that my split had failed to achieve status as even the most shocking story of the week only aggravated the tenderness in my chest.

I'd always believed my husband was more likable than me. That being married to him upped my likeability factor. As in, if this great guy loves her she's got to be awesome, too. I wasn't thinking about the fact that Mary Ellen and I had been friends through numerous men. Or even that she'd just offered to let me and my dogs or even just my dogs, stay as long as we needed. In that moment I suspect Mary Ellen thinks Geoff did the right thing. All I can see and hear and feel is how easy I am to leave.

"You gotta remember, these guys don't know anything about dogs, and they don't wanna touch 'em," my friend Paul says. A veteran of overseas living, he's taken his dog through Korea, the United Arab Emirates, and now Qatar. He knows the ins and outs of all the systems, and is sharing this knowledge with me in the Dunkin' Donuts parking lot. We'd stopped to pick up snacks for our weekly gathering.

"You just make sure all the papers are right where they can see 'em and you won't have any problems," he says. "If it looks like they're hesitating in any way, you offer to bring your dogs out of the crates. They'll do anything to avoid that. When I left Abu Dhabi some guy questioned Barrett. You can bet the German Shepherd's on their unacceptable breed list. They woulda destroyed him. So I offered to bring him out. The guy's eyes went like saucers. Bam! Bam!" Paul hits the hood of his Nissan Patrol with the side of his fist, simulating the stamp hitting the papers. "Approved."

This leaves me with one problem. How am I going to move both dogs around the Ministry without taking them out of the crates?

"I'll help you," Michelle volunteers.

I haven't actually seen Michelle since the previous year, when our little sober community had thrown a Christmas party. I'm not seeing her now either. It's later that night and we're talking over the phone.

"What about work?" I ask. I'm reminding a workaholic about her job?

"This is a no-brainer," she says. "We leave first thing and I'll go to work straight away afterward. I'll just call in. Let's go tomorrow."

Which reminds me, I have someone to call, too.

The next morning I phone Emma to tell her I'll be in late on the way to the Ministry. I thank God, again, for having bestowed these people on me.

Michelle and I have decided to meet at the Parachute

roundabout — so-called for the weird sculptural assemblage at its center. I take it as an excellent sign that I find my way in one try. Maybe this will work, I dare to think.

When Michelle arrives I follow her to the Ministry where we make a game plan in the parking lot — you can't just take dogs around out in the open, on a leash. I drive us up to the door with the dogs, and we hoist the crates out; she waits with them while I park. Inside, we slide their crates along the marble floor.

The kids are oddly silent throughout this process. Grandpa's heavy, but Michelle is surprisingly strong. It's early yet, so it's only blazing — not yet inferno — hot out. We keep our jackets on for the duration.

"The Minister is on the second floor," I say. Not that there's a sign or anything. I know this from an article I'd read in the local expat rag, *Marhaba*. As we slide the crates down the hallway to the elevators, then back again toward the Minister's office on the second floor, I can't help but notice the building is deserted. Have they seen us coming?

"What if the guy I need to stamp the papers isn't there? What if he's at the Mall drinking tea? I don't have an appointment." Why hadn't I thought of any of this before?

"Oh, no," Michelle says. "They come in for these jobs. Government. It's all Qataris."

I take her word for it. I'll find out soon enough anyway.

Michelle stays in the hall with the crates, while I walk into the office to find three men. The two in Western clothes are tea boys, and I'm hoping the guy in the thobe — with the matching white headscarf, sitting at the Minister's desk — is the Minister. Can't be sure though.

None of them even looks my way until Michelle starts pushing Grandpa's crates in the door with her foot. The tea boys scatter instantly. The thobed dude looks at me with a big smile. How can he help me?

I explain that I'd like to take the dogs with me when I go home to the States, and that my flight is less than a week away. He begins to shake his head. Now Michelle is pushing sophie's crate through the door, so I go for Grandpa's door saying, "Oh but you must look at him. I can bring them…"

I can't finish the sentence before the Minister opens his drawer, pulls out his seal and starts stamping. Not counting the crating up, driving over and hoisting the cargo to the room, the whole thing takes less than thirty seconds.

Thanks, God. I think. Then I have to laugh. I've made fun of this exact phrase as a malapropism for thank God. It occurs to me now that maybe the right word all along has been thanks.

Michelle helps me get the crates back to the Jeep, we hug and part. Back at my villa I don't bother with the crates, just take the dogs right out on their leashes. I'm on the compound and fuck it. What's the worst that can happen? I get deported? The guards stare at me wordlessly. No smiles. No waves.

With only a couple of days before my flight, I'm trying to keep as normal a schedule as possible, especially now that the dog situation is under control. And so, as has become custom, after Friday yoga I go to Val's to sit on her patio, sip tea and smoke. We'd discovered our secret vice some time back, when I'd just gone ahead and lit up in front of her. Everyone, even the yoga teacher, smokes in Doha.

In a low voice, I tell her about the wakeup call and taking the dogs to Pittsburgh. Her villa, like mine, is surrounded by our colleagues. Her neighbor, Adam has his window open, and I wonder if he's trying to eavesdrop. Gossip is Doha's primary leisure pursuit. Neck and neck with shopping and getaway planning.

"You two did seem very careful with one another," are the first words out of her mouth.

That's her comment? I am completely taken aback. "In what way?"

Now she looks off guard, as if she thought she'd been relaying a fact.

"Mmm, very solicitous of one another," she finally says.

I don't know what that means. I know what solicitous means, as in overly eager to please, but how is that a bad thing? And again, what is she talking about?

"Maaahm!" one of her daughters yells, interrupting our moment.

It's just the break I need. I light another cigarette and survey Val's back yard. Her compound, though just around the corner from mine, is a world apart. It has a few years on our place so the plantings are better established, but mainly it seems better planned. First off, her back yard is actually something like a yard, square in shape and anchored by a separate unit that serves as the maid's quarters. (Her I don't fault for having a nanny — not only is she a single mother with two daughters, a dean's-level job and the whole yoga thing, she's working on her Ph.D.) She's placed ficus trees, bougainvillea, cacti and hibiscus around her borders. All of it grows wild. There's even room for a trampoline.

"I can't believe you've gotten the dogs' paperwork sorted in such a short amount of time," she begins as she returns. "But how can you not see Geoff while you're in the States? You need to find out what happened."

Why is everyone so obsessed with this? "I know him well enough to know his mind is made up," I say. "I just don't understand how I could've missed it. That trip we just took was like a second honeymoon, was he faking that?"

Then Surya is at the sliding door, wiping sleep from her eyes and squinting against the day. February is Doha at its most beautiful — brilliantly cloudless skies, low humidity, temperatures in the 80s. Mere weeks earlier, on one of the four days Geoff had spent in Doha that year, we'd taken our families and dogs and a picnic lunch out to one of the abandoned stretches of beach together, past where Qataris tore up and down the shore on three-wheeled ATVs.

"Why are you taking your dogs away?" Surya asks.

I shoot Val a look. I'd brushed it off when she'd told them I was planning to leave that summer — with so many people coming and going all the time the news couldn't have seemed too remarkable — but now this? *She tells those kids everything.* How, at the ripe old ages of 7 and 11, are her daughters supposed to appreciate my need for discretion? Then, too, her girls had liked Geoff. I don't want them to lose their faith in men entirely.

"I told them," Val says, taking her daughter onto her lap. "About the dogs."

I try not to look too visibly relieved.

"Of course I'm going to miss them, but you know from Poochie and Silver how hard it is to find someone to watch dogs when you go away."

I'm trying to convince myself. This is a story I'm going to need again, and most people will figure out that the responsibilities haven't changed in the weeks since Geoff left. "I travel a lot for work."

Surya nods. "Plus I bet Geoff misses the dogs."

I can't even imagine the look on my face as I try to recover from that blow. *Does he miss any of us?*

"Paperwork?" Paul asks, going through the checklist as we pack his SUV on the way to the airport. Besides the fact that traffic near the terminal is horrific, my flight is at midnight. Yet, Paul hadn't hesitated to offer a ride.

"Right here," I say, holding up a folder that contains the papers the dogs need for travel.

"No," Paul says with a frown. I blanch.

"Don't give me that look. Geez. Nannette!" he yells, ducking his head around Grandpa's crate, calling to his wife inside their house. "Do we have any tape, honey?"

If he had told me to tape the folder to my forehead I would have, but the vet's papers just need to be taped to the top of the crate. With the Ministry certificates in hand and health certifications duly affixed to each crate, we're on our way to the airport. Paul and I ride in the Patrol, with Sophie and Grandpa behind us in their crates. Nannette follows in Geoff's Jeep, with my luggage and their one-year-old daughter Janet in tow. I'm glad to have Paul in my corner; I don't want to lose my faith in men, either.

"Wanna make God laugh?" Paul asks me at the red light just outside the terminal. "Tell him your plans."

If only I had some.

At the airport it's assumed that Paul is my husband, and that his daughter is our daughter, and that his Filipina wife is our maid. Hence, all four of us surround the dogs' crates at check-in, well beyond security. Sophie is out of her crate.

The British Airways official is shaking his head. The kennel is a smidge too small; he's about to deny travel. Before I'd gotten the paperwork together, Paul had offered to watch the dogs while I was away, but I'm not about to leave the kids behind now. Before the agent can finish his sentence, I protest. Loudly. All the emotions I've been holding in for the last ten days come burbling out, though I'm not saying anything comprehensible over the tears and snot. Paul's daughter starts to cry. As if on cue, the dogs begin to howl. Paul sinks his face in his hands, I'm pretty sure he's suppressing laughter.

"Ma'am, ma'am," the representative says. "Oh my goodness. Ma'am. Please. It's OK. See? OK." he pushes Sophie into her crate, stamps the papers on top of both — bam, bam! — and puts the both dogs on a conveyor belt.

"Bismillah! Shukran!" I say. God is great. Thank you.

In London, I watch as my dogs' crates are moved between terminals. Sophie's crate has been replaced with a larger, plywood construction that must have been made by British Airways. The guilt I feel is minor in comparison to the relief that we'd all made it out. And the anxiety over the question, now what?

TWENTY

YELA

Yela:
"Get a move on, let's go, speed it up," but _not exactly the same as_ _"Hurry."_

WASHINGTON, DC
March 2006

A T RONALD REAGAN International, I push Sophie's crate next to Grandpa's before I realize, _I'm home!_ I can take them out of their crates and put them on their leashes. Except I need a luggage palette. In addition to the two crates, I'm dragging along my maximum weight limit, in case I decide to stay. The baggage metaphor is not lost on me.

"Hey, do you need some help there?"

It's a random strange guy with his wife. It turns out to be the first of many offers.

At every turn, someone appears to lend a helping hand. This is not the kind of world I'd grown up with, but it's the kind of place I've always wanted to live. The kind of place I always imagined Geoff calls home.

My husband always had tremendous confidence in other people's generosity. In marrying him, I'd hoped to get access to this parallel universe; I didn't. It took many years and many yoga mats to see that making it Geoff's job to engender goodwill on our behalf had actually strengthened my feelings of isolation.

There in the terminal, however, I begin to see the universe conspiring to help me. This is not to suggest that our experiences are entirely self-determined, but we do play a role in the kinds of energetic exchanges that draw and repel others. What I'd long viewed as "me" was in fact mutable.

All I have to do is ask, and sometimes not even that. Mr. Rogers was on to something when he advised, "You will always find people who are helping." The bigger surprise is how hard it is for me to let them. But I have no choice, I can't possibly accomplish this feat on my own.

Getting to Pittsburgh means moving me, my bags, and the dogs into a rental car, driving four and a half hours from D.C. to the Steel City, then immediately turning back to our nation's capitol for the team building seminar I'd signed up for. Against my own inclinations, I take all offers of support.

It's mid-morning of the next day, and I don't know how I'm even awake after all that driving. I've been to corporate seminars like this before, I know the questions that will be coming.

Yes, other people sap my energy. I'm often tardy. I have poor impulse control. What I've actually had to learn, however, is that these are not the characteristics of a successful business type. Some might have thought a career change in order; I learned to lie better. I mean, *enhance* my responses. The next session opens, snapping me out of whatever I'd been thinking, and into a fresh new hell.

"My name is Homero Bayarena," he says.

Not only have I figuratively heard what this guy's got to say before, I've literally experienced it. I had a seminar with this same man back when I worked at Ketchum. Of course, he asks us to write down our overall Life Aspiration! Blech.

I scribble away, barely cognizant of what I'm putting on the page until I read it.

"I want to help other people find the light within and make it shine."

Really?

My life is so far from anything like that, I can't even imagine the steps it would take to get there. I'm in danger of crying. *Again.* I am a crying machine.

I can't quit my job. Who'd hire me in this state? That would be even more depressing, proof that I'm worthless. Over the next two days, as I move from session to session, my plan becomes clear in my mind; I know what I'm going to do. Nothing. I will stick to the original plan and leave at the end of the school year.

———

B ack at the airport. I'm heading home to Pittsburgh when I get a call from Mary Ellen. "I don't think I can keep Sophie. I'm afraid she's going to eat SweetPea," she says.

From anyone else I'd think this overdramatic, but Mary Ellen knows animals, and I know Sophie. Like all salukis, she's a sight hound. I'd seen her catch a fish and swallow it whole while running in the water at the beach.

In desperation, I dial Geoff again. Again, he doesn't answer.

I don't leave another message. If he's read my emails or listened to my voice mails, he knows I'm here and that I've got the dogs. I push down my resentment at his total disregard.

Think, *think.*

I dial Geoff's mother. She picks up right away and I launch into it.

"Geoff needs to get in touch with me asap," I say.

"Well I don't know where he is," she says. "And I don't want to be in the middle of this."

Great. Geoff has circled the wagons and I'm on the outside. Despite that being vulnerable has been working pretty well, my anger flares. Why doesn't anybody ever have my back? I'm in an airport, Geoff is missing in action, and I'm supposed to just make everything work? I want to be able leave on a whim, goddammit. "You tell Geoff he better answer my calls, because I can't take the dogs back to Qatar," I say, flummoxed. I don't know if I can't take the dogs back or not, but I don't know what else to say. "There's no one else who can take them. If he doesn't do something, I'll have no choice, I'll have to have them destroyed." She replies with a totally noncommittal promise to do her best.

It will be much later before I learn this is the first she's heard of our divorce. I get on the plane bound for Pittsburgh, flipping through my mental Rolodex. Who can keep the dogs?

PITTSBURGH, PA
March 2006

I get Grandpa and Sophie from Mary Ellen's, and drive toward my dad's gym. Both my parents work there, but the place is emphatically my dad's. "Your father knew I didn't like to exercise when he met me," my mother used to say while sitting at the reception area, taking a languid drag off her cigarette.

Thwap! *Thwap*! I hear, the sound of racquetball being played in the background. A sound that always takes me back to being a teenager and makes me want to leave wherever I am.

"Lisa, have you seen this email?" my mother asks. I haven't.

"Well, you might want to have a seat."

I don't want to sit. The dogs are in the car. And there's the thwapping, reminding me that this business had changed all our lives in ways I'd never liked. The company car disappeared, no more family vacations, and we all got jobs.

Noticing I'm not moving, Mom flips her computer around to face me.

"Hi Mary..."

Begins an email from Geoff.

Why is Geoff writing an email to my mother?

"Hi Mary, I have just written Lisa expressing again my regret for this painful situation between us, which is my doing, and my regret that she has allowed her anger at me to put the dogs in such jeopardy. I'd like you to know that I had no idea she was bringing them until the day before she left, and begged her not to do so yet. I also did not know for certain that she had brought them until yesterday."

Put the dogs in such jeopardy? By bringing them home? By not leaving them in Qatar? Like he did. And what's this disingenuous yesterday and today bullshit? Firstly, I'd concocted this entire trip only to see him and planned it before he'd left. With the amount of effort he's put into ignoring me, he has to be aware. Could he not show some small amount of cognition of the fact that indeed, this may be what I've been trying to reach him about? Thus far I've been angry, but not at Geoff. Mostly at myself. I deserved to be left; I blew the best thing that ever happened to me.

Until now.

Now I'm so pissed off at Geoff, I want to throw Mom's computer terminal across the reception area, smack into the glass wall of the racquetball court. It's bad enough he turned his mother against me, but trying to turn mine?

"The only way you could match his level of irresponsibility would be to have left the dogs in Qatar to rot," my mother quips. "Obviously, it's too late for that."

"Would you write that back to him?" I ask. "Please?"

But I know she won't and I let this fuel my anger, so much more powerful than vulnerability.

Back in the car I crank on WDVE, the local rock station. Fuck NPR. It's two-fer Tuesday, and I catch the second Guns 'N Roses selection. "Welcome to the jungle baby," I scream as I drive. "Now you're gonna die!!!"

The dogs yelp from the back seat. *Gratifying.* I'm eager to get to my parents' house so I can check my email, but I'm not exactly in a hurry. My parents live in Murrysville, a small suburb outside Pittsburgh. Though I'd graduated from high school there, it hardly feels more like home than Qatar.

Growing up, my family had moved every year or so; naturally I thought of Murrysville as just another stop along the trail. Until the start of our second year there, when my father sat us down for The Talk. Yay! We were gonna blow this town!

We gathered on our green woolen couches in the living room— my sister, mother and me. The same woolen couches that had moved with us almost every year since I could remember. I pictured pulling the encyclopedias off the bookshelf as we learned where we'd be moving next. Only we weren't going anywhere.

"I've bought a gym," he told us.

It stretched the bounds of even my dysfunctional notion of family communication, that he made this pronouncement to us simultaneously. Leaving the steel industry for the health club business may have turned out to be prescient, but at the time, I thought he was insane from a business perspective. He had two daughters who would soon be matriculating, and he'd just given up his career to open some harebrained small business? Plus, there were way too many people strewn around town I was hoping I'd never have to see again— I was used to blowing in all shiny and new, year after year. To suddenly have to stay in one place? Learn to get along beyond ritual gestures?

Then there is the house itself; my least favorite of all our abodes. Despite that its centerpiece —a room addition abutted at one end by five-foot high stone fireplace, and topped by a cathedral ceiling — is lined with picture windows, the place is best characterized as a dank, ranch number. Even with those high ceilings and glass walls, light itself dies inside.

Maybe it's the clutter. Every surface is littered. As interiors go, it's not evening-newsworthy for hoarding. The house suffers mostly from neglect. They'd lived there close to twenty years before replacing the sectional couch the previous owners left behind, and then only after one of the sections caved in. Being in that environment unleashes a kind of chaos inside that renders me incapable of rational adult behavior. Just to free up the square foot of space I need to make room for my laptop I have to move change, envelopes, reading glasses, candy, notepads and a couple of books.

And there it is, the email from Geoff. I've been copied. I go outside to smoke — my parents also pretend I don't— and ruminate.

Seated at the decaying picnic table that's been there as long as I can remember, I look out at a small stand of trees, smoking and ashing into the base of a clay pot. In the grass behind that was the first place I'd ever made love. It was the summer between my junior and senior year of high school, and the first time I made the connection between adoring someone and expressing it physically. Suddenly, I am seized with the need to find my parents' wedding pictures.

Throughout my childhood I'd spent many an idle hour poring over these images. My favorites remain etched in my mind: my mother looking into the mirror, chin tucked, hands adjusting the veil atop her pillbox hat; my father running through a shower of rice, devastatingly handsome in formal wear; both in the backseat of a limo before being whisked away, hands clasped victoriously around shiny new jewelry. There is one particular photograph I want to see, a shot of my father gently lifting a slice of cake to my mother's mouth. In it, his fingertips graze my mother's tiny waist where, impossibly, my sister rests inside. That gesture had always filled me with longing in the way it said, *I will look after you, I know*. In my teens, I'd looked at these shots and wondered what had happened to that love, where they'd gone wrong. Now I feel the need to see them again, to see if I can figure out what they've done right.

I can't find them anywhere.

There is one change my mother has made to the family manse, she's claimed my old bedroom. This puts me in the guest room in the basement, where I have my own fridge, bathroom, phone, cable, internet, rogue exercise equipment, and a semi-private entry and exit vis-a-vis the garage. Set completely underground, the room has no windows, no source of natural light or air. The perfect lair. For days I go nowhere and see no one. I mostly sleep. This was supposed to be our rendezvous time. Then one day, I open the laptop and there's a note from Geoff. He's coming to pick up Grandpa.

Only Grandpa.

———

The day comes.

I'm out walking the kids when Geoff arrives for the big pick up. He's brought a strange car and I see it in the driveway as I approach the house. My knees buckle slightly as I wonder whose it is. Everyone has been asking, "Is there someone else?"

I say no. I don't think so. But really, I don't know.

Geoff is seated in the green woolen couches in the smaller living room; it's all positioned exactly as it had been when my father announced his new life plan. My parents watch TV in room with the cathedral ceiling.

Just short of groveling, I ask Geoff to reconsider. I still do not want a divorce. I can leave Carnegie Mellon. Or not. I even attempt to ply him with sex.

"Let's," I say, touching his neck. "If I stay in Qatar, we could even sleep with other people. But please, can we just stay married?" Where this came from I have no idea. up to that moment, I would have told you I considered extramarital sex unforgivable. But the idea that Geoff may in fact be with someone else is in my head, and I realize I don't care. I don't want to lose the intimacy of our relationship. Maybe that doesn't have to mean living together or having sex. But I can't imagine life without Geoff. I miss the man I've shared every day with for the past seven years. I miss my best friend.

He declines the offer.

"Why are you still wearing your wedding ring?" I finally ask. I mean, really. There it is on his finger, driving me to distraction. It's true, I'm wearing mine as well, but it's *for* this occasion. In Qatar, I'd stopped wearing it, and there anyway, I'm trying to pretend we're still married.

"It doesn't make any difference," he says.

Much later, I learn that he had not told anyone about the divorce, and I retrospectively assume he's kept his ring on so he doesn't have to tell anyone that he's abandoned us. I'd made it so easy for him by freaking out on his mother. He's certainly clever enough to have orchestrated that.

But in that moment? I have no such ground for purchase. "Do you still feel married?" I ask.

He shakes his head no.

"I don't understand. Why are you doing this?" I ask.

"It has nothing to do with you," he begins.

It's one thing to say that to a prospect, someone you've just met and decided reminds you too much of a loathsome auntie. It's something else to say that to someone to whom you've professed for years— right up to the wake-up call— to love.

After that statement it's hard to listen, although he does go on to tell me exactly how his decision has everything to do with me. "You're not a trusting person," he says, "and I am. And I don't see how we can reconcile that."

I don't need Victoria to understand why this hurts so much. Part of being in recovery is being fully aware of my defects of character. As I had gotten to know Geoff, and slowly exposed my very worst self, I had come to believe he, like Jeffrey before him, had seen and known and accepted me with all my imperfections. Now he's telling me, in no uncertain terms, that I was wrong. That my ugly is too ugly.

Yet somehow, in that moment, I do not feel shame. It will come, just not then. I stay in my most vulnerable self.

"We're just going to get to this place again in another relationship, and I can't imagine meeting someone else I'd rather get through this with than with you."

I can't quite believe this is coming out of my mouth. It's true and it's not mean and it's how I feel. But it changes nothing.

"I just don't feel like being married anymore," he replies.

And that's it. Geoff has rush back to Buffalo. Very Important Deadline.

If this is all the time he's willing to give me— it's been about an hour— there really is nothing more to say. Though I do bring up the storage.

"When do you want to get your things?" I ask.

"Later," he says.

He means never. As in yanni, Insha' Allah... Bukara! Mafi mushkilla.

What I will discover, *later*, is that he'd removed what he wanted from storage the previous fall, during his Ramadan trip.

———

Geoff has to pick Grandpa up off the couch. He won't get up. Doesn't want to leave.

I don't want Geoff to leave either.

"I'm afraid I'll never see you again," I say. "That we won't be in each other's lives."

He grins at me. Those dimples. The sparkle in his eye. I am still in love with him.

"Of course we will," he says. And then he is off.

Sophie and I spend the night on the green couch. As we cling together, I have no idea this will be another last. My friend Julie has agreed to watch Sophie until I come back in the summer, but Sophie will keep running away. From Doha I will arrange a home for her through the saluki rescue league; a farm with all the room she needs to roam. I never see her or Grandpa or Geoff again.

I meet Kyle for dinner. Since we last met her divorce has finalized and she's gotten a new job. She'd been forced out of the university. I find it gratifying to know the constant fear of losing my job wasn't just in my head.

"The Qatar campus was the nail in the coffin," she says. "If you have to choose between getting the job done and building the relationship, pick the relationship every time."

Naturally with all this confessing, I tell her about the divorce. She doesn't say she's sorry, she doesn't feel bad at all. In fact, she's delighted.

"You were too much for him, you know that, right?" I have no idea what she's talking about.

"Lisa, he moved back to his hometown," she said, flicking her now strawberry-colored hair over her shoulder. "You took him across the world, expected him to grow up. He didn't. This is great."

I don't know what to say, so she moves on, telling me about her new job.

"Look, I don't love it like I did Carnegie Mellon," she says. "But that also means I'm not obsessing. That now I have a job that fits my schedule instead of the other way around. I needed to give my daughter more time, she just turned 15."

"That's the thing, Kyle," I say. "Did your husband down-grade his job? No. I hate how it's always women whose careers are de-railed by children and divorce. This is why I don't even want to mention this at work."

"I can't blame you," she says. "I wouldn't want to give that fat bastard Mohamed the satisfaction."

Kyle does seem to get exactly where I'm coming from, though it will be a long time before I can see what she means about Geoff.

"I did tell Robbie that I'm getting divorced and want to leave at the end of the school year," I say.

"How'd she take that?" Kyle asks, an unusual look of surprise flashing in her face.

"That's the weird thing," I say. "She doesn't want me to mention this either. She was totally supportive — she even admitted she wouldn't want to live in Qatar herself — but she's got so much going on, she wants me to work with her on the departure date. To me that means she'll keep quiet, too. So I agreed."

"She's pushing for a flexible departure date? What? As in, you may go when we say you may go?" Kyle muses. "Classic Robbie."

There had been something so affirming about feeling like she needed me to stay, I hadn't thought of it this way. Now I won't be able to think of it any other way. *Great.*

W here are those pictures? I look in the usual spots, the drawers of the built-in desk under Nana's ornate ticking clock. The marble-topped end tables in the living room with the green couches. The desk in the kitchen. Nowhere. They wouldn't have thrown them away, would they?

I want to scratch the itch and compare their actual pictures to my memory of ours, inexact as it might be. Whereas we'd eloped, my parents' photographs featured family prominently. Mom was the eldest of seven, and the first to wed at twenty-three. Her parents look relieved, though they're never quite looking at the camera; their eyes searching the corners of every frame, tracking wayward aunts and uncles. In comparison, my father's mother struggled with her smile. Her hat was askew and

—if the photos are conveying it right —she wore her coat all day long. Dad had been the youngest, the last to wed, the only boy. Only my parents look confident and relaxed.

Our wedding pictures are beautiful — a Bahamian beach at sunset after a storm, we even had a rainbow — but the image that sticks out in my mind is one we attempted at the photographer's behest, a high five. We tried three times, but couldn't quite do it.

Our hands failed to connect.

DOHA, QATAR
March 2006

I return to Qatar with one suitcase. In addition to the dogs and crates, I'd left behind an entire wardrobe of clothes that, for the most part, no longer fit me. I have lost weight, but what I'm starting to notice is that — besides the dogs — I will miss nothing.

My appearance is about to undergo a radical overhaul.

Today is my fourth wedding anniversary.

On the night of our honeymoon, we'd begun a tradition that would come in oddly handy. We'd written love letters to each other, then sealed the envelopes to open the following year. Last year's letters are sitting on the shelf, waiting in a box with years zero, one, two and three. I read them all in search of clues, but only come up with more questions. How? Why? What... It doesn't matter, there will be no more.

I put the letters in a bag. To this I add every photograph of Geoff, Geoff and I, and Geoff's family, save for one: a picture of us at a friend's baby shower, taken in the first months we were together. Geoff is standing behind me, looking on lovingly as I perform for the camera. We look so happy. I don't want to lose sight of the fact that, once upon a time, we had been the answer to one another's dreams.

In the gaps left behind, I mount new snapshots of my most ardent supporters, Mary Ellen, and Valerie my yoga teacher. My sober friends in Qatar, Michelle and Paul. I have no idea where I'm heading or what it's going to look like, but these are the people who are going to help me get there. I put the bag in the hutch in the dining room, and call Valerie to tell her what happened with the dogs after all.

The next day, I'm back at work.

TWENTY-ONE

THE LAND OF MILK & HONEY

The Land of Milk and Honey:
Old Testament reference to the place to which God would deliver those who had served him; a place overflowing with abundance. Milk and honey: also, popular ingredients in spa treatments.

Saloon:
In Asia the word "salon" becomes "saloon"; a fact that caused yours truly no small amount of confusion for an embarrassingly long period of time while living in Qatar.

Riyals:
Qatar's currency.

DOHA, QATAR
March 2006

I T'S TIME TO REUNITE with one of my longtime loves, the Dairy Queen Buster Bar. This means tripping into the congested heart of Doha's traffic. There's a DQ at the Landmark Mall closer to my house, but they don't sell this particular snack bar. I keep asking, hoping they'll sense potential profit, but profit doesn't seem to be a concern for anyone. This is a country the size of Connecticut but with fewer people, and fewer still who can afford the many luxuries on offer. Food vendors have to close all day for the month of Ramadan every year. The ruling family *must* subsidize these businesses, just like they support the university.

As I inch past earth movers, orange construction barrels and piles of concrete slabs, I push down the bubbling self-pity. *Driving was my husband's job! Ex-husband.*

I'm still so lost that, before Geoff left, I'd asked him to make me a map. He hadn't, and I'm suffering because of it. But not today. Perhaps the Buster Bar has seared a spot in my memory, but today I arrive at my destination without error.

Next up, I know I must pull up to the drive-thru window directly — to speak at the intercom is to know frustration.

Maybe I should stay... I start thinking for the millionth time that day. I'm just getting the hang of life in Qatar. Almost before I finish the thought, I stop myself. There's no way I'm staying past the end of the term. Come May, I'm so out of here.

"Buster Bar, please," I say to the Filipina at the window.

She smiles and blinks against the slanting afternoon sun. "Finish!" she chirps.

"Finish" is a translation of the Arabic "helas," a sentiment much closer to "no" than mafi mushkilla, but still not no. She could be telling me they're out of Buster Bars, or also, no more, never again.

This is unacceptable. Never again would mean I am cut off from Buster Bars altogether. I deserve the cold comfort of my non-dairy treat. Nay, I need it.

"Helas Buster Bars?" I say, slashing my hand in the air between me and the steering wheel.

"Oh no, ma'am," she replies. "No more chocolate. More is coming. Insha'Allah."

Whew. Except. That could still be a while.

Summer, not yet in full force, is on its way. The winds, that make it feel as if you are standing in front of an open clothes dryer, have begun to blow through, swirling up the dust, but also keeping the oppressive humidity at bay. Soon my glasses will fog each time I step outside. The massive yard sales — held indoors for safety's sake — will begin. People will start leaving town in droves. Shipments of expatriate supplies — such as Dairy Queen chocolate — will grind to a halt. I'll show them. I head for the Mega Mart across the street.

This means making a right, going through Doha's traffic light to the roundabout at the next block in order to double back, about a 15 minute ordeal. Torture. The gratification of finding Dove Bars — on sale — is so intense, I buy three boxes. Once proud to eschew over-consumption, since moving to Doha I've started buying like it's Communist Russia. We all do, as those yard sales make abundantly clear. Gold lame tissue box cover? Better snatch that up now. At any time, anything could disappear.

My first jaunts to the grocery store had been fun-filled larks. "Oh look, honey, they've put shaving cream next to Preparation h and... What on earth? Clothes pins? how adorably weird!" They became a phantasmagoria to be endured. "I am sure bread was here last week."

This wasn't just about delivery issues. Back in Tunisia, I

once tried to make brownies for our group. This was not an "add eggs to the mix" endeavor; there were no mixes. Thus, I found myself in a dark, cramped aisle, staring at shelves and wondering what in the hell I was looking at. Was that baking powder or baking soda? And how exactly was I going to communicate this question? In Qatar we had mixes and Western brands and even English and Arabic labels, but neither language was necessarily useful to the workers stocking the shelves.

Once, for two weeks, I couldn't find coffee filters. It might not sound like such a long time, but after seven or eight days of making do with paper towels, it started to feel like forever. I checked the usual suspects, the Carrefours, the Megamarts. And when the gleaming expatriate grocery stores failed to deliver, I started hitting up the hole-in-the-wall grocers, places where you drive up and order from a runner who delivers your goods to your window. But I was never sure if they didn't actually have them or simply had no idea what I was asking for.

When five miscellaneous boxes appeared at MegaMart I snatched them up. All of them. They weren't the right size, so I cut them down each morning and kept my eye peeled. When the right-sized filters did arrive, I bought every box on the shelf. Of course, I kept the oversized filters, too, just in case. It won't be until my yard sale that I finally let the #6 paper cones go. A woman clutching the two remaining packages— one of which is open— will ask how much. I will tell her to take them. "Free." But that's getting way ahead.

There in the MegaMart checkout with my ice cream bars and a couple of packages of razors, my mobile rings. It's Michelle. After three years of waiting, her big promotion has finally come through. She's moving to the U.S. in two weeks. Fourteen fucking days. I pull a bar from the box right there in the store and suckle it all the way home.

I need a salon. Or, in local parlance, a saloon. Thanks to Aya, my Qatari graphic designer, I finally have access.

Aya has a heart-shaped face, almond eyes and latte-colored skin and — like all Qatari women I ever met — is always immaculately groomed. She drives a brand new BMW SUV, and talks about summers in europe. I'm certain that at some point she's visited the real thing — a salon — in France.

She's told me about a place called Al Mashata, but I have no idea how to find it. I text her.

Hun, wd u send directions to Al Mashata please?

She calls right away, and agrees to meet me. I'm floored with delight, in part because I'm worried I won't actually be able to find the saloon, but mainly for the chance to hang with some Qatari women. Maybe, like Geraldine Brooks in *Nine Parts of Desire: The Hidden World of Islamic Women*, I'll find my "in" with Qatari culture through the women. Then, I think through the whole story. That Brooks and her husband, Tony Horowitz, had moved to Egypt together and both written books about their experiences. Why weren't Geoff and I able to make it work?

I have to laugh at myself. Talk about compare and despair. Wow, now I'm really reaching, finding some couple I don't know and have never met to make myself feel bad.

Just allow yourself to feel happy.

A ya meets me at the Ramada roundabout and I follow her; I never would've found it otherwise. Al Mashata is a stand-alone villa that's been converted into a house of beauty, set back from the main road behind a gated wall. The only sign reads, 'Children not allowed,' which assumes that whoever shows up with a child will have not only a driver on hand, but a nanny to deal with strays. I park, and Aya pulls up next to me. "I'll be back with my cousin," she says, then drives off.

Inside, the scene is as familiar as any salon I've ever been to, yet still completely alien. The reception area swirls with black abayas, appointment-making, the pressing around of riyals, and chatter. The check-in counter sits in the grand foyer, the list of services hung behind. It's written exclusively in Arabic. I've grown completely accustomed to the fact that most signage in Qataris bi-lingual, even English only. I stand there mute and illiterate, hoping Aya will arrive soon. But a friendly Indian woman behind the counter notices my confusion, and pushes a sheet of paper my way. It's a list of their offerings in English. This does not solve the problem entirely. Threading? Foot henna? What?

"Pedicure, please?"

She shows me to a back room that has ten massive leather chairs built onto blocks, with sinks below. I slip into my comfortable seat and am shown my choices in nail color. Not a massive selection, but a massive improvement over the Ritz already, and less than a third the price. I am so coming back to this place. I pick up a magazine on the side table and start to browse.

I love the way it's someone's job to go through all magazines sold in Qatar with a big black marker, and "cover" plunging necklines, shoulders and knees. Al Mashata has only Arabic-language magazines, so I amuse myself with trying to find bits of skin they might've missed. I can't. Much as I loathe censorship, it's depressing that the words are never redacted. No one is reading them.

In walks our Education City colleague, Jameel, trailed by Aya. Cousins.

They greet me and take their seats opposite mine. I'm so tickled I don't know what to say, but pretty soon it's obvious it doesn't matter. They are chatting away in Arabic and I cannot break in. I understand. I've avoided hanging out with co-workers outside office hours whenever possible, because it quickly turns into work. Then there's the expatriate curiosity factor, on top of that, probably even more taxing. But there's so much I want to ask about, like, why is it that she and Jameel are both wearing their abayas?

I look around the saloon, no one has removed her abaya. They have clothes on under there, I can see sleeves and jeans poking out. Only the shaylas, or headscarves, have been removed, and not by everyone. We're in a testosterone-free zone. Aya doesn't wear her abaya at work. Why would she, or any of them, stay covered? I will never get this place.

Later that evening, looking at my toenails and smoking, it occurs to me that Aya must've pulled some strings to even get me that appointment. I wonder if there was yet another sister she bumped for me to be there at all. The next day, when I thank her for taking me, I can't help but comment on her abaya.

"Why was everyone wearing their abaya out like that, when they don't have to?" I ask.

"We're not always wearing designer clothes!" she laughs. "It's just easier. Like throwing on a baseball hat when you're having a bad hair day."

"But you don't wear it here, and you're not wearing designer clothes," I say, but then notice that actually, yes, her jeans are Guccis, her shoes are definitely not cheap. "Are you trying to set an example?"

"For the students?" she asks, with a smile creeping into her voice. "No, it is for me. I am more comfortable this way at work."

And our conversation on this topic is closed, and I'm only half-satisfied.

In my idealized version of life in Qatar, I'd pictured myself as setting an example. But as my employer Sheikha Mozah shows, I'm not the proof I thought I was. I'm certainly no longer bothered by the fact that she's but one of the emir's three wives. Considering that marriages are essentially contracts engineered for extending the family lineage, keeping households together beyond child-bearing strikes me as actually kind. Marrying a person you have sex with outside of your marriage shows more accountability than we require in the West. I don't think this shift in my thinking owes to my impending divorce, but I can't be sure.

Lest it appear I'd lost my mind *and* soul, I continued to believe, in principle, in the Education City's mission. The way the mullahs in Saudi Arabia took over education underscores the point — when religious leaders control the knowledge in a society, epic disasters (like the Crusades, to name another) ensue. I believe that secular education matters. Even in my brief tenure I'd seen changes.

Our first freshmen were afraid to raise their hands in class — they'd not grown up in an education system that encouraged a dialectical experience. Now, students are actively participating in the Doha Debates, an internationally-broadcast, BBC news program where they not only stand up in a room to make their points, they are broadcast on television. This will, I believe, have a net positive impact on Qatar, and perhaps even the region, in years to come.

And this is when it hits me. I've been operating with this vague sense of discontent because of Doha's ever-changing landscape. This mania to transform has felt in opposition with spiritual ideals of being, as opposed to doing. But purchase is the illusion. Things change all the time. If I can learn to live harmoniously here, I can do it anywhere.

C*an u take me 2 hospital?*

It's a text from Cindy. She is 8 weeks pregnant. This cannot be good. I call Emma and cancel my appointments for the day.

At Hamad we wait for miscarriage to come. She's been going to the American hospital, but since her husband is out of town she figures she might as well take advantage of Hamad's free services. She seems fine, but I am a wreck.

"It's not really a baby, just a clump of cells," she says.

I don't know what to say. Maybe not being able to have a child makes the idea of losing one seem crueler. I haven't said a word to her, or anyone else, about my own infertility or my husband leaving, and now is not the time for my crises anyway.

"I was told I probably would never have children in the first place," she says, brightening. "And we have a beautiful daughter, so you never know. Anything's possible. We'll just try again, that's the best part."

Her comments were not directed at me, and yet I felt a sharp sudden stab of pain.

Will I ever have sex again? Will I ever want to have sex again? How will I ever learn someone new, take on their relationship biography?

Then came the thoughts beneath that.

I've failed to fulfill my gender identity.

And then.

I need a new mantra.

The next day at work there's an email to all staff from the dean announcing a death. The deceased was one of those uber-healthy types to die suddenly, a heart attack while jogging.

He was 48. He's attached to our community through his girl-friend, a colleague who takes my yoga classes. I might not have known him or her well, but I know the sting of unexpected death. There is no one new to come. Just different someones.

And yet, as I write out a card for the bereaved, shock. I expected to conclude with a line about remembering that life is precious because it is short. Instead I urge my friend, the one who was left behind, to remember that life is good.

I wrote that?

My husband's just left, my dogs are gone, my best friend is leaving town, and I feel on the verge of losing my job. But yes, I not only wrote that, I meant it.

Before he died, Jeff was fond of saying there is no life instruction to stop and beat yourself. I could spend the next God-knows-how-long torturing myself with everything I've lost, or I could focus on what to do with the life I had. And thus comes my new mantra.

Pain may be the touchstone of spiritual growth, but that doesn't make happiness a waste of time.

———

At home I go back into the hutch in my dining room and remove the bag I'd filled with pictures and letters. Without peeking, I stuff Geoff's winter coat into the bag. On my way to the dumpster in front of our compound I take the coat out of the bag and offer it to the guard at the front gate, who gladly accepts. Maybe he has relatives in Northern India.

———

A fter the funeral service Rima invites me to her place at the Four Seasons (despite the project's name change, we all still call it that). *Maybe I should move here*. Although, as my other colleagues have gone on to tonier compounds, living at Valley Rose has felt more private. Now that the bougainvillea and hibiscus I'd planted when I first moved in cover the entire front of my villa, I can sit there and smoke in complete privacy. But Rima's made her apartment so beautiful. To the already gorgeous interior, she's added tribal rugs and paintings and photographs. I'm not moving anywhere but out of Qatar.

Over a pasta she's paired with red sauce, we talk about work. "Thank God, Mohamed is finally getting some staff," I say. "It's so much easier to process invoices."

"I know," she says. "It used to feel like trying to get the car keys from dad or something."

"So it wasn't just me?" I laugh, but I meant this in the deepest way.

After our meal Rima produces a crystal ashtray. Smoking was a behavior I'd always tried to hide, but lately we've both been letting down our guard, to a certain extent anyway.

"How are your sons?" I ask, genuinely curious. I'd often wondered what the children of such an accomplished woman would be like.

She tells me her older son had just completed his doctorate, and the other is about to have a child.

What I really want to ask about is the rumor that she's sleeping with a colleague.

"And what about your husband, how is he?"

"He's good. Busy. And yours?"

"Good. Busy."

After dinner I drop in on Cindy. Considering what we've just shared at the hospital I'm thinking I'll tell her about my divorce. She's still recuperating, but she's clearly wound up from spending so much time alone. I tell her I've just come from Rima's.

"You've never noticed?" Cindy asks. "The eyebrows are painted on, she wears a wig — a good one, but it's a wig. The woman has no hair."

"I wonder if Rima had cancer or something," I say.

"I wonder if that's why her husband left her," Cindy says.

"What? She's divorced?"

"God, love, don't you know anything?" Cindy starts. "This isn't even news. She and her husband have been apart for 20 years."

Rima, a woman possessed of a working knowledge of three languages and at least as many passports, is divorced from the man she still referred to as her husband?

"No wonder she's sleeping with that guy."

"So you do know *some* things," Cindy laughs. "But get this, she has every reason to call that man her husband. They're still married."

Once more I'm creeped out at how Cindy's willingness to reveal details from the personnel file. There's no way I am telling her about my divorce. What was I thinking? In Doha we live for these juicy tidbits. We are our own celebrities.

"Why would her husband leave her for having cancer?"

"Can't have kids after that."

"But they already had two sons." "Maybe that wasn't enough for him."

Oof.

DOHA, QATAR
April 2006

Michelle and I meet for the last time at the Costa Coffee near the Ramada Roundabout, not far from my favorite DQ, which still has no Buster Bars. Curiously, in the parking lot there's a stand with the words "hot" and "dog" written on one side. What in God's name could they be selling there?

The first and last time I ever visited Doha's Chili's — the place for ribs — I'd been disappointed to learn they didn't even do a beef version of ribs. It was basically an Appleby's. Now you can buy hot dogs? Emphatically uninterested in hot dogs, I don't even check. Rumor is they might start selling pork when the Asian Games blow through town. I will be gone by then.

Michelle arrives in a deep blue, button-down shirt, khakis and a pair of Bally flats. Her hair is down and looks amazing, soft curls framing her face. She is carrying the latest Louis Vuitton handbag, with a cherry blossom pattern, the very portrait of a successful professional. Meanwhile, I'm wearing Capri jeans and a tight T-shirt with cap sleeves. My money is balled up in my pocket. I just don't care about looking conservative enough anymore. Go ahead, deport me!

Unlike most people, Michelle never asks "what happened" in my marriage. It isn't that she doesn't care, quite the opposite. She knows. In our many discussions about the complexities of our marriages we'd discussed how, along with deep love, there could co-exist equally deep feelings of animosity. Or maybe this is wrong. She and her husband were still together then, but they wouldn't be much longer. What I recognized in the moment, however, was that this was why I loved her so. Michelle had a unique ability to accept conflicting information without judgment.

She does ask me what I've learned in the months since Geoff's been gone.

"Months?" I say. "That can't be right."

"It's April," Michelle says. "He's been gone since January." My answer surprises me even more.

"I feel relieved," I hear myself say. "I wake up glad he's not there. He never asked me to, but I kept making decisions based on what I thought he wanted. What music to play. What shirt to buy. In this box I defined, I kept packing myself into smaller and smaller spaces. Now I get to unpack."

What? I had no idea I was even thinking these things, let alone about to say them. But it's true. I love waking up in the morning and playing music and reading and smoking and surfing the internet. When Geoff was there he'd always try to wake up with me. I knew he was trying to be sweet, but I had a low-grade resentment about it. He was a night person, and I could never last with him. But I had no problem going to sleep and leaving him to his own devices. It surprises me to realize how much I'd missed having time to myself.

"Good girl," Michelle says.

And that's when I really feel the loss. Things will always come and go, but Michelle, with whom I've shared Buster Bars and coffee both, will be gone for good.

"It's a different story when I go to bed."

Even if we didn't always go to bed at the same time, I knew he was there. Now I fear there will never be anyone there again.

"Doha didn't invent deprivation, you know," Michelle says. "You can find it anywhere."

"I know, I know. The land of plenty comes from within and all that," I say.

"Or perhaps," Michelle says, "it's your turn to be there for someone else."

And this is one truth I've learned in sobriety. So much self-help talk is about learning to love yourself before you can love others. My experience has been one of learning to love myself by loving and doing for others first. It's basic self-esteem building, doing esteemible acts.

We hug.

"You look amazing, by the way, so happy," I say. "And your hair. Did you get that done when you were in Bali?"

"Oh, no! There's a new hairdresser in town at the Intercon. You must go see him," she says, handing me the number. "You need to make an appointment, so call."

An appointment?

Weird.

Most places you just walk right in.

Doha *is* changing.

TWENTY-TWO

SHWAY SHWAY

Shway shway:
"Little, little." Depending on context, it may mean anything
from *"I speak a little bit of Arabic"* to *"Slower, more gently."*

DOHA, QATAR
May 2006

I'VE GOT A NEW routine down.

On my trip home, my friend Julie— the one who'd
been unable to keep Sophie contained— is horrified when
I tell her about Qatar's lack of bookstores (and no, I don't count
the departure terminal at the airport or the sad little selection of
travel books that had recently appeared at Jarir's). She has sent
me back to Qatar with a suitcase full of reading material, and it's
as if I've re-discovered reading. I'm going at it like I did when I
was 10. At night I read till I can no longer keep my eyes open,
then when I wake up I put my nose right back in the book until I
absolutely have to leave for work. When I get home, it's back to

the book. I repeat this cycle until I come upon one particular title, Waiting for My Cats to Die. Our protaganist has just turned 40 and asks, Will I ever get laid again? Or have I had sex for the last time ever? What gets her through this crisis is her place at the nexus of a web-based community. She's a blogger.

Up to this point I'd held a low opinion of blogs and blogging. Behind the wall of online anonymity, people could say whatever they wanted regardless of the truth.

Now it occurs to me, *I* could say whatever I wanted. And remain anonymous. Unlike the rest, however, I would camouflage my identity, not to present a better version of myself, but to tell the truth.

F or the first time in months, I crack my computer in the middle of the night, naming my website The Years of Sleeping.

Thursday, May 25, 2006 Is optimism doomed?

At about 9:30 p.m. last night Val actually had to wake me up to tell me to leave. She offered her couch, but I wanted to brush my teeth.

"I used to have spare toothbrushes," she said. But she's not that optimistic anymore.

Neither am I, though there had been a time when I carried even travel-sized dental floss (hyperlink to great moments in science: dental floss).

That was after Jonathan, my first fiancé. In an early phone conversation he kept taking these long pauses. I had to ask. He was flossing. That he was peering intently into his own mouth while courting me should have been a sign. Instead I said, "I like a man who thinks oral hygiene is important."

What a dolt.

Thus read my first-ever blog entry.

But concealing details about my identity and location, at last I found a place to share the uncensored truth about what was going on in my head. What a relief. Even with people I'm close to I've been pretending.

"We're having a very modern divorce," is how I put it to the few whom I do tell the story. "Doing the whole thing over email."

I'm joking when, in fact, I don't find it at all funny that this is how it's going down.

"Now might be a time to break down, Lisa," Mary Ellen says.

I smile. Nod. "I'll have to think about that."

What I'm thinking is, *what the hell does a healthy break-down look like, anyway?*

"I can't believe how you just keep going," Val tells me.

Attempt to smile and nod, but really, just look wistful. *But how should I look?*

Then, with people who don't know about my impending change in marital status, I'm even more obtuse.

"Are you alright?" the dean, Chuck, asks. "You've lost a lot of weight."

"Thank you, I'm fine. Unless you're saying I was fat before." I'm joking but also not joking about that.

W hat I do feel is unmoored. One of the things I'd loved about being married was the idea of my life rooted by its effect on another. untethered now, I often feel as if at any moment I might float away and it won't matter one whit. My life has taken on a surreal, conditional quality, the feeling it will start "for real" later. If I can make it here until the end of my contract, then I can travel the world. Or get the next job. Or, you know, be happy!

Worst of all are the friends who tell me they envy my freedom. It's all I can do not to scream when such sentiments are thrust my way. I certainly can't seem to explain that, no, finding myself swiftly and unexpectedly single is not like being set free as a kid in a candy store. It's more like when you're sick, and standing in the drug aisle, trying to decipher which combination of symptoms you have so you can choose the right pain reliever. My decision will show the world not only my competency, but tie directly to my immediate, near-term level of suffering.

I take all this to my blog, and take to blogging with a passion. Between the reading and the blogging and at least showing up for work, I seem to have zero spare time. I don't miss the TV— that was a good money-saving decision, Geoff was the one who watched — but the maid's another story. I'd figured it'd be easier to clean up after myself alone, but with all this typing and reading it's not quite working out that way.

The summer winds leave a fine layer of dust throughout my opulent, if shoddily constructed villa. It's cockroach season, the time of year these critters flock indoors to die. I cannot connect broom and dustpan and time to simply sweep them away. The mounting corpses remind me of the summer of Fleas, the months that followed Jeff 's death.

My recollection of that summer, is sitting for hours in front of my Mac Classic, journaling and spooning down Frusen Glad-je's Swiss Chocolate Almond ice cream straight from the pint container, swatting absent-mindedly as fleas nipped away at my shins. It wasn't until September, after my neighbor claimed my cat for her own, that I finally set off a flea bomb.

As soon as I think it, I type this thought into my blog, forgetting again about the cockroaches.

When I run out of books my routine shifts slightly, with typing taking over for reading. Whereas the books had to be confined to lunch hour, I find I can write on my blog and appear to be productive at my desk.

I begin to actively appreciate my job.

TWENTY-THREE

GOING BLUE(TOOTH)

Mobile:

No one calls it a "cell phone" outside the U.S. It's "mobile," with "bile" pronounced like the stomach acid.

Blue:

American slang for "dirty," as in dirty comedy.

DOHA, QATAR

May 2006

A REUTERS REPORTER CALLS about a story he wants to do on campus. "They call it Blue-toothing," he says.

"A Blue-whaa?"

"Bluetooth is a feature on your phone that allows you to communicate wirelessly with other Bluetooth-enabled devices." Though it's haram, or sinful, for members of the opposite sex to speak to one another, Udai explains that the young men and women of Qatar circumvent this hadith by using the short range devices on their cell phones. They aren't speaking, they're Bluetoothing. At least unlikely to get caught.

He tells me that, when you see someone you like, you hit "browse device." That sends a message that asks for a connection. If accepted, you can begin a conversation.

"This is why everyone is always charging their phones," he says. "Discoverable mode runs down the battery."

Not bad, I think. Possibly on par for efficiency with actual dating, even with the difficulty actually identifying yourself or your target. You're at a mall, what do you write? *Im the 1 in black?*

Udai, a Lebanese man who'd been raised in Vancouver, already knows how it works, he just needs color for his story. That's where the campus part comes in. Of course, I can't grant his request, but personally I can't wait to read the story.

In the absence of my husband, my mobile (another word I'd adopted from the Britpats) has become increasingly significant. Attending to its beeps and vibrations, when I'm supposed to be doing something else, helped me believe that I was needed in Qatar. For the most part. At times I'd find myself surrounded by texters and talkers, longing for the sound of my ring tone. (I'd set it to "Continental," like the phone sounds in Pink Floyd's "The Wall.")

Sometimes, I pretend I've heard it and fish for the phone in my bag. Sometimes there's even a message. Like an automatic verification of deposit. *Awesome.* But I'm not sure you can live in Asia and not turn into a complete asshole with a cell.

I'm not sure when I turned. There was that early business meeting where the cigarette-smoking designer's cell phone had gone off with a plaintive pop tune, "Habi-i-i-biii!" (Dear one!). I'd been shocked when he took the call during the meeting, without leaving the room. But by the time Udai visits, I'm so on board with this behavior I've become the kind of person who not only takes calls in meetings, sometimes I place them. Texts, anyway. I never was quite so brazen as to start the talking. (Though many others did.) Most of the people I wanted to talk to— or about— would be in the meeting anyway.

ME: *wot wd u call R's hairstyle 2day? I'm going w/geo washngtn*

DONNA: *how did u c past that outfit? tangerine NIGhTmare!*

I invite Udai to come at lunchtime.

"No, you absolutely cannot officially interview our students," I tell him as I lead the way to our student cafeteria, so he can grab an unofficial bite to eat.

———

"I cannot imagine dating again," I tell Victoria.

"Luckily you don't have to worry about that here," she says.

Very funny. "But seriously, I've been in this blissful state of not having a sex drive. But that Udai's visit got me thinking. He spoke English and Arabic fluently. He was wickedly smart and handsome. Not once in our interactions, however, did I get the feeling that he'd rather be in my pants than conversing, that mere circumstance was blocking a more passionate encounter.

"In fact, I can't think of a single instance of a man expressing unwanted interest in me during any of the past six years that Geoff and I have been together."

"Did you ever cheat in your relationships?"

"Not sober," I say.

"Me neither, and no one's ever come on to me, either. You give off signals that say you're not available."

That seemed too easy. "I'm totally available, even if technically I'm still married," I said. "I'm worried it's the menopause. That *that's* the signal I'm sending out. That I'll never get laid again."

"But didn't you say you haven't been in the mood for sex?"

So? I shrug.

"So stop telling yourself that story."

Easy for her to say. I set my mobile on discoverable. For exactly one afternoon.

I leave Victoria's and head for the carwash, an all-male bastion I'd previously left to Geoff. But fuck it. The Jeep's filthy, and dirty cars depress me more than I fear going to an unwelcoming place. I've been here long enough to know that nothing bad is going to happen.

My phone vibrates. A message!

No. Someone wants to connect with me on Bluetooth. What?

I look around. There is only one person remotely close enough to have sent the message, an older gentleman in a dirty thobe, sitting in a plastic chair opposite mine. He's staring at his phone, sucking his teeth. I decided to go outside to wait, and shut my Bluetooth off. So much for nothing bad happening. Is that what I can attract these days?

PITTSBURGH, PA
May 2006

The day of Carnegie Mellon's commencement is gray and rainy. The Qataris I've traveled to the States with *love* it. "Hamdullilah!" God is great!

When you come from the desert, rain and cold are miracles.

But the weather reminds me how nice it is to burrow into Geoff's side. His warmth. His smell. The whole trip is like this, I am in and out of moments while I'm supposed to be running interference for Her Highness.

On the phone with Theresa Heinz's office. "Does she eat meat?"

I'd be shocked if she didn't, but I don't know. *Will a lover ever cook for me again?*

Then with the hospital at Pitt. "Where is she?"

Where indeed. *That's the million-dollar question I'd like to ask.*

After applause in the library. "Can you get her to do a photo with us?"

I can't make anyone do anything. *Geoff remains incommunicado. I need to find a lawyer. Not in Qatar, that's for sure.*

Commencement. Her Highness is speaking.

Did she just call for a jihad on ignorance? *Who decides what's ignorant?*

There is one lone protester in the audience with his back to Sheikha Mozah as she addresses the assembly. Considering the number of angry emails we'd gotten from human rights activists, this is a working out well. We'd been expecting an angry mob.

They are furious at the exploitation of labor. They're not wrong, but also, the U.S. was built on guest workers. It's not OK, but I wish my fellow Americans could be less sanctimonious. Of course, most of my compatriots haven't spent the last two years realizing just how similar our cultures really are.

I need to get out of Qatar.

The next morning, coverage. The lone protester is not mentioned. No one mentions the guest workers, or the jihad on ignorance, or how difficult her English was to understand. The Today Show provides rapturous coverage.

The blind spot in the coverage may be great on the professional front, but it's exactly the kind of soul sucking moment that made me leave the corporate world the year before I met Geoff. Are people that easily conned? Or is it about the money?

The elevator door opens to the lobby of the William Penn hotel in downtown Pittsburgh. There she is — Her Highness and her entourage.

I can scarcely recognize some of these women with whom I have been working very closely these last months; everyone is wearing a suit, including Her Highness. Everyone seems much plainer, despite their beautiful clothing; the abaya mystique is broken. I'd found the garment terrifying before I lived there — anyone wrapped in black in the blistering heat of the desert surely has something to hide, no? — now I see how weirdly sexy it is. More hypocrisy!

As I walk toward the group, seated on couches, I think back to what Rima said about Her Highness early on. "If she doesn't like you, it's bad. If she does like you, it's worse." Now I'm on my way out, it's time to take a chance. Show what I've learned about duplicitous charm from them. Maybe something like, "What a delight to have someone such as yourself bring ignorance to our attention in your speech yesterday, well done!" Move over, Saladin! What the hell?

"Excuse me, your Highness," I begin.

In one eternal second she locks me in her gaze. The chatter around her stops, as do I.

Her slow, steady, sure movements — and she is not really moving, she is sitting on a couch, but just the looking is enough — convey power and strength with femininity such as I have never encountered. There is nothing masculine about her and yet, you do not want to fuck with this woman. Clothing be damned! Everything changes to match the pace in her orbit, including me. I can't even imagine what she's been through to be this woman. I fall instantly, irrevocably, in love. These are the only words that dare to form.

I introduce myself and tell her my job. "What an honor to finally meet you."

I do not reach out my hand; this is bad for royals and for Muslim women in general. No touching without permission. You must wait.

"We are delighted to be here," she says.

And then it's over. The chatter resumes and I am, without word or gesture, somehow thrust out. Gently, but surely.

That's how I want to be a woman.

My next big meeting is with Hilary, a divorce attorney. She terrifies me too, but in a different way.

"You wanna do this thing fast, before he establishes residency in New York," she tells me, tapping the desktop with a pencil.

How come?

"Because New York laws favor the dependent spouse," she says. "You could end up paying for your ex-husband to get another degree, alimony, his lawyer's fees, plus half of everything you have."

But Geoff wouldn't do that to me.

"Didn't you say you weren't expecting the divorce?"

I start the paperwork. I'd worked too damn hard for that 93 percent.

Later, I will joke that getting divorced was exactly like being married. "He said what he wanted, and I made it happen."

Is it the money that gives Sheikha Mozah — or if I thought about it, every Qatari woman I'd met — her surety? Whereas I'd been raised to believe that becoming a bag lady was a very real possibility, these women never worry they'll wind up alone and stuck with a mortgage at 39. Or any other time. Even if they do divorce — and it happens a lot more than I'd imagined — they simply returned to the family compound. Not that this is a choice they get to make. There is no option for not living with your family. A Qatari woman does not simply rent an apartment somewhere. She either lives with her husband's family, or her own. Yet they manage to project this air that they are complete.

Then again, what exactly is so free about my circumstances?

I am by no means rich, but I have all the money I need to pay my bills, take care of my health and put something away. But only if I stay in Qatar.

My presence isn't required elsewhere, I have no interest in returning to Pittsburgh, and I can't imagine being hired by anyone in my current state.

Victoria would say this is disaster thinking, but if this isn't a disaster, what is?

———

I reach out to a former lover, tell him I've just been to the divorce attorney. He doesn't really ask any questions. Never did. I do not tell him of his place in the pantheon. The first after. I just want to get it over with. I like that I won't have to ratchet up the count of men I've slept with to take this man on board. The most thrilling aspect of our coupling is that I get a period right in the middle of it. At least he'll think I'm still fertile! yes, I think this. But otherwise, our encounter is lackluster. Still, it hurts when he eschews my embrace the night before I leave Pittsburgh.

"It's not like we're building something here," he says, taking off his glasses and shutting off the light. Simple as that. For him.

I am hating being this person. I want to dump someone.

TWENTY-FOUR

YANNI, INSHA'ALLAH... BUKARA!

Yanni:
A breather word, like "like." Used liberally, but always ahead of Insha'Allah bukara.

Bukara:
"Tomorrow." An oft-bandied promise.

Yanni, Insha'Allah... Bukara!:
Literally, "Like, God willing, tomorrow!" Though there's a pause between the second and third words, the phrase indicates *a shifting, Wile E. Coyote point in time*, especially when following the words *mafi mushkilla*, at which point you're being told something closer to "not now, probably never, God willing!"

DOHA, QATAR
May 2006

DRIVING HOME FROM THE airport I'm overcome with the awareness that I'm surrounded by dog hair and my husband's dander. Why am I still driving Geoff's Jeep? And like that, the scale is tipped— my desire to purge finally outweighs my inertia. Doing anything around cars has been traumatic since landing in Doha.

DOHA, QATAR
June 2004

Upon arrival in Qatar it was clear, with temperatures soaring over 110 degrees four months out of the year (and topping 120 for another two), your car had to be tough. It was also immediately obvious you were surrounded by locals with nothing to fear from the police and for whom road rage was a hobby, you had to be tough. Thanks to the carsickness I suffered on roads that spun in circles every 300 yards or so, I had to ditch the driver and find a car more quickly than I'd have like.

I was unwilling to get trapped in the golden handcuffs of being an expat in the Gulf, but options in my price range were these nasty, low-end models I'd never heard of, like the Nissan Sunny, the Honda Jazz, the Skoda. These reminded me of the cars I'd grown up with, like the Pacer, the K Car, the Yugo. Not a one in the bunch gave me the requisite confidence. Then too, unwilling was not the same as impervious.

Our little peninsula was home to Rolls Royce and Bentley and Mercedes dealers. In the past I'd looked down on people who chose such vehicles. What were they trying to prove? But then... here in Qatar, no one walked anywhere. You knew people by their cars. Who was late for work. Who was at the party. Even the Emir (highly visible, speeding through Doha's roundabouts in a phalanx of black BMW SUVs while traffic was stopped for his passage). Given the local conditions however, suddenly these automobiles seemed practical.

Though a road safety campaign had recently begun (bizarre billboards reminded drivers "do not take your life in your hands") and red lights and stop signs had begun to appear, car accidents were the leading cause of death in Doha.

I sought advice.

"If you don't half a Lahnd Crooszer," my co-worker Fawzi intoned in his inimitable Yemeni accent, "You're a looszer."

A quick look at the roads showed this sentiment was taken to heart by much of the population. The Toyota land cruiser was the vehicle of choice, admired both for its on-and off-road capabilities, as well as a hefty tolerance for abuse. But it was well out of my price range. Unless I bought used, an idea Fawzi vetoed immediately.

"If there is any breakdown on the road, the police?" He hinted. "The police here are bad."

"What do you mean, bad?"

"They are men," he said, as if his clue should have been obvious. "For some women it is okay to drive around with their hair out," he grinned, letting me know I was just such a woman, as he drove us to lunch with my uncovered head. "For my wife it is safer with a driver."

The best part of having a driver, I reckoned, was always knowing where to find your wife. Women may have had the legal right to drive but, like the right to travel, their male guardian had to approve. The only reason I could be alone in a car with Fawzi was because we were co-workers and I was a godless Christian.

"A used car is the way to go," Mohamed advised. "You'll find something at the used car souq for sure. It's over by the castle roundabout."

I took this as a compliment. The car souq was not a place most lady expats went, and Rima, my running buddy in those early days, had shown no interest. When Geoff got there he was all over it. Better yet, he could find it.

Thinking I was being clever, I tried to memorize the souqs on the way over. Unlike the ever-shifting landmarks, retail areas didn't move. There was the fruit and vegetable souq. The cell phone souq. The car wash souq. All very specific.

"Geoff, did I tell you about the time a group of us went to the animal souq? I saw camels mating," I mused as he drove the rental car. "And yes, it was as terrifying as you'd think. Their penises are the size elephant trunks."

As we drove on my mind wandered. *God forbid we get a flat.* Where is that souq?

When at last we arrived, I'd lost all sense of where I was in relation to where we'd begun. But there was no mistaking the used car souq.

Extending through four roundabouts was a sea of used sedans, trucks and SUVs. Wealthy citizens cast off vehicles with scarcely any wear at all —a cherry red BMW convertible, last year's Porsche Carrera, a Land Rover sedan. (Who knew they even made them?) There were also well-worn makes, miles of Jeeps and Fords and Nissans.

Tucked in between the lots were garages and food stalls, fronted by men in blue jumpsuits and dirty thobes drinking tea. It was the first time I'd ever seen a dirty thobe. Even with Geoff at my side, I felt vaguely uncomfortable poking around. There wasn't another woman in sight. Would we have to come back?

But it only took one look to find the car I never knew I

always wanted, an Audi A8. After a lifetime of economy—minded vehicles, this desire surprised me as much as Geoff.

Seven years old, she still looked brand new —black and gleaming inside and out. Leather interior. Fully adjustable seats. Bose stereo. An eight cylinder engine that responded with an alacrity that made me feel I could take on the traffic around me. Her handling was incredibly tight.

"I want this car," I told Geoff.

He looked puzzled. "But it's so...big."

True, a small family could have nestled inside her trunk. But she was lithe. I couldn't get her out of my mind. We looked around more, checked out more new cars in the budget. Ugh.

"I still want the Audi," I told Geoff.

"Are you sure?" He asked. "It's old. And so big."

Finally I realized that this was the selling point. Deep within her ample frame, I felt safe. When we signed the papers, the salesman at Platinum Motors told me she had once belonged to the Syrian ambassador.

"Is that the Middle Eastern equivalent of a little old lady?" I asked.

Blank stare.

Right. Not funny in Qatar.

On the way home I felt compelled to point out how great she was.

"Hey check this out," I said, pushing buttons to adjust my lower lumbar, leg and neck rests.

"This car is almost a decade old," Geoff said, unimpressed with my discovery. "So is the technology."

"You gotta admit," I added, trying not to sound too desperate for affirmation, "riding her feels like we're floating on a magic carpet."

"Yeah, her suspension is a dream," he agreed.

Ha! I thought, adjusting the seatback to full recline. "I

wonder if we could ship this back to the States." Always pushing.

Doha, Qatar
May 2006

I call Paul for his opinion on whether I should try and fix the car. Not because he is a man and it's a car but because this is how my "friend-dependency" works. I have to talk everything through. After spending most of Ramadan at the dealer, I had yet to learn what exactly was wrong with the car.

"I can't even think about a driver, can't deal with the car sickness," I tell him. "I can sell the jeep and use that money to rent a decent car for the next couple of months. Just leave that stupid Audi in the garage."

"Weren't you still *driving* it?"

"Yeah, the car still moves on the road, but the engine started skipping and I'm afraid it'll stall and I'll end up on the grill of some Qatari's Land Cruiser," I say. "And I want to get rid of the Jeep."

The next day Paul and his wife are at my door with a wad of cash. Apparently she'd really liked driving the Jeep to the airport. This sale feels too fast, but summer is coming and departing expats will be offloading newer, shinier Jeeps. The raft of new purchasers will not come along again until the summer is over, by which time I hope to be gone myself. Better to take his offer than miss the possibility of a sale altogether.

And so, like the divorce I seem to be organizing, I take the best advice Mary Ellen ever gave me. "Accept everything and move on."

Then Paul and his wife are gone. It's Thursday evening.

Unless I want to be stuck in my villa for the next two days, I need to do something about the car situation right away. I'm not even sure I have enough food in the fridge to tide me over and I don't want to miss yoga.

I walk into the garage, a cement carport, really. Because it's open on one side, the car is coated in desert dust, a fine beige silt that makes its way up and out of the sand and infiltrates all crevices. I open the door and the light comes on — thank God the battery's not dead —but I can't see out the windows. Rather than try and start the engine, I wheel her onto the driveway to hose her off. Both rear tires have gone flat. I've been worried enough about the transmission. Now this?

I could go over to Robert's, my neighbor and Geoff 's former boss. He'll have food or at least be willing to go out to eat. But I'll just be creating a worse situation later because the tire place won't open again till Saturday, a day where it will be crowded, a press of bodies consisting of me and other people's fixers and drivers. Tonight? The place will be empty. There's a place less than a mile from my house and, worst-case scenario, I can call Robert to come get me.

I drive slowly, a/c off, windows down. Sweating and smoking, though I don't typically smoke in the car, mostly because I don't want to be seen smoking, but also because of the smell. In this situation, the smoking is a defense; I don't want to catch the scent of the engine burning.

At the tire store I'm surprised to learn that I need to replace *three* tires. Apparently we'd been riding on the spare. The regular full-sized tire was in the trunk and it was flat too. When did that happen?

Having four full-sized tires lead to an immediate performance improvement. Part of the "sputter" was the uneven surface we'd been driving on. I'm not sure about the car's overall health, but I get a little cocky on the drive home. Turn on the a/c. Then the stereo! Behind the Audi's tinted windows I laugh and sing along with Neko Case.

"They're all so happy... now that I done wrong. I'm surprised they don't come up and thank me."

———

Sunday at work.

I still want to sell the Audi, I don't trust it. Plus I don't really think I can just leave it in the garage at my villa and depart Qatar. The car *is* registered in my name.

Maybe now I could stomach a driver. Or maybe I'll go back to renting?

How am I gonna sell a broken car? *Time for more advice.*

Soon as I'm done debriefing Mohamed on our upcoming ad campaign, I lay out my car troubles.

"I'm not sure if I should fix it or sell it."

"What's wrong with the Audi?" he asks. "I love that car."

"I do too," I say, feeling touched by our moment of solidarity. I tell him how the car had begun to choke on the roads and how, fearing a breakdown, we'd taken her into the dealer. Mohamed is not surprised to learn that, even after spending all of Ramadan at the dealer's, I still don't know what's wrong with the car.

"It's still drivable, right?" he asks.

"I think?"

"Then you can sell it at the monthly car auction," he says. "The prices are low, but so are the standards."

"Do women go there?" I say, startled at the idea.

"You could ask Fadhel to help you," he says with a grin. And he's back. Bonding over.

But maybe Paul will come with me. First I have to get the oil changed.

My grandfather owned a garage, and in turn my father knew nothing about fixing cars. The only wisdom ever imparted to me was this: change the oil every 3,000 miles. Now, I don't think I put 3,000 miles on the car the whole time I lived in Qatar, too small a place. But because of that desert dust we'd been getting the oil changed every three months and when I say "we," I mean Geoff.

On my own, I have no idea how he accomplished this task, so once, again, I ask. Robert this time.

We're sitting on his stoop—I've taken Geoff's place in these nightly gatherings. I smoke, he drinks, and we gossip. We don't speak of Geoff and more than we speak of his wife and kids. The main difference being I haven't met his family; he's here without them. Who knows what the real story is. And I haven't mentioned I'm leaving.

Robert is the perfect go-to because everyone else I know would've gotten their driver or their employer's fixer to do it for them. I still have a fixer problem in Fadhel. Luckily, Robert lives like a monk. He doesn't have a driver and I just don't see him paying a fixer. He'll know how oil changes get done.

"There are a couple of places nearby," he tells me. "On the far side of the Landmark Mall, opposite the Mercedes dealer. Or you could try the gas station at the Burger King roundabout. But why did you get rid of the Jeep if there's something wrong with the Audi?"

Think fast.

"Geoff has signed onto that consulting position permanently," only a white lie. "And I never really liked the Jeep anyway." Totally false.

"How is Geoff?" he asks.

Really? Now?

"Good. Busy," I say. "Hey, did you notice they've started using the word waqf in place of the word 'charity.' Weird, huh?"

"Indeed. Historically it's meant keeping Arab lands in Muslim hands. Has that jihad connotation, doesn't it?"

"Right, like, give us money or else!"

And on we riff.

Does no one think it strange *they* haven't heard from Geoff?

The following Saturday I go to the nearest oil change station first. They don't have the right filter, so I go to the one by the mall, same story. By the end of the day I've gone to five different garages, but am still driving around with the same old oil. Geoff had never mentioned having this kind of trouble. I can't believe how I'd insisted on these oil changes. This is why my marriage ended: I behaved like a spoiled child.

I'm driving home in defeat when I spy a place called Rapid Oil Change. Reassuringly, it looks like an American oil change shop. Most of these places look nothing like oil change outlets from back home, they are holes in the wall with no signage, hence the asking where to even go.

But Rapid Oil Change had a large, bright, red-lettered with three double-wide metal doors in front of changing bays. I'm so thrilled to find it, I don't mind having to loop back around the roundabout to accomplish the left-hand turn. Or that I take the wrong slip road. This is the madness of driving in Doha, oftentimes the roads in front of shops don't actually lead to the shops themselves. Like a local, I ignore road rules and just drive over the low barrier, half on the sidewalk, right up to the front door. Let's do this thing. Who needs a Jeep?

"Tch tch tch," the guy behind the counter says, shaking his head. "La."

"La?" I ask. "Why la?"

And what's an Arabic speaker doing working the counter at an oil change shop?

"T'faddal," he says, extending his right hand. Allow me to show you.

I follow his arm out the front door, where I see a giant gaping hole, complete with orange construction barrels and netting, capped off by a giant sign that reads, "Sorry for disturbing." The place is either closed for renovation or still being built. He's not an employee, probably the owner.

Later that night Paul breaks the news.

"To get the right filter you're going to have to go back to the dealer," Paul tells me later that night. "Industrial Road."

He offers to come if I can wait until the following Saturday, but I don't want to risk driving to and from work all week. The car, though driving much better, is by no means perfect. And anyway, by the following Saturday I want him to accompany me selling the car at the auction. Besides, Sunday morning ought to be nice and empty, too. An excellent reason to go in late. *Aim low!*

Calling Emma to say I'll be late, I savor the moment. *I have someone to call now.* As I'm inching toward Industrial Road, I make out Khalifa stadium going up in the distance, one of three new arenas being installed for the Asian Games.

The imminent athletic event baffles me; the closest thing Qatar has to a sporty national pastime is driving. Nonetheless, the ruling family has spent $15 billion to ready their country for these Games I'd never even heard of before living in Qatar. Apparently, they're trying to woo the real Olympics.

The amount sounds outrageous, but moving toward the

stadium and thinking about the sheer volume of what's being brought in for these games—from the printing presses to churn out the giant vinyl wraps coating the city's skyscrapers with logos, to the athletes to man their teams—the reported dollar amount seems almost conservative. In a few short years they'd be rewarded with the FIFA World Cup, but sitting there in the traffic with the Games mere months away and construction at a fevered pitch, I wonder if they will pull it off. The construction is definitely making commutes more hellish than usual.

When I finally make it to the dealer they tell me they can't change the oil until the next day at the earliest. Yanni, insha'Allah, bukara. But I don't get my hopes up. Mafi mushkilla, they add, meaning, *maybe never*.

I'm sick to death of the passive/aggressive invocation of God. Helas.

"You had my car all of Ramadan and still can't tell me what's wrong with it," I say, even though I know this guy has no idea what I'm talking about. "Just give me a filter so I can get out of here."

On the way out the door I worry the job might require special Audi tools, but I'm not turning back now. I call Emma and cancel the rest of my appointments for the day.

Not knowing where else to go, I return to the place originally recommended by Robert—if worse comes to worst I can get a ride home from him. They take me right away.

I'm checking email on my phone and feel I've only been there about a minute when a man in a greasy blue jumpsuit—why always blue?—emerges from the garage carrying my car's oil filter—it looks like a smoker's lung. "This?" the man says, shaking the old oil filter a couple of times.

"Finish."

I smile. Big. This has not been a complete waste of time!

"You must come back after one week and we will replace the oil again," he tells me.

My eyes go wide. I can't go back to the Audi dealer again!

Now he smiles. "This filter is too much old. The engine is cleaning for one week. We use again same filter after. New oil."

We run through these lines a few more times before I understand what he's proposing. We're going to change the oil and the filter now, run on that for a week, then drain and replace the oil. We'll re-use the same filter. It's news to me that you can change the oil without changing the filter. Is this why Geoff never mentioned having trouble? Like the flat tire, it was all mafi mushkilla to him.

But I can't get up much of a lather about it. Maybe there is nothing seriously wrong with the Audi, after all. Unlike my marriage, here is a problem I can solve.

Later I'll realize that, also like my marriage, the story exemplifies the clear signs I so readily missed.

───────

Monday night I'm leaving the yoga class I teach when I see one of my students at the Sheraton's roundabout.

"Nice car," Kara says, as I pull up to her at the roundabout.

"Thanks," I say. "Where's yours?"

"Don't have one," Kara replies. "And I sent my driver home for the day. I was just going to grab a cab."

There are two kinds of cabs in Doha, those registered with the Qatar Transport Authority, and those not. I feared the latter, unlicensed orange and white minicabs; but those are the only kind that will come along here at this time of night. I insist she get in.

"Oh that's bullocks," she says as she tucks into the passenger's seat. "They're much cheaper, that's why I walked away from the hotel in the first place."

Kara is one of the Britpats at Education City, brought in from an ad agency in London to help establish a much-needed local design firm. In her early 30s, she's dirty blonde, impossibly petite, and boasts a wicked sense of humor.

"I'm over by Doha Cinemas," she tells me. "God, don't look like that. Traffic shouldn't be too bad now."

I must explain that, despite living in Qatar for two years, I still don't know how to find my way around town. "Geoff did all the driving."

"No worries, love, I can guide you. The cab drivers never know where they're going either."

And so, between directions, Kara begins her story.

A little over a year ago, Kara's partner of six years wanted to move to Qatar. They aren't married, but share a flat which, in London she says, amounts to the same thing. Their unsanctioned union is why her partner wanted to move. Since they aren't husband and wife, they could each find a sponsored position, meaning they'd be entitled to more benefits. Cha-ching!

Kara finds a job first and relocates. The partner keeps looking. Weeks turn into months—he visits!—until finally it's Christmas. She returns home for the holidays and they have a lovely time back in their shared flat. He drops her at the airport with a teary farewell. When she lands back in Qatar she rings him right away. She doesn't want to keep separating like this.

Almost immediately she senses something's amiss. The ring tone tells her —her partner is not in the U.K.

"When I finally do reach him, he tells me he's snowboarding in France! 'You told me you didn't have any money to go on holiday! Where were your bags? In the boot?'" she laughs. "How did he get another woman to support him? He's not that special."

We reach her place and she asks if I'd like to meet up at the Four Seasons' Cigar Bar for happy hour Wednesday.

"I'd love to," I say, "though I don't drink."

"God, is that some yoga thing I'll have to watch I don't get that far into it," she says in one breath. "Surely you'll drink something. And anyway, you'll be in better shape to help me reel in a new man. Hey how's Geoff?"

She's reeling in men? Already? After six years together, she was moving on? Geoff and I hadn't been together that long, and I couldn't imagine being with someone else. Of course, we weren't yet divorced. On paper anyway.

"Oh, he's good. Busy." I say. "Got to run. Early meeting tomorrow. Work."

The parallels in our stories are astonishing, but for one major difference: That woman has bounced right back.

———

D riving home I realize, even trying to abide by the laws of self-preservation, to drive in Qatar is to break every road safety rule I've ever known. Furthermore, if I aim right *at* the roundabout, push the pedal to the floor, release it as I round the corner, then hit it hard again as I go into the turn — I don't have to slow down either. Like calculating the flicker of green lights, if I time it right, I almost never have to stop.

With access to gas at just 65 cents a gallon and an 8-cylinder engine under my hood, I realize what there is to love about driving. The curving roads become my own Nascar oval. I am in love with my car.

TWENTY-FIVE

FLY ME TO THE SALOON

Saloon:
In Qatar, a "house of beauty," a "beauty parlor."

Fly Me To The Moon:
A love song popularized by Frank Sinatra.

Fly Me To The Saloon:
My version of the tune, which I kept reinventing, "Darling take my hand, in other words, paint my nails, make me look like springtime in June, fly me to the saloon!"

DOHA, QATAR
June 2006

MY EYES AREN'T EVEN OPEN and there's that familiar pang. Dull though it may have been, having sex again had reawakened me and I'm thinking about shagging all the time. I'm blaming Qatar as I grab for the vibrator.

Somehow I'm single and childless in a culture where women are valued primarily as wives and mothers. And in three months I'll be forty.

Enough.

At least I should get up before hopping on the shame spiral. The mood is ruined anyway. I toss the vibrator back on the nightstand. I'm not coming any time soon, only getting later. Repeating my newest mantra — pain may be the touchstone of spiritual growth, but that doesn't make happiness a waste of time — I push out of bed for Friday morning yoga. Not that this is exactly a happy-making activity. Valerie's class still pushes my physical limits, but that hour and a half on the mat allows me to shut off the commentary on the life behind the new mantra. On the way to the Sheraton's gym, I huff down a coffee and a smoke.

The room is packed with overstressed expats, but I squeeze in next to an Education City colleague, Jeff. Beautiful, kind, Canadian Jeff. Okay, maybe I don't totally lose awareness, but I'm not going there. Not with him. He's married and worse. I have a Jeff problem and I'm swearing off. Being near him will have to suffice. More than anything I miss having a masculine presence in my daily life. Is it my imagination or does the sex segregation exacerbate the feeling of deprivation?

Banks have separate entrances and areas for women. Restaurants partition off "family" sections where women can sit and eat, fully covered of course, scooping food underneath their niqabs (the face scarves). Five-star hotels are like mini-embassies, lawless zones where you can buy booze, expose your shoulders and, I imagine, take your illicit date up to one of its rooms. They are the hub of expatriate life. Much as I'm enjoying working up a sweat in the Sheraton next to Canadian Jeff, I'm anticipating the afternoon's rendezvous. My appointment with Rene, the new hairdresser in town.

I've always loved getting my hair cut, any beauty service really, with its promise of passive transformation. After class, I'm rolling up my mat quickly so I can get home and get a shower before my appointment, when Canadian Jeff pulls me aside. "Can you talk?"

When he puts it like that, barely. God he's cute. Do I really care what his name is? That he's married? What do such things matter if we are meant to be together? I may have needed a haircut and a shower, but true love would see the real me beyond such surface imperfections, like Jeffrey had. And Geoff. Nothing's happening here, nothing's happening here, I tell myself.

"Sure," I shrug, all casual.

We drag our mats from the studio to the deserted bar, rank with the smell of last night's cigarettes. The odor does not deter me, as Canadian Jeff lays out his troubles, from wanting one badly. To scratch myself from the inside out. It's hard to keep from crying uncontrollably. I keep my mouth shut and just try to listen.

Since giving birth his wife had become depressed and difficult. He'd been doing everything he could—more chores, therapy, yoga—but to no avail. She's still despondent and it's breaking his heart. They're moving back to Canada to save their marriage. So he hopes.

They're thinking that family and friends and familiar surroundings will help, but what if it doesn't? Unable to offer up reassurances about the enduring qualities of love, I ask questions. Keep him talking. I can barely breathe. Considering that my husband walked away from our marriage because he didn't "feel like being married anymore," and I'm still adjusting to the fact that I'll never have my own children, Jeff 's troubles look good to me.

"How is your husband?" Canadian Jeff suddenly asks, snapping me out of my internal monologue.

"Fine. He's busy," I say quickly. Same thing I always say. "How's work?" Same thing I always say next.

There's no time to go home and shower before my haircut, but there's no way I'm missing it. Though unusual to have to wait for any kind of appointment, Rene is in high demand. The Filipinas who comprise the ladies hair-cutting cartel in Doha haven't known what to make of my limp American locks. Like many of the Western women in town, I'd taken to pulling my hair back in a French twist and, horror of horrors, coloring it myself. I'm ready to put those days behind me.

At the salon I'm greeted by a woman who fastens a gold lame cape around my neck, and leads me to the chair in the center of the room. A paunchy man with delicate skin and flushed cheeks flounces in and right away I know it's Rene. It's not just his curly golden locks, but the way he commands the room. Ever on the lookout for potential smoking buddies, I wonder if that what he was doing. His doesn't look like smoker's skin, but then, neither had my husband's.

Rene is taking his time, chatting with his employees, three very attractive men who seem to be his old and dear friends. There's a playful banter in the room, that combination of French and English and Arabic that is so particularly Lebanese. Umm Rene, mother of Rene, I hear one of them say to the woman who'd fastened my cape.

How adorable! The hairdresser brought his mother!

When at last he approaches, I get Rene's his full attention. I tell him I love what he's done for Michelle, as he massages my head. I'm amused to feel aroused by his caress. Clearly, the man is gay. Considering the state I'm in, however, I imagine I'd feel the same had it been his mother palpitating my scalp.

Rene is calling one of his assistants to wash my hair, when a beautiful woman walks into the shop. Heavily made up and stuffed into a tight t-shirt and jeans, she is the consummate example of Lebanese style. Rene bounds toward her for three kisses (hello, hello, hello, very Lebanese), then quickly introduces us. She is his girlfriend.

The assistant is leading me toward the sink, but I'm doubting myself. Not that there's anything wrong with *them*, but a bad experience with a straight male hairdresser had made me vow never again.

Unaccustomed as I was to the undivided attention of a heterosexual man taking scissors to my head, I'd paid scant notice to what he was doing. He'd know what would make me sexy, *right*? I ended up with two dangling tendrils on either side of my face, dairy goat-style. Not that I could blame him; I'd gone along every step of the way. Considering my current state, I trusted myself even less now. Given how I'd arrived at this state I also wondered, *Had I ever improved? Deep breath.*

It's become increasingly hard to ignore that my preconceived ideas have never served me well. Is it *my* view of how men and women "are" that created these troubles? Hadn't my impulse to come to Qatar in the first place been driven by the deepest lie of all cultural norms, that the man should be head of the house? Didn't the women here seem strong as fuck without my imposed ideas of feminism? Could I resolve this cognitive dissonance before the haircutting begins?

Mary Ellen often said to me, "When you don't know what to do, don't do anything." It's why—six months since the husband left—I'm still in Qatar, it's why I stay in Rene's shop.

Returning to the chair, I face the mirror with my wet hair and force my eyes onto the British Vogue that's been put in my lap. But I keep checking out the chummy antics behind me. The girlfriend seems to want something and she's not getting her way. She's alternating between pouting and chiding. I want to understand the act and what Rene is thinking. By the time she leaves and he starts snipping at my hair, I am in another dimension.

What is it about her that makes him care enough to put up with that behavior? What makes people decide to be boyfriend and girlfriend anyway? Am I really going to have to get to know someone new? Figure out how they like their coffee? Learn how he feels about his mother? About my mother?

The next thing I know the hair dryer is out. An hour and a half has passed.

"Now you are more you," he pronounces, fingering through my hair. "Beautiful and a little bit wild."

A ridiculous thing to say—how could this guy know what's more or less me?—but I lap it up. My hair does look fabulous, and he's gotten all the red out. I'm super blonde. I'm blushing in the mirror as I try to think of a pithy reply. Always good to practice.

Before I can come up with anything Rene unfastens my cape then moves his hands to my neck and jaw, tilting my head back to kiss me, if kiss is the right word. He employs an odd suction action which calls for him, rather than opening and exploring my mouth with his tongue, to clamp onto my lips and vacuum them into his maw.

The salon is now empty, but for one of his employee/friends rinsing something at the sink in the back. Rene releases me just as the employee/friend rounds the corner. I see in the mirror I'm thoroughly red, and Rene is back by the cash register, talking with the employee/friend.

From the waist down I know exactly what I want. Moving up from there it gets murky. It's one thing to sleep with a man

I've slept with before, a man who lives eight time zones away. But someone nearby? Someone new?

I'm caught between thinking how weird it was and wondering if I liked it. If I want him to do it again. If that's how all Lebanese men kiss. If he'd do the same between my legs. I go into auto-pilot.

The next step in the process is typically payment, so I grab my bag and move to the cash register. Rene accepts only a fraction of the cost. He's paying me for the hoovering? And why *some*? So the employee/friend doesn't get suspicious?

He asks for my phone number and I tell him he already has it, pointing to his appointment book and smiling mysteriously. *Now I'm flirting with this charlatan?* Is it working? I'm actually wondering if I'll hear from him again.

His relationship is not my concern. Not that I'm *un*concerned about it, but those two obviously have problems with or without me in the picture. On the positive side, Rene is unconnected to me socially; the girlfriend gives him as much incentive for secrecy as I have. This might be the perfect solution to quelling my unrelenting sex drive. If only I found him attractive like Canadian Jeff. If only thinking about this didn't make me miss Geoff. Maybe not being attracted to him can work out to my benefit. Good Christ. Wasn't getting married supposed to make all this go away? Absolve me from ever having to manage ambiguity with the opposite sex again.

Footsteps approach. Since I've been in Qatar, I can't recall the last time I heard the sound of someone overtaking me. The air rarely dips below body temperature. No one walks anywhere. It's Rene.

Now, in the U.S., this would be call-the-police time. But we're not in the U.S. and I know this guy is pretty much harmless. Even after he follows me into my car, I'm not worried. I know what he's after and in those brief moments between panic, recognition, and opening my car door, I decide I want Rene to maul me a little bit. I'm holding the car keys and if it comes down to it, I can take him. "Drive," he says.

OK, but where? No matter where we go there is the problem of being seen. There is no pedestrian traffic, people are known by their cars and mine is quite distinct — a big black Audi A8 in a land of SUVs.

"Anywhere," he says. "Just drive."

I pull out of the lot and slip through the roundabout that heads toward Aladdin's Kingdom, an amusement park I've never seen open. We stop, but keep the engine running. Rene rubs his thick yet nimble fingers over my clothes, across my breasts and between my thighs. As he suctions and paws, my internal stupor continues.

Do I like it enough that it's worth it? Should I blow off the dinner I'm supposed to be going to? For what? I'm not about to have my first *first* since Geoff left take place in my car. And I sure as hell can't take Rene to my compound. Maybe there's someplace else? Is this going to bruise my lips? Suddenly his cock is out and in my hands.

Not since high school has a man's dick in my palms felt so weirdly out of place. Much as I want to move on, I'm not ready for some clod who doesn't know me well enough to sense my hesitation.

I go with the truth.

"Ohh, hey, I have to go!" I tell him, looking at my bare wrist like it has a watch. "This was great fun, but I have a dinner party I'm supposed to go to."

"Finish me," he pants. And that does it.

Finish YOU? What about me? Didn't I just meet your girl-friend two hours ago? Get her to do the job. Then you can finish ME. Except, nevermind, because you just showed me everything I need to know about you.

"Listen," is what I say. "Be a good boy and show me you know how to draw out your pleasure and wait for it. Because right now, I have to go."

Being that we are in Doha, this works. I drive Rene back to his shop. There was a time I would have booted him out the door and made him find his own way back in the blistering heat. At least slapped him. What happened to that chick?

From the hotel drop-off I race to my villa, peeling out of my clothes the minute I shut the door. Since Geoff left I'd turned the bottom floor into a pass-through zone I mostly ignored, other than beelining to the kitchen. Upstairs in the master bedroom I flip on the portable CD player. "Live through this," I sing along with the Stars, a disc I had in heavy rotation at the time. "And you won't look back." I am making that dinner with my colleagues if it kills me.

After a quick if careful shower—don't want to muss the hair —I grab some jeans and a T-shirt off the floor and slap on some makeup. I check my watch, late but not too.

On the drive to the Mövenpick I catch my reflection in the rearview. *Damn, I look great. Is it too weird to go back?* And that's when I know what happened to the throw-the-drink-in-his-face girl. She'd rather not to make a mess she doesn't want to clean up.

Why not have a fling with Rene? Am I going to have to figure out my marital implosion before I allow myself some regular carnal pleasure? That could be never. Meanwhile, all around me are Qataris getting it four or five times a day. With multiple partners. Why should they be getting so much more action than me, when it was their laws that made even holding hands in public taboo?

I'd never been the type to line up a new man before cutting ties with an old one, but even if we weren't done on paper, we were done. I sure as hell wasn't going to get better at relationships by being single.

———

The group is already tucked into their meals, the infamous weekend buffet I'd scoffed at when Rima and I first went. I'd spent most of my life avoiding meals involving a sneeze guard, but in Doha even the Ritz-Carlton regularly offered up meals from a food trough. Since I'd only recently even been invited to join this weekly gathering, I wasn't about to turn my nose up at the food itself.

It's a smallish group tonight, just Cindy, Bob, Natalie, and Ben, colleagues from Education City. Before marching over to fill up a plate, I lean in for hello kisses. We all do that now.

"Nice hair," Cindy says. "How's Geoff?"

"Fine. Busy." I say. "Hey, did you get the chance to look at those business card proofs I sent over?" But I don't wait for an answer. "Oh God, sorry, let's not talk about work."

Heaping tabbouli and pasta onto a plate, I remind myself there is a reason I'm still here. Victoria and I agree, maybe I should take a look at how it is I found myself alone and heartbroken in a Middle eastern desert. Twice. The first time I'd been on the verge of 30; I lost years. I don't have that kind of time to lose anymore; I sure as hell don't want to see what this pattern will look like at the half-century mark.

Maybe if I stay, I'll learn whatever lesson I missed the first time around.

"Hey, Lisa," Ben says, rising to pull out a chair for me. "Glad you could make it."

Ben is a relative newcomer to campus, in town for a quick

project. It takes less than one split second to figure out how he wormed his way into this group so fast—his thick dark hair, square jaw, and muscular build.

As we sit he leans toward me and lifts his hand to my face. Did I mention his charm? And youth.

Has Rene made me irresistible?

"Is that a bruise on your lip?" he asks.

The next day I make an appointment at Al Mashata.

New houses of beauty had begun popping up all over Doha, but I remain faithful to Al Mashata. Since I don't have kids, saloons are my main inroad to local culture and this is a place that locals go. In keeping with my spirit of adventure, I decide to go for what I think is a local's treatment. Since then, I've since seen this same offering in the U.S., but prior to living in Qatar I'd never heard of a threading.

Al Mashata's procedure chamber features a row of back-to-back mirrors running down the center, each flanked on either side by padded chairs. En route to previous facials and pedicures, I'd peeked into this room and watched as a room full of women lay placidly, their black abayas billowing over the chairs while techs appeared to comb their faces with thread. An air of serenity pervaded the room. Until I went inside.

About one second into my treatment, I could see that threading was an acquired taste.

In this hair removal process, the technician skims the skin's surface with twisted thread, somehow yanking out the offending hairs with a laser-like precision.

As my face flushes and tears roll forth, I ask for a break. I sneak a look around to be sure I'm getting the right treatment. It appears the same as what the women around me are being subjected to, only they remain calm. Between breaks, the surrounding chairs empty. My eyebrow starts bleeding. Should I call off yet another treatment?

Then my tech sits me up, "See? Very nice?"

And it is. Maybe for the first time ever, I have two perfectly shaped eyebrows. I ask for ice. My threader laughs and tells me it's the kind of pain you got used to.

Like childbirth? Or maybe I'm just a wuss. The price list shows you can do arms, legs and full body. FULL BODY?

"There is a room there, you see?" she said, motioning to a closed door. "But this is mostly for the weddings."

I was going to have to do some research for more intel, try and understand why. The purported *why* anyway.

What is it about the hairless female body? I find fake tits less unnecessary. At least they convey "adult," whereas hairlessness is a quality found only in pre-pubescents.

"This hair thing is actually a hadith for men and women," I'm telling Val and Adam on Val's porch that night. It's a school night but it's late, so cool enough to sit outside. Am I turning into a night person?

She and Adam drink wine, I, tea. All of us smoke prodigiously. "Something about maintaining the original state of purity in which we were created by Allah. Um, aren't aging and growing hair also natural states bestowed by God?"

I notice Val is smirking into her wine; Adam is looking away.

No!

"I like having a Brazilian," she says.

"Is this mandatory these days?" I ask Adam. He's Val's student on and off. On when he's not dating someone, off when he is. He's been on again recently, though he's still in a relationship.

"Well, I don't know about mandatory..." he trails off.

"Why, are you worried?" Val asks, looking right at me. She's been pushing me since I'd asked her opinion on my marriage.

Victoria and Paul and Michelle knew only my side of the story, but Val—being a colleague—had seen us together regularly. "You two did seem like you were walking on eggshells a lot," she'd said.

Though offended, I'd believed Val was referring to all the ways I responded in reaction to my fear of Geoff's depression. "You need to start talking about this more," she'd said. Again, I'd felt injured by her admonition.

That night it's clear Adam knows about my divorce, and that she's told him. Rather than feel offended, I let myself lean into the openness.

"Don't look at me," I say. "Half the reason I got married was to avoid ever having to date again."

"Right, well, I suppose getting a date's the first step," Val says.

"A date? How does that even work? One minute you're talking, then...kissing? How?"

"There's loads of single people in Doha," Adam says, interrupting our laughter.

"That's easy for you to say, Adam, you have more to choose from," Val says. "I know loads of vibrant, single women."

Val's a good example. Why aren't men beating down her door? In the U.S. the statistic is something like 86 unmarried men for every 100 unmarried women—yeah, I'd looked that up, too—but here the ratio must be just the reverse. Adam confirms my suspicion.

"Oh, c'mon, Val," he says. "This town was built on oil. There are way more single men here, and plenty of those men express interest in you. That guy from yoga? This morning? He asked you out for coffee, didn't he?"

Then there's you, I think. How is Valerie so oblivious to the torch Adam holds for her?

"Tch. I'm not attracted to him at all," Val says. "And I don't have time to go out just for the sake of going out."

"That's not the point," I pipe up, feeling at last that I can contribute. That I'd made a fire-y train wreck of love doesn't matter. Once a professional yenta, always a professional yenta. "You have to be open to meeting someone. Why not go for coffee with him? Maybe he has a friend. In fact, I'm sure he's got several. Help me out here, Adam, you've dated half of Doha."

"He's more worried about hurting you than you hurting him, trust me," says Adam.

Interesting. Adam, with his slender physique, closely cropped brown hair and blue eyes had never struck me as attractive. Until now. But he's way too close. I can *talk* relationship, but I'm nowhere near ready for one. No point in piling up the carnage on my own doorstep. But I am curious.

"Tell me, Adam, as our representative male. What is it that makes a man stay with a woman?"

Looking back it's clear; I'd become so deeply embedded in the Byzantine machinations around me, I'd forgotten about love. Nor was I wondering why women stayed with men. No, I was utterly mired in my own melancholy.

"When I find out, I'll tell you," Adam says. He's trying to extricate from his relationship, hence the return to yoga. "There's something missing, I'm just not sure what it is. Kate's great."

I roll my eyes and look at Val.

"Adam, it's 11:30 at night and you're sitting here with us. If you're not dying to be over there getting into her pants, I've got a pretty good idea of what's wrong. Don't do her any favors. End it."

Adam laughs nervously and shoots a glance at Val before looking back at me, "Who are you?"

I widen my eyes in a kind of mock fear, "Qui, moi?"

"Oui, toi," he retorts.

Are we flirting?

"You're just different since Geoff left," he says. "It's like you were invisible before."

Invisible? Walking among swaths of women wrapped head-to-toe in black, I'd disappeared?

Within the confines of my marriage, I had changed. Unbidden, I tried to minimize anything about myself that I thought might grate my spouse and cause the unthinkable to happen. Thanks to the friend about to enter my life, I'll finally start to wonder why I hadn't been thinking about getting a divorce myself.

S ame scene, the following week on Val's patio. Only now we learn that Adam's girlfriend is leaving town.

"We're going to try and make a go of it," he says.

Weren't you just trying to break up with her? I want to ask but don't, afraid my crush on him will be obvious.

Then Val starts talking about some new man.

I'm the only one left here who needs to move on, and I certainly don't wish my unhappiness on them. But I feel a little betrayed by them both.

TWENTY-SIX
SOUQ IT UP

Souq:

A "shopping area," maddeningly grouped by function: you could find car stereos in one location, but God help you if you need gas.

DOHA, QATAR
June 2006

IT'S SATURDAY AFTERNOON and I'm at the City Center Mall's Starbucks on 1, about to meet Eddie, a National Public Radio correspondent. We'd met when the campus first opened and he came to do a story. He's back now working on a book. "Geography is underrated," he's telling me. "All that happiness comes from within crap is crap. It's *where* you live that matters."

As someone who'd spent her whole life moving, I disagree vehemently.

"It doesn't matter where you go, you take yourself with you," I argue. "A change of scene might make you temporarily happier, but ultimately geographic cures don't work."

But he begs to differ, and he's done the research to prove it. "Some places cultivate unhappiness," he says. "Like Moldova. Just the name and you know they're miserable. Whereas, in Bhutan, right up there with GNP is GNH—Gross National happiness."

The premise is clever, but I'm skeptical. Much as I want to fault Qatar for the breakdown in my marriage, I'm aware this is a way of not looking at my problems head on. It will be years and another relationship—where I take Geoff 's passive role to a boyfriend's aggressive —before I'll see that there was no way I could have caused, or changed the problematic co-dependent dynamic we'd gotten into on my own. But there in Starbucks, I feel like I've ruined everything. Pointing the finger at a place is too easy.

"On a scale of one to ten," he finally gets to, "How would you rate your happiness?"

When Eddie had first written saying he might be returning, he'd mentioned looking forward to connecting with Geoff and me. Hard I'd been avoiding the we're-getting-divorced conversation face-to-face, it was easy to leave the news out of an email. He probably won't come anyway. Now here he is, and I'm supposed to be helping him find possible interviews.

His question takes me by surprise—I'm not a subject, after all—but the man is a trained journalist. I find myself telling him everything, more deeply and in more detail than I have, even with Victoria. Soon I'm even dredging up my Peace Corps days.

"Still I came back for more!"

We laugh.

"I was more looking forward to seeing you than Geoff," he says.

I'm floored. I always assumed people liked my husband more than me.

"He was kinda boring."

Sunday morning, I wake up and notice a gecko looking at me from the corner near my dresser. The cockroaches must've drawn him in, but I put my music on at a lower than normal volume so as not to disturb him. I like having geckos in the house and hope he'll be back.

Soon as I get in the car I blast the stereo. Another reunion the split has made room for—music. When it came to song, our overlap in taste was by and large at the blandest extreme. (Exception: Wilco.) Since I don't listen to music while I work, most of the time I had for listening to music was time I spent with Geoff, and we'd gotten into a habit of silence.

"Holding out, for that teenage feeling," I sing/shout along again with Neko Case on the way into the office.

Aya's already there. She's not a morning person. Oh dear. She follows me into my office and shuts the door.

"Is it bad news?" I ask. "Can I get coffee first? or sit?" "I've just sent my driver," she says. "Venti, black. Just how you like it."

I nod and smile and wonder what could be coming. Someone must have really pissed her off.

"I'm afraid I have to quit."

Not what I was expecting.

"Is it Fawzi again? Do you want me to have Mohamed talk to him?"

She smiles and shakes her head. She is so lovely... and that's when I notice. She's covered.

"I'm getting married," she says.

I pull out a chair for her and slump into one on the other side of the table. What am I going to do without my secret weapon? *Pull it together, Kirchner!*

"Mabrouk!" I say, remembering a hair too late to smile. "When? I didn't know you were..."

But I trail off, unsure what to say. Of course she wasn't dating. They don't. Date.

"Shukran, habibti," she says into the void. Thank you, dear one. They are charm machines. "We are getting married in October."

I am still at a loss for words. *Please, let me be gone by then.*

"He is good," she says, "and I love his mother. She is my aunt. Aunt Roodha."

I've never been described as having a poker face, but I'm doing my best not to convey what I'm thinking. My best is not very good. Her *aunt*? She's marrying her fucking cousin?

She doesn't look so happy either. But she always does what her family wants, and I know this will be no exception.

"Why so..." sad? She won't know what I mean if I say 'long face.' But again, she fills the unspoken space.

"It's an adjustment, now I must always cover," she says. "And I have to quit working. Here. With men."

I tell her she can stay on as long as she wants. Good God, I'm awash in flexible departure dates. It's been four months since I told Robbie I wanted to leave, and I know for a fact they haven't even posted my job. *Maybe they have an internal candidate?*

Aya tells me she thinks she'll stay until Ramadan is over.

Clever. I doubt I'll be seeing much of her after it starts.

The next morning I see the gecko again. *He* likes me. I post his picture (I've decided the gecko is male?) to my blog before heading into work.

"Aya's not coming in today," Emma tells us at lunch, flashing her phone. "She just sent a text."

Ahh, this feels more like normal.

We're eating subway sandwiches at the table in my office while Noha translates the news. She's lived in Qatar all her life, but her family is Egyptian. She dresses in clothes that cover her wrists and ankles, with headscarves to match. Her makeup is so thick, I wonder if it's meant as another layer of concealment.

"You would be surprised at how unwomanly you feel without your hair," she'd explained one day.

I once saw her hair, lovely, lustrous, long and thick. *So show your hair*, I think. But what I say is, "Isn't that the point?"

"I want to find a husband who appreciates my virtue," she says.

That I get. Loud and clear.

"When is Ramadan this year?" I ask over our six-inch subs. "Approximately."

"End of September to end of October," Noha says.

Oh, God. My birthday? Can I please be gone by then?

"Aya says she's staying till then, but if she makes the end of Ramadan her last day, we'll want to have a little party for her before Ramadan," I say. Plus I should be here for it. "Did any of you know she was even thinking about getting married?"

"She's at the age," Noha says.

"But, her cousin? The woman has a college degree. She's knows Weill Cornell is doing that study on birth defects from inbred populations right here on campus. Can't she get out of it?" I ask.

"Their families are close," Noha says, "and it's very good that she gets along well with his mother. She has to move into his family's house."

"Try and be happy for her," Emma says. "It's not what we'd do, but it's exactly what she's used to. If anything, my guess is she's nervous about the sex. Can you imagine?"

"It would provide incentive," I say, not too eager to go into this realm. Noha might feel the same and I would not want her to feel uncomfortable or judged. Then again, she does have that deliciously catty side.

"Oh, I don't know about this," Noha says. "Qatari women have a bit of a reputation in the Gulf.

They *do?*

"And it sounds like he will let her get another job, but in a traditional office, maybe with the government. He gets to decide. She knows this. It's better here than in Egypt. There was a case in the paper last week. A man was divorcing his wife after he lent her to his boss. Not because she cooperated, but because he didn't get the promotion he was hoping for."

I insist Noha dig up the clip. She does. Jesus God.

That night on Val's porch after I teach yoga, Val explains what Noha meant about Qatari girls' reputations.

"Anal," she says. "That's how the girls go off to college and live their lives as young adults and still say they're virgins."

"Well they are," Adam points out.

"I did not have sex with that woman," I joke to blank stares. "Bill Clinton. It's what he famously said after the sex scandal." Still nothing. "You know, the ex-president and the blow job."

Adam shakes his head. "You Americans are such prudes."

Tuesday I'm at lunch. All the mobiles are out and I've got nothing.

Im bored.

I text Ben, the new young, hot colleague who'd asked about

my bruised lip. It's not exactly innocent, but I'm in no way expecting his reply.

Wanna fuck?

Sex with Geoff—bone-crushingly dull, though it had become—had continued without interruption right up until he left. I'm suspicious may've been a ruse on his part. If we'd stopped having sex I'd have had a conniption. Geoff had never been as adventuresome as I in bed; I'd long feared if I unleashed what I really wanted, we might stop getting it on altogether. It's one thing for sex to leave you adequately satisfied as opposed to blown away, but quite another for it to stop entirely. We had our whole lives to work on this, was how I'd reasoned it out in my mind at the time.

Now, my libido is back with a vengeance. Of course I wanna fuck.

I shoot my head up to see if anyone at the table noticed my world just changed completely, but everyone's glued to their devices. What to do? I must act quickly. Can't look like I'm taking too much time on this.

Of course, I write back. Answering, but not answering, his unstated "me?"

He obliges with a speedy reply.

Sux that Geoff's out of town.

Oh, right. This is going to be more difficult than that.

———

I meet Eddie for dinner Tuesday. He is now my confidante; I tell him everything. When I asks what he makes of Adam continuing a relationship he professed *not* to be interested in and long-distance to boot, he chides me.

"Nobody who wants to be married wants to be in a long-distance relationship," he says. "But you're just being ridiculous if you can't see he's flirting with you."

We're at Assaha Village, a new Lebanese restaurant in the style of American chain restaurants, except the kitschy flare reflects the Arab world—coffee urns, camel saddles, jewel-toned pillows and rugs. Unlike their American counterparts, the food is incredible.

Over platters of hummus, tabbouli and kebbeh, Eddie opens up a bit, as well. He loves his wife, but misses being single, the ability to go anywhere whenever he wants.

"I'll kill you if you tell me you envy my freedom."

"But I do," he says. "Married people can be unhappy too." He goes on to tell me that his strategy for success is frequent travel and remaining 99 percent faithful.

This is what an enduring relationship looks like?

D riving home I call Paul.

"What the hell is that supposed to mean, 99 percent?" I ask.

"Sounds like the guy isn't faithful," he says.

"But get this, I start wondering, while we're talking, why hasn't he lifted a finger in my direction? What's wrong with me?"

"Oh, my God, when are you leaving for the summer? You need a break."

"You're right," I say, putting thoughts to words for the first time. "I need to see if I can attract someone who isn't legally bound to bed me."

"Enjoy it while you can," he says. "Do I miss Nannette's body from before the baby? Absolutely. I may never lay hands on a pair of 17-year-olds' breasts ever again. But that's not why you get married."

I don't ask, I already have. *Exactly why does a person get married?*

———

Wednesday morning and my gecko is still in the same spot. That's when I notice the cockroaches feeding on his curling body. I take another picture and title that day's blog entry, "My Future ex-husband is Already Dead." I'm so proud, I send the post to Kara. I'm going to have to tell her about the divorce now.

"You might wanna think about cleaning your villa," Eddie tells me later when he calls. He's been following my blog. "But that's not why I'm calling. I want to go duning."

To dune is to drive out into the desert, let the air out of your tires and then tear through the country's one natural beauty, its sand. It's nothing to these drivers, these regulars of the desert, to fly at the lip of a 100-foot dune, dangle on its edge then snake down like it's a sheet of ice. The driver's on their cell, speakers blaring in the background, "Ha bee ee yeh bee!"

In its uncensored form the sport was quite dangerous. The Qataris held weekly races, secret affairs conducted in remote areas of the desert. Aya once told me that casualties were a near weekly occurrence.

I went out dune bashing several times, but in an anaesthetized, corporate version of the pastime where professional drivers would crawl up, over, and along the rim of a dune, rest precipitously at its crest, then make their way down at slow speeds. It is the only activity I can think of that's left me feeling simultaneously endangered, bored, and guilt ridden.

Naturally, all tourists want to go, and since Eddie is a

reporter, I can take the rest of the day off to accompany him. I invite Udai, the Reuters reporter who wrote the story about Bluetooth romance, just to be sure it looks legit.

Because we're in Qatar, Emma can arrange all this for us in an hour. And so we begin, like all good Gulf adventurers, by shopping. My list of provisions comprises the following:

Pocari Sweat. (Japanese version of Gatorade, pure sugar. Check.) Pringles. (A snack curiously prevalent outside the U.S. Check.) Dark chocolate. (Check.) Condoms. (Please?)

———

Condoms weren't actually on the list, but when I saw them on the shelf, I wanted them for the summer vacation I had yet to plan. Nay. Needed them.

"You have to buy them for me, Eddie," I insist. "Please?"

"Why don't you just buy them yourself?"

"I'm still married. I can't have someone I know see me buying these. My husband's out of town. Ex-husband. Whatever."

"No way."

"But you're a guy!"

"But I'm married, too."

"But you don't live here!"

"Lisa, people will think we're sleeping together."

That hadn't really occurred to me. And what does Mr. 99 percent care?

I pluck the insulting item from the shelf, force the package into his hand and push him toward the counter while I slink away. I doubt this is accomplishing much in terms of subtlety, but it is the best part of the trip.

We join Udai and his brother Sami, in from Vancouver, and head out into the desert. While the driver lets the air out of the

tires—which apparently enables greater control on hot sand—
Udai asks how Geoff is doing. I brush him off with the usual fine
and busy and how's work, garnering a look of disbelief from
Eddie. I slip into the front seat and let the boys talk journalism
shop in the back. I think about where I might go to escape. The
whole town's abuzz with vacation plans.

We're going to Geneva. We're going to Turkey. We're going
to Beirut. We we we. I need the respite, but thinking about
going away feels more medicinal than relaxing. It will be my
first solo vacation in years, which makes it feel more like something I need to get over with more than something I'm looking
forward to.

It had actually been our trip to Thailand—a place Geoff and
I arrived at without a map or an agenda—that had convinced me
we could pair for life. We both scorned people who needed to
organize their vacations, worse still were the people who needed
other people to organize their days off, group tourists. *The poor
unfortunates.*

My travels were never about monuments or tourist destina-
tions. I liked to sit in a coffee shop and watch the locals come
and go. Experience a movie house. Go to the grocery store.
Pretend I'm inhabiting a new life.

Thinking about a loose itinerary now, however, I imagine
dreaded down time on a beach or a coffee shop, or market.
Stewing. If there's one thing I don't need it's unstructured time
to think.

My mobile beeps. Someone needs me?

I dig it out. Kara.

I read your blog. WTF?!

Showtime.

TWENTY-SEVEN
SHOUF

Shouf:
"Look!" Often intended as, "Watch out!"

DOHA, QATAR
June 2006

I T'S FRIDAY AFTER YOGA and Kara and I head to the
pool at the Intercon. Nothing has been said about my blog
post and under the shade of palm trees, I relax and look
out onto the emerald green of the Doha bay.

"It almost feels like we're on vacation," I say. "I should get a
membership here."

"Don't be daft, I get this free from work and you can come
as my guest anytime — they hardly pay attention," she says.
"The water used to be much nicer but when they started
dredging for The Pearl it got all mucky on the bottom. I don't
even paddle in these days."

"What exactly are they thinking with that thing?" I ask,

thinking about the plans I'd heard to create *another* luxury retail area surrounded by high-priced high rises. "It's like they're trying to compete with The World."

"I don't think they're trying to compete at all, there's going to be gambling in Dubai."

"What!"

"You heard me," she says with a smile. "After all, it's not Arab land, is it? It's man-made." I'm flummoxed, and that's when Kara pounces.

"That's their problem," she says. "What about yours, what the hell? I thought Geoff was just off on some job."

And so I tell her, leaving out the menopause and the failed attempt at artificial insemination. Baby steps.

"I'm gobsmacked," she says. "Geoff? If he were any more laid back he'd be asleep."

It is still a shock to me that anyone could've had a negative perception of my husband. Ex-husband. *Whatever*.

"Don't worry, love," she says. "We'll get you sorted. Starting with those swimmers. Why in the name of God are you wearing a one-piece with that body? And it's baggy to boot."

I look down at my brown swimsuit; I love the cut, but she's right. I'd bought it for the Bahamas, when Geoff and I had eloped. I don't know about switching over to a bikini, but maybe it's time I get rid of this. For the first time I let myself think, just maybe, with Kara at my side, my future ex-husband is going to be *hot*.

DOHA, QATAR
July 2006

A group of students is sitting on the couches we'd placed outside the office. They're giggling and enthusing about getting married. They don't know about my impending divorce, so I figure I might as well make an attempt at my empowerment agenda.

"You don't have to rush," I offer. "Not right away after school at least. I didn't get married till I was 35; I couldn't possibly have picked the right person before then."

The girls pass a look between them.

"Live at home till I'm 35?" Abeer says. "No way!"

"And children," Maha whispers. "No children?"

They giggle, a bit more nervously it seems.

Headway?

"You'll live at home anyway," I persist, thinking I have the ace card. "I'd rather live with my mom than my mother-in-law."

"Then you didn't pick the right mother-in-law," Radha says, and they all burst into laughter.

These women didn't need my fairy tale any more than I needed the university's God squad to teach me about my higher power. Who was I to show them anything, anyway?

The fear I'd expressed to Geoff — that he should leave me to find a real woman when I found out I'd gone through menopause—had been very much a part of my consciousness of late. As in, how will I ever find a man now?

If I believed my value as a woman was so directly tied to my fertility, how was that any different from the way they looked at it?

An idea began to take root in my head.

What if my ambivalent feelings about feminism weren't a personal failing. What if there was something deeper?

"There is nothing natural about equality," Victoria says, plain as that. "Evolution favors the killers."

"But isn't that the point to society?" I begin. "We temper our primitive inclinations."

"Well, of course," she stops me. "But that doesn't mean it's going to be your first impulse."

"See? No man is going to want me."

"That's not what I'm saying at all. People are complex." She shifts in her seat. "Nothing fits into tidy categories on the individual level. So here's my assignment for you."

I'm ready.

"Don't do something if it makes you feel bad. Whether it's imagining a conversation with someone, or just eating something you don't think tastes as good as you'd like it to. Just cut it out. The minute you start to feel that something isn't right."

Whoa.

That evening I'm over at Robert's riffing on the latest initiative launched by Sheikha Mayassa (yes, that's her real name and yes, the pronunciation is as ridiculous as it possibly could be). She'd recently begun a charity to help tsunami victims, Reach Out to Asia, and he's been tapped to help with some publicity for their upcoming trip to Pakistan.

"I'll say, if they really wanted to reach out to Asia, they needn't look further than our back yard," Robert says. "But no, they're going over on a first-class junket."

It's good material.

Then Adam drops by. It's a little odd, but not entirely, and I like watching his swimmer's body. He'd stand to make a point and his shirt would lift ever so slightly, revealing taught muscles wrapped around hips. I hadn't seen Geoff 's hips, well, ever. I want to get home to my vibrator and blog, and around midnight I say goodnight and head for my identical villa across the street.

My phone beeps — a text from Adam.

Tnx a lot. He can keep drinking for hours.

Adam's not much of a drinker. I like that.

Tell him you need to call your gf.

It seems like he's at the door before I hit send. I'm not the *gf*, why is he here?

"Aren't you supposed to be calling your girlfriend?" I ask. He tells me it's too late to call her, she's in Spain. They're having trouble connecting.

Finally I confess; tell him about the phone call that ended my marriage. The lingering mystery. The gaping hole in my body. I cry.

He's sweet and listens and touches my face and says, "I'm sorry, baby."

Then he leaves.

Of course he can't stay, Robert would definitely notice that. But also, he'd not made any kind of a move. How the fuck does this work?

I send a text. *Tx 4 listening.*

Then another. *And I liked it when you called me baby.*

He writes back. *I know.*

———

We carry on a torrid text affair for about ten days. It feels good, though I don't mention this to Victoria. She's gone on holiday anyway. Then one night, as Adam and I are leaving a press conference for the launch of Raz Gas, we meet in the parking lot. We'd arranged this in one of a dozen texts we'd sent during the event.

"Let me drive you to your car," he says with a grin.

We sit in his Honda CSV and talk about how text messaging is all the further this will ever go. I'm disappointed, not because I want a relationship, but because I am wired for sex. I still don't want it known around campus that I'm getting a divorce, and he's got as much reason as me to want to keep it quiet. Then, one night at Val's I text him.

R u home?

His reply is instant. *Stop by.*

We both know what's about to happen. That morning I'd sent almost exactly this scenario via text.

I sneak into ur villa at night, snake my way up ur sheets and tease you w my tongue.

First, though, I drive off and then return, parking farther away. No one can know, not even Val.

Our sex is the first glimpse I've had at how the intense style of yoga I've been practicing has affected my body. I'm stronger, leaner and more pliable than ever before. Adam presses me into a backbend and then into a posture approximating a handstand. I come upside down. Then we do it again. And again. It's been years since I've had a proper hat trick. Thank God I'd gotten the big box of condoms.

———

Alone in my villa the next morning I feel indentations of his fingerprints all along my body. I lay still and review where his tongue and his breath had caressed me. I feel like it's the first time I've ever had sex. Like I've never been touched before. Like I'm in a Foreigner song. I email a friend—Adam's a nonsmoker—maybe I can finally quit smoking! Again!

The next day I jump into the pool at our villa, and the water feels like the massage of a thousand tongues on my body. I text Adam.

Why aren't you fucking me right now?

I'm coming over.

Damn, this is going to be fantastic.

Maybe I can even stay for the rest of my contract. Only, I don't want him coming to my place. I tell him I'll meet him at his.

That's when he tells me. He and the gf have broken up.

This puts me in a bit of a panic. He broke up with her because of me?

But, no.

"I want to see other people," he says. Quite reasonably.

But it's too much. This would put me in a situation where he can date and I cannot. I feel like this will make me filler while he's looking to meet the person he actually wants to date. I don't have it in me to get emotionally involved with this guy, but I know it would crush my self-esteem to watch him get involved with someone else.

I end it.

This does not give me the relief I'd hoped for, when I'd come to the conclusion in Pittsburgh that I needed to dump someone. I go upstairs and throw the condoms Eddie bought me in the trash, making a mental not to pick up new AAA batteries.

DUBAI, UAE
July 2006

I meet with my team in the terminal. We'd scheduled this trip very last minute, so our seats weren't together but all over the plane.

Noha, Emma and I will be in Dubai for a couple of days. Aya can't join us.

"I heard that her new husband doesn't want her traveling," Noha tells us in the car en route to our first appointment. "And her brother is going along with it."

I can't imagine how this relationship is going to work. Aya's family is more liberal than her betrothed, but her father is dead, which makes her younger brother her male guardian. That kid must be a real douchebag I think, but do not say. And where does Noha get this information anyway? Anyway, the point of this trip is to have some fun. Yes, team building. And we do have a bona fide work purpose.

I'm laying the groundwork for our real inaugural event, a celebration that will be held when our building opens; we're still squatting in Weill Cornell's building.

I don't *plan* on being on campus for that, but will I? To my knowledge, still nothing has been done to recruit my replacement. I let myself fancy that my boss is trying to think of a way to beg me to stay, though I believe this is as unlikely as a reunion with Geoff. Still, I hold out hope for both.

I n the lobby of one building is a giant touchpad floor; as you step the squares light up and emit various notes. Dubai has all the event wizards.

"Web cams? Live web cams?" I ask in disbelief as the vendor is talking up the technology they can offer. "We've had enough trouble just trying to use the internet live in presentations, no way."

He insists.

"There's nothing like it to bring two separate events together in real time."

He's British. And dashing.

"My wife was recently in Boston at a trade show."

Of course, he's married.

"I was missing her terribly."

Happily married.

"When she called me from a web cam display." He softens visibly.

"I'd been so desperate to connect with her and when she called it was almost as if she was in the room with me. Absolutely brilliant."

His story hits hard, spotlighting the lack of communication from my husband. It's always there, like a constant thrum, but now it's like a knife to the back of my throat. How can he have stopped caring about me so completely? So much for team-centric fun.

The day plods on, we have several appointments scheduled, then we're spending the night before heading back to Doha the next day. I'm on the verge of tears the whole time, but can't bring myself to confess to what's wrong. Not even over our fancy girl-bonding dinner when Noha tells us about a boy she likes—he works at Al Jazeera, definitely marriage material.

Not even later, at the diamond souq, when it gets serious and Emma tells us she's having trouble getting pregnant. I need to hold onto the feeling that these girls just think I'm an awesome boss with a relatively put together life, although my brusque responses do not support this. But I can barely talk. I feel like I have pneumonia, my head and body ache, and it hurts if I breathe too deeply.

I get Kara on the horn as soon as I get back to my villa.

"He's had the papers for over a month now," I say. No matter thatI know it's not true, I can't help but say it out loud. "Maybe he's changed his mind?"

"Aw, love, why don't you just call him?" Kara says. "You need to know what's going on."

She and Victoria have been absolutely steadfast about telling me to call. I *have*. He doesn't pick up. Though he has responded to a few emails. But before I can ask about a strongly worded letter I want to send instead, Kara blows me out of the water.

"I've been accepted to that school."

A few weeks ago at the Intercon she'd mentioned applying to a prestigious, difficult to get into school. Of course, I was encouraging, it seemed so remote. She will be leaving before Ramadan starts. Fuck.

I call Geoff. He picks up.

We talk for close to an hour, almost the same amount of time he'd granted me in person when he came to pick up Grandpa.

I have to ask.

"I haven't changed my mind," he says. "I've just been so busy."

This is so dismissive I cannot bear it. I cry.

He does not.

He says he will always love me. I do not say the same, though it's true.

"Please sign the papers and send them to Hilary."

This turns out to be the last time we speak. The last of our three conversations.

Talaq.

Though it will be months before he actually does sign the papers, my call has that little effect on him.

What I can salvage from the interaction is this—the satisfaction that I did know my husband. I need to start protecting my intuition. I suddenly see my secrecy for what it is. Keeping this mess quiet has been nothing but false pride, an attempt to prove he means as little to me, as I to him. Helas.

K ara eyes my new bikini with approval. "Much improved, love," she says.

"Have you ordered fries yet?" I ask as I set up on my chair in the shade. Book, sunscreen, water spritzer. It's Friday after yoga and we're at the Intercon again. Gotta love a "gym" that has a swim up bar and restaurant. I feel like I'm among my people. "And a Coke."

Kara hands me her mobile: *If u mean to torture me with this yoga business, u better be able to give a good massage.*

"That text is from Dan," she says. "How has he not yet figured out that I have no interest?"

"Wow. It's hard to imagine a lack of correlation between a man's come on and his coming. That dude is showing one strong desire to be serviced. If all you want's a massage it's called Thai Lady, you numty. And while you're there, pick me up a gift certificate. Isn't he married?"

"I have no idea why people get married. Like I say, we don't do it anymore in London. Would you hand me that sunscreen?"

I tell her about my recent conversations with Eddie and Paul.

"Maybe for kids?" I suggest.

"Perhaps it might help us with this dating thing if we knew what we were looking for."

I've not mentioned the fling with Adam. We may be only as sick as our secrets, but does that really mean we can't have any? No one in Doha has ever seen Kara or Val with their partners, making it impossible to superimpose ideas about what had gone wrong, wherein the fault lay.

"Ach," I make a face. "My list pretty much begins and ends with one thing, I'd do him!"

"Mine too!" she cries. "This might explain a lot."

I whip out the Montblanc planner I'd gotten at the launch of Her Highness' website. Pen poised and cigarette lit, I announce we've got to make a list, and start with an item I'm sure should be on it.

"He must not be able to move into your house from his car, even if it is his own car."

"No!"

"Yes. After Jeff died, my future boyfriend stopped over to say goodbye before moving to Seattle. He unpacked instead."

"Absolutely one for the list. I have another one," she says. "You've got to dump him if he won't take you to a friends' wedding."

"What?"

"Yeah, I think that should've been my first clue," Kara insists. "Last year I offered to take a holiday to attend a mutual friend's wedding, and my partner insisted I not waste the time or money."

"Oh, I've another," Kara cries. "If he employs his left pinky finger in the service of toilet hygiene, it's a no," she laughs. Muslims have a hadith around how far one might stick one's finger up one's ass in order to clean without overmuch pleasure, but she doesn't mean she's opposed to dating a Muslim, just a super religious one. Not that this would be a problem, but she's on a roll.

He must make you laugh. He must find you funny. He must be able to flirt; if you catch his eye and put a finger to your hip he must without hesitation shoot a look that tells you he wants to slide right up your skirt. Soon enough, she's blathering on about successful, driven, ambitious and playful...my mind wanders. She has definitely ventured into boyfriend material and I'm not there. She really has moved on. Suddenly, I realize we're sitting in silence.

"You know what, love?" Kara says. "Being in a real relationship means taking on another person, their quirks and their needs, their expectations. And I just can't be fucked."

Thank God.

"Pick you up from work? MAKE DINNER?" I ask. "Are you on crack?"

"What's wrong with could-I-do-him topping the list?" Kara says. "Are we to leave it off the list entirely?"

I shake my head no.

"I just can't take all the fuss," she says. "And I don't want to have to teach him how to treat me, in bed or out."

"Right," I agree. "So here's the list. No training. No drama. The end."

"Don't forget—I could do him!"

"Oh absolutely, that's always right on top."

"Unlike me!" she says.

Good call.

———

Back home I pluck the condoms from the trash again. Even if it has to be alone, I'm going somewhere to escape the summer heat.

I crack open my laptop and start searching.

Lolling on the beach in Mauritius?

Still don't trust myself not to go maudlin.

Moscow?

That'd be great, but I can't figure out how to sort the visa.

Maybe Iran?

But they'll be doing Ramadan there, too.

Then I find it.

A tropical jungle paradise with arts and culture and markets. There are longboat rides and trekking and cave expeditions. One drawback— it's a group tour.

I dither for days.

What about Israel? But I can't deal with the possibility of I'd get my passport stamped and then be unable to get back into Qatar.

New Zealand?

Too far for a few days. *Fuck it.*

The jungle trip is through an eco tour company that has rated this tour a "5"—the most extreme challenge they offer. I still dread the idea of getting stuck someplace I don't want to be, with people I don't want to be with, doing something I don't want to do.

But on such a tour, there will be men. Men with the means and ambition required to take an extreme holiday. This feels very good. I'll miss the worst part of summer in Qatar and be back in time for Kara's leaving party.

TWENTY-EIGHT

MY MISADVENTURES WITH A BORNEAN TRIBE

Massaalema:
"Goodbye." A too-frequent occurrence in Doha, *goodbyes.*

BORNEO, MALAYSIA
August 2006

BORNEO. THE NAME ALONE evokes lush rainforests and exotic wildlife, a land where the wild things are free to roam. Nestled to the south of the Philippines and north of Java, the world's third largest island is home to one of the most ecologically diverse ecosystems. In one 25-acre-plot, you can find 700 tree species co-existing, more variation than in all North American forests. Then there's the wildlife—orangutans, flying squirrels, the world's smallest deer, and some 10,000 insect species. Best of all, it's one place I've never been with Geoff. I'm hoping to make it a destination that reminds me of someone else. We meet in Miri.

Assembled in the lobby of our three-star hotel, I find a group of ten women, two of whom are retired librarians from New Zealand. Even the group leader, Dee, is female. So much for the troupe of men with the means and wherewithal to handle an extreme fitness holiday. This will be my tribe for the next two weeks. Back in my room I wrap the condoms in tissue—I don't want my roommate Liz to see—and toss them in the trash.

I decide on another challenge, a long-standing conundrum of mine. Why is it that people behave so badly on reality TV? Given the challenge I've just been handed, this seems like the perfect opportunity to experiment. This group of strangers does not know me, or my husband. Exactly who am I without him?

Liz, a doctor from the U.K. who's in her early 30s, is up and packed and out the door before I'm out of bed. So much for bonding.

I get ready in about 10 minutes, including shower and packing. As I'm closing the door behind me, I stop. Pull the condoms out of the garbage. Maybe.

—————

Much of Borneo's terrain is impassable except by longboat, low, narrow canoes built from a single tree. I'm glad for the chance to drift. I'd found myself in many developing countries before, trapped on poor roads in cars with even poorer shock absorbers, fearing for my life from oncoming traffic and/or vertiginous drops. Gliding down the river, I lie back, marvel at giant stands of bamboo.

We spend the night at Gunung Mulu National Park, a very civilized place with wooden-planked boardwalks and didactic materials on the flora and fauna. I'm emboldened for our coming adventure — the Pinnacles Trail. This is the part of the tour that's pushed this trip to the company's highest rating. In just 2.4 km the mountain peak rises to an elevation of 1200 m, with the last section near vertical. It takes six hours to climb. First we have to get to the trail. That's another longboat ride. And then, a warning. Note the order.

"The leeches from the ground are just your normal ones, but watch out for the canopy," Dee, our guide tells us, as we step out of our canoe and into the mucky jungle shore. Her Australian accent makes it sound slightly less terrifying, but leeches? "They're tiger leeches, they sting a bit. Don't try to pick them off when they're drinking or you'll bleed uncontrollably."

It's enough the idea that some creature might latch onto me and try to suck out my life force, but she's telling me these guys might just fly at me from the trees?

The longboat pulls away, headed back to the base camp where the librarians had stayed behind. It had not occurred to me to take an adventure holiday and skip the adventure, but now I envy their wisdom. I'm on the bank of the Melinau River facing a two-to three-hour walk blood march.

yet, there's a part of me that's pleased with myself. I'm actually disappointed when not a single leech descends. Liz, my roommate, is not so lucky. Or unlucky?

The next day, only Liz and I take the trail. Even Dee stays behind. "Infested with mozzie bites," she tells us. I'm thankful for the 95 percent DeeT solution I've brought along, but as we begin our hike, I regret my sole companion.

Beep.

It's another text. "It's my ex-," she says. "We just broke up."

We're in a jungle, and this woman is texting her boyfriend. With all the stopping and starting to send and receive, she's easy to lose in a hurry.

Would I lie in my reality show cutaway? "I needed to keep

an even pace." Would I go bitchy? "She's a physician? She has the emotional maturity of an infant." or would I tell the truth? "How is it that everybody but me has enough sway over supposedly former partners to keep a relationship going?"

The first hour is torture. The dense jungle overhead crowds out the view, leaving just a relentless uphill climb. My heart and lungs pound, my limbs twitch. The sweat pours off me. Somewhere into the second hour I'm thinking of turning back—this is my vacation, I don't need to prove anything —when I come upon a couple taking a breather. He looks apologetic, she looks apoplectic. I know I could be her, that somehow, in the context of my relationship, I'd been quick to blame. Had I been too quick to give up? I push on.

As has happened so many times in my life when I've moved through fear to step into the unknown, the reward is almost instantaneous. Patches of sky poke through the leafy awning. Hills surround me and fog touches down in spots. I and the clouds, one. When I finally reach the Pinnacles, otherworldly, stony outcroppings that top a nearby peak, I am triumphant. Small though it may have been, I have accomplished something I'd set out to do, and for no one but myself.

Liz is not far behind and, after a round of congratulatory photos, we make the descent together. We can't dally. The downhill climb will be much faster, but we don't want to take any chances that darkness will fall. The way down looks entirely different. Whereas on the way up I felt as if I'd seen nothing, now every inch of ground presents something new — armies of marching ants, bright orange lichen, moss-covered trees, even the musky scent of wet, rotting leaves. Qatar never smells like anything.

Back at Mulu the park manager explains how the pinnacles were formed, something to do with limestone, water and shifting tectonic plates. These geologic tendencies also produce caves, and Mulu has them in spades. Home to the world's most extensive cave system, it boasts the world's largest cave chamber, and the following day we set out to see them. All. Four or so hours into looking at stalactites and stalagmites, I wonder about finding my way back to base for an ice cream sandwich and a nap, but I'm shy one longboat. It turns out to be a good thing because, yes, Virginia, there is a bat cave.

Deer Cave is home to some 12 different species of bats, which doesn't sound all that impressive until you see them come swirling out of its interior. Each night at sunset anywhere from 2.5 to 3.5 million bats spew forth in bursts, each group with its own unique flight pattern. I shot more photos of this creepy spectacle than anything else I saw on my trip. Bats terrify me, so ingrained in my psyche like a leech, so flying rodent, so upside down. I reveled in the power of watching from a safe distance as the bats spilled from the cave, in search of food that was not me.

The next day we hop into another longboat, heading further inland to meet an Iban tribe. Infamous as headhunters, the Iban have long since forsaken this practice in favor of doing business. They offer accommodation— their homes are called longhouses, separate units under one roof that shelter entire tribes — and wares to visiting tourists.

We pull up to a dock with a hand-lettered sign that reads "Skandis." The caterwauling of chickens greets our ears. There must be hundreds of them. What is daybreak to be like?

I regard the longhouse, high upon the riverbank, with suspicion. Constructed of what looks like salvaged materials, the whole pile sits atop rickety stilts. I doubt it can withstand our group's combined weight. Once again I'm struck by my sense of smell —a foul animal stench: part dander, part rot —permeates the air. This will be our home for the next two days.

Our first treat is a bath. In the river. Dee has cautioned us about Leptospirosis, a water-borne bacteria. Comes from rat urine. "Just keep your head above the water and be very careful not to swallow any." I am grateful I didn't get any leeches, after all, though Liz jumps right in.

The ritual would be simple enough, except that we're supposed to bathe fully clothed. First we change out of our clothes underneath a sarong, which we must then keep in place during said bath. Afterward, we must struggle back into our stinking duds, still keeping the sarong in place. Then it's time for afternoon tea. Then another bath. I am in desperate need of a shower.

Finally it's time to present our "gifts." I'm embarrassed by these items —staples, really —that we'd picked up the market in Kuching the day before —onions, garlic and dried fish; tooth-paste, dish soap and tobacco. This awkward moment is accompanied by a smattering of applause from the 13 families who gather to divvy up the goods. Then the drinking game begins.

The ritual goes, one for me, one for you, but our group is not terribly interested in sampling the tuak, or potent rice wine. The disappointment is palpable among the group of young men who mysteriously appear as the fun begins. When the night finally ends — earlier than most, they tell us — we are shown to mats laid out on the porch that fronted the length of the longhouse. For most visitors I suppose the experience is mitigated by the evening's entertainment. Not so much for us. I squirm on my mat for a bit, then pull out my New Yorker. The magazine confronts me with a resort ad featuring a scented strip. I lie still, inhaling alternating currents of the magazine's "Green Tea" and the resident's "Eau de Cur." I think longingly of the 5-star Hilton just 20 km downstream, and am almost willing to take my chances floating there, especially now that the chickens have been joined by the shrieks of mating cats. "It does help to be drunk," Dee whispers to me. Liz laughs.

The three of us spend the night exchanging love stories. Dee had recently become engaged. Liz is getting back with her ex-. I tell them about my divorce. Mostly, I'm glad to feel genuinely happy for Dee and Liz. That my own sadness isn't pure poison. That our stories unite us.

The next morning we're lounging by the river —it does do wonders for mitigating the smell —but it feels like I'm bailing on my journey. As I vigorously apply more DEET, I ask my companions if they'd like to have a look around. All decline.

Then a great splash comes from the water. I look over to see about a dozen children, running down the path from the longhouse and into the water. I look back at my fellow travelers, pale and inert, then back to the river. Unsa, the tribe's chief, is joining the kids.

Rather than spend the day wishing I were elsewhere, I walk to the water's edge where Unsa has begun bait to a home-made fishing rod. His English is surprisingly good, so I ask him about the families living at Skandis.

He explains that the many children running around are the offspring of his generation's children, young men and women who had been born in the longhouse but had moved to Kuching to earn a living. Though he planned to be around for at least another 20 years or so—he wasn't sure how old he was—he didn't think his son would want the job he'd inherited from his father back in the mid-1970s.

"They don't know how to grow rice, they don't know how to check the rubber tree, they don't know how to plant pepper," he says, listing the daily chores of the longhouse. "Some of them like it, some of them don't. Most of them don't like it. Maybe this is gone in the future. The lifestyle nowadays always changes."

If he could adapt, maybe I could, too.

The fact that my own marriage failed to produce offspring left me feeling as if my future were more tentative than other people's. Yet here was this father of many children openly discussing his uncertain prospects, directly within his familial enclave.

I see the place anew, as an elaborate daycare setup. Even if they rarely saw their actual parents, these kids are safe and nurtured by their large extended family, free to spend their days alternately playing in the river and bothering their grandparents, the sounds of their laughter echoing off the rocks and trees. Surely, it is not how he'd planned his life would go, but he's happy.

As he pushes off to go fishing, I grab a toddler from the riverbank and run with him into the water. We wave goodbye to Unsa's disappearing frame. Maybe not having my own children actually gives me the opportunity to be there for *more* children.

That night Unsa invites me into his place. Despite that he's chief, his unit at Skandis is the same size as everyone else's. Smaller than a New York studio apartment, the room houses Unsa, his wife, his mother-in-law and their grand-daughter. But they do have a TV.

Each night they get a few hours of electricity, and right now that time is being devoted to World Cup soccer. I am the honored guest. I marvel at ads for shaving cream, and think about the university's "sustainable green architecture" projects I'd spent time promoting. Unsa has a TV, but he uses chairs, plates and utensils carved from local trees, and baskets made from river reeds. That's sustainable architecture.

We sit watching together in silence, until his mother-in-law's penchant for hand rolled cigarettes drives us both back out to the porch. Later that night, the tribe members lay out a market of their handmade goods on the front porch: baskets and decorative wooden carvings. I spend all the money I've brought.

A s we're leaving the hotel in Kuching, I'm presented with a bill. "Seven dollars for a local phone call?" I cry in disbelief. "Are you kidding me?"

At some point in our exchange I realize I have failed my own "Survivor" question. This is truly ungracious behavior. As we wait for the cab to the airport roadside, however, Liz comforts me.

"That is a ridiculous charge," she says. "They think you won't notice because we're all so rich."

"Compared to them we are," I say.

"But it doesn't help the tourist trade to be known for ripping off tourists," she says. "You did the right thing."

I think back on the conversations I've had with Victoria about how I was always forced into the role of "bad cop" with Geoff, and how it was made worse by his inevitable ensuing criticism. Remember what it feels like to be supported by a friend.

DOHA, QATAR
September 2006

I see Victoria as soon as I'm back in Doha.

"I can't believe I took condoms!" I say. "I mean, how in the hell am I gonna meet a Boy Scout if I'm the one who's always prepared?"

Barely a beat goes by before I add, "like I'm ever going to date again."

"That's a poverty mentality," she says. "When you tell yourself that, you need to correct yourself immediately. Of course, you will date again."

I wish I felt that sure about it. I'm still not divorced. Is Geoff ever going to sign those papers?

———

K ara's going away party is on a Thursday night. I go with Robert Baxter. She looks beautiful in a skimpy black dress. She's laughing and dancing with Kaleem, her latest Lebanese fling, whom she has plans to try and continue to see long distance after she leaves. I silently hope that someday I will stop feeling left behind by the plans my friends make with their lovers.

"Crazy" by Gnarls Barkley comes on and I join her on the dance floor. We've done this many times at Doha's various five-star hotels, and I'm sad that this will be our last dance. It's only been a few months we've been hanging out, but it's become so important. There isn't even any eye candy to fantasize about; I stay till the bitter end. I seem to be turning into more and more of a night person.

"Get laid already, will you?" Kara says as she's giving me a final hug at the end of the night. Though I had finally told her about Pittsburgh, I've not mentioned Adam. She hates him.

"I wish my sex drive would disappear instead of my friends," I say. I mean it.

———

B efore Ramadan hits, I need to take my staff out to lunch. I need to tell them.

TWENTY-NINE

THE L.E.A.N. TEAM

The L.E.A.N. Team:
Like all PR people, we loved an acronym. This one stood for
Lisa, Emma, Aya and *Noha*. Presented to me by the ladies of the
CMUQ marketing department; I still have the t-shirt.

DOHA, QATAR
September 2006

AFTER DINNER AT the Mövenpick I repair to
Robert Baxter's stoop. Robert isn't part of the buffet-
going set.

"How's Geoff," he begins as he sips some disgusting liqueur
that I believe was a gift. He's not even expecting an answer to
this question, doesn't wait. "Are you sure you don't want to try
this?" he asks, proffering his tea cup.

But I'm bored with my own charade.

First I tell him I don't drink because I'm a recovering alcoholic. That I'm getting a divorce. That I'm going to quit the
next day.

I am?

"I dare say, I don't think it will be a surprise," Robert says. That's it? That's what he has to say. What a fucking asshole.

True or not, I'm hoping to hear something more along the lines of, *That's terrible, you and Geoff were such a great couple.* Or even.

You can't quit! You're so great at your job.

Mostly, I'm angry I haven't fooled him for one minute. But I have to face facts. It's been almost nine months since I told Robbie I wanted to leave. In that time I could've given birth, but here I am in the same old place having the same old conversations.

Just as suddenly, though, I think of Victoria telling me that I've been looking for validation in the wrong places. Or, as Mary Ellen had said many times, "Everyone's in their own movie, hon. Just be the star of yours."

"I'm going to tell Chuck tomorrow," I tell Robert.

Really?

That's gonna piss Robbie off.

My team is going to lunch for Aya's going away party, so it's perfect. She'd insisted we not throw her a party, and this was a day we were all available before Ramadan started to celebrate our co-worker. I have a meeting in the morning, so as soon as I drop my bag I call the dean, Chuck. I may have told Robbie, my boss in the States, about wanting to leave months ago, but I've not said anything to anyone on campus. Do they all know? Like Robert?

Chuck is just back from a family vacation and I hope he's not too busy to see me. By the end of the day I want everyone to know. His phone goes right to voice mail, his admin's voicemail

—Ruth, formerly my admin, the solitaire-playing whiz. I leave a message about needing to see him urgently.

Emma and I make a coffee run, and I'm back just in time to meet with a designer about an upcoming issue of the campus newsletter. When he leaves, I go online to a page I'd bookmarked when I was looking for a trip earlier. A yoga course in India.

The perfect time out while I plan the next phase of my life. India offers six-month visas; plenty of time to sort myself, or so I think. It won't be, not by a long shot.

Most importantly, however, the course imposes a deadline: November 6. I click "confirm payment."

Where the hell is Ruth?

I walk over to the dean's side of the building. Still no Ruth but Chuck is in. I walk in and shut the door.

"Uh, oh," he says smiling. "She's closing the door." I know he's trying to be light, but I feel trivialized. We sit and I tell him the whole story.

He doesn't ask me to stay either.

"That doesn't sound like the Geoff we know," is what he says.

This comment is shattering. On some level I recognize Chuck is responding to me. I still love Geoff. But really? Chuck himself is a good man, but in that moment, he chose to be a total dick.

"The heart has no mind," I say, convoluting words I'd read on a spiritual website earlier.

I walk out more determined than before. Before anything can stop my, I compose an email to all staff announcing my resignation at the end of the semester, with a cc to Robbie. I grab the keys and head around to Cindy's office. Her head's in the computer.

"Come with me for a coffee?" I say. I need more caffeine

like I need a hole in the head, but I need Cindy now. "I need to tell you something."

On the short drive to Landmark Mall, I tell her I'm getting a divorce, something that didn't really fit into the resignation letter. I can see she's hurt that I didn't include her on this aspect of my life, and I feel terribly guilty. I've sold everyone short. At the same time, I know I can't bear to keep having this conversation and I figure our one conversation will work like a press release. It does. Later, at TGI Friday's with the team, we recount stories of Aya's contributions. Noha is grateful she'd railroaded Fawzi.

"He was driving me crazy, always arguing my Arabic translations were wrong," Noha laughs.

"Remember when Nour's father wanted us to take down the video we made in February?" Emma asks. "Aya got him to see that she was helping other women feel comfortable, and that she looked so modest."

"My personal favorite has to be from the first week you were here," I say. "I'd been pestering Mohamed for months that our office needed a Mac—on the main campus they insist on tech savvy across platforms—but you got one right away. Nice."

I don't want to take away from her moment, but I know now's the time. These women have saved my ass for the past six months—from bringing me premium coffee, to letting my foul moods pass without comment, to simply continuing to show up when none of them actually need to have jobs. And so I confess. The girls are stunned. Then I am.

Noha says she doesn't want me to go because she has more to learn from me. Emma wonders who will make doing great work as fun. Aya says God has other plans for me.

By worrying that life was not as good without my husband, I'd almost missed the life I'd created without him. A good life. Am I making a huge mistake?

"You're forgetting what you want," Victoria says. "When you were in DC at that conference, you said you wanted to help other people find the light within and make it shine."

"So corny," I say.

"Yes, but that doesn't make it untrue," she says. "The point is, you can't be there for other people when you're not showing up for yourself."

"Oh, not you, too," I say. "Why does everyone seem to think I need to have some kind of breakdown? I don't want to be miserable."

"How's that working out for you?" Victoria asks.

I look at Victoria like I want to kill her, because for a moment I do. Then I have to concede. Because this isn't working out so well for me. I still have no idea what I'm going to do with the proverbial rest of my life, and can't let go of the idea that my presence is not really required anywhere.

"Do I need to remind you, you quit your job?" she asks. "And no one has asked you to stay. Allow yourself to move toward the path of least resistance."

The good feeling this talk gave me wore off over the next couple of days. Right to the nub of "no one asked you to stay." standing in front of Dunkin' Donuts on Sunday night, I'm hoping Paul will right me.

"I always say, if you feel like you're constantly banging your head against a wall," he says, "You're probably going in the wrong direction."

"But haven't I put up those barriers?" I ask.

"Ahh," Paul says. "You think life is a self-improvement course? one long march to perfection?"

"You're right," I say. "I thought I realized this when Jeffrey died. Life can be brutally short. Over in a flash."

"Or it can go on and on," Paul says. "Either way, there's no reason to stop and beat yourself up. The only person that's going to suffer is you."

That's it. I decide to throw myself a birthday party.

M y birthday has always been fairly traumatic. Coming as it does at the beginning of the school year, and that we moved all the time growing up, and that my sister and I were born two years and three days apart, it sucked enough that we held joint birthday celebrations. To top that off, no one ever came. No one goes to the new kid's party.

I can't have that on this birthday.

It's bad enough I'm turning 40. In Qatar. During Ramadan. Single. God help me if I'm alone, too. So before Rammers gets underway, I run out with Robert Baxter to buy some booze beforehand. The month before Ramadan, just to ensure no one can get too upset, expats are allowed to buy twice their monthly allotment of liquor. Since I don't drink, I am going to stockpile the shit out of my bar and thus get all the expats I know to my party. I'm excited to be going to the booze souq, Doha's most modern, gleaming store. We pick up beer and whiskey and wine. I let Robert make many of the selections, I don't know what to buy anymore.

"Is Adam coming?" he asks.

"Of course," I say. I haven't said anything about our liaison to Robert. "This is the big 4-0. Everyone's invited."

"I hear he has a new girlfriend."

So much for "seeing other people." I definitely need to move on.

"I hope he brings her," I say, trying to sound chippy. Did Robert know something? Had Adam said something?

B esides the Ramadan factor, my birthday falls on a school night. I think about moving the party to the weekend, but decide against it. I'm only turning 40 once, and if there's one thing I want to avoid it's feeling sorry for myself. I've had enough of that.

On the actual day of my birth, Mary Ellen emails me an iTunes gift certificate. "You'll love this!" she writes. She's right. I spend most of the day at work putting together the playlist for the party, sampling a lifetime of my favorite music, from X's "Los Angeles" to the Arctic Monkeys' "Dancing Shoes." *Aim low!*

So many people are out of town, I'm surprised at the number who do show up. What if I run run out of supplies.

We expats are nothing, however, if not expert guests. As the night rolls on, the food and liquor supplies multiply on the dining room table. Despite my plea that no one bring gifts, I get a number of things I know I'll take with me when I leave— a phone card, a scarf, a travel towel. But my favorite is a birthday card from Donna, my subversive co-worker with whom I'd shared the many texts about the sex lives of Qataris.

It's actually an anniversary card that appears to have been given to her by her husband. The word "wife" is scratched out and replaced with "You." "I" is "we," and so on, so it looks like they're professing, in the purplest of hues, their undying love to me. Not only is this a send-up of the idea of birthday cards (I'm not a card person in general), I love that she's making fun of the fact I no longer have a spouse. She is officially the first person to make me laugh over my divorce. Regardless of her intentions, I'm buoyed with fresh confidence.

***

Adam comes alone. We're cordial. See? I'm fine.

"What's your spread?" he asks as I'm bent over a platter, replacing grape leaves.

I shrug my shoulders and look from side to side slowly, as if to say, does anybody know what this man is talking about, though at that moment we're standing alone.

"Mine's four," he says. "That's the number of different decades the women I've slept with were born in."

From the corner of my eye I see Cass, a newcomer to Education City. Nothing but intuition tells me she's the new girlfriend, which must've added another notch to Adam's decade belt. I can't believe I slept with this asshole. Kara was right.

"Oh look," I say. "More guests."

I skip over to the door and there's Emma and Cindy and Ben.

Ben would change my decade spread. *Down, girl.*

The night goes on. When Paul and his wife leave, I am the last remotely sober person in the room. I kick out the disco and Val starts dancing with Robert Baxter. Donna and her husband sway in time and murmur sweet nothings. Even one of the priests from Georgetown University is sweating to the beat. The playlist finally ends around 1, Donna summer's "Last Dance." The room clears and the only people left are Robert and Ben and I.

"Where's Cindy?" I ask.

"She got a cab."

Oh really?

But Robert doesn't get the hint.

The three of us repair to my front stoop. The bougainvillea and hibiscus have filled in, making it the perfect place to sit undetected. We're sitting and talking and smoking — Robert goes for a cigar — and it seems like forever passes. I learn Ben moved a lot when he was growing up, military family. He's also taken over DJ duties and has great taste in music. Finally, Robert bids goodnight—*he's still here?*— and crosses the street.

I'm scared and excited all at once. This is almost like a one-night stand. I wonder when's the last time I had a one-night stand. College? Have I ever had a one-night stand?

"I guess I should go too," Ben says. *Is he fucking kidding me?*

"Okay," I say.

"I'd rather kiss you," he says.

"That would be okay, too."

Then I remember, we're not invisible. "As long we go inside."

We talk and kiss and smoke on the couch. Sure we're smoking inside. When we finally do fuck, Ben puts Adam to shame. We're not doing calisthenics, but his motor skills are extremely well-honed. He finds my g-spot in about one second. Does he have an extra hand? After several goes, I long for my condoms—but he's packing. *My Boy Scout?* We actually come at the same time.

"If you have time before you go," I tell him at the door, "let's do this again."

I head right for the shower. Not that I'm trying to scrub him off, I know already I'll want to sleep until the last possible second before I have to head into the office. Yes, I had my party on a school night, because that was the day my birthday fell.

Morning hits hard and sooner than I expect. I grab clothes off the bedroom floor — beige Capri pants and a rumpled, black linen shirt. A mirror check on the way out the door reveals whackjob hair—I went to bed with it still wet. I'm wearing glasses and no makeup. The 4 a.m. lights-out doesn't wear so well at 40. I look back into my demolished living room. *Take that Adam*, I think. Then I laugh out loud, delighted. For a moment I wasn't thinking about Geoff.

N oha is out of town and Aya won't be in the office so I can make coffee for myself and Emma only. It grows cold on her desk till I finally drink it. I'm dying. Thank Christ I don't drink anymore. She rolls in around 10:30 a.m., looking about as good as me. "That party made my hubby one randy little bastard," she laughs. "I got no sleep, you twat."

We burst out laughing.

"I'm going for lunch," I say. "Yeah, I know it's not quite 11 a.m., but I'm just so thrilled the cafeteria is open this year, I can't stand it." The ban on eating and serving food is still in place around Doha, but Education City mess halls have been granted a reprieve. I show her where I stash coffee beans and the French press, in case she wants some caffeine, but she's not feeling that coordinated.

I'm crouched over a pile of lamb and rice, alone with my orange tray and a magazine when I hear Cindy's voice. "Lisa, look who's hee-yah," she says. I look and see her bounding toward me with Ben. Jesus H. Christ.

She doesn't know. *Does she know?* Oh, what the fuck do I care?

"Haa-aay," I say, drawing out the word and scooting my tray a little closer. "Join me."

Ben smiles. I smell the soap coming off him as he sets his keys down across from my chair. Yeah, 4 a.m. looks a lot better on a 27-year-old. Yeah, that did change my decade spread.

Ben makes his way over to the steaming trays of food. Cindy sits down. "I'm not eating," she says. "Not after last night." She goes on to show me where the acupuncturist put a needle in her ear. This is the guy Victoria had recommended to me; after a few visits I'd begun sleeping through the night, and found that if I went after a trip I didn't get jet lag. But I'm skeptical when she gushes, "this is supposed to make me lose weight."

I wonder how she has all her energy. She was up late with me, yet she's wearing makeup, she got her daughter to school that morning, and apparently, she'd been to the acupuncturist.

Get back in your own movie, I remind myself. It was more fun there.

Ben returns to the table, he's playing it so cool. If I hadn't been there, I never would've guessed we'd slept together. I don't think Cindy notices as she's doing most of the talking. Is Ben embarrassed? It's almost noon, I've been sitting there long enough, I can leave without seeming terribly rude. Then in walks Adam. With Cass. Jesus.

What are *these* two people doing eating lunch at my office? They don't work here. OK, I hardly work here, but that's another issue. It's Ramadan, no one's even supposed to be in town, and yet, here we are. All in the same cafeteria. Together?

But the question is the answer. It's Ramadan, and there is

just about nowhere to get food, and there are only about five people in town. Of course, we're all in my cafeteria at the same time. I feel like I'm in high school. Am I doing any better now than I did the first time around?

Or worse, am I the 40-something divorcée who flounces around night after night, staying out too late in optimistically youthful outfits that, often as not, miss the mark? Is the next stop on this train meals grazed from happy hour specials, lipstick smeared across my cheek and a wickedly incomprehensible mumble?

"Oh," I say, looking at my wrist. I'm not wearing my watch, I guess it wasn't on the floor. "I have a meeting with Robert at... 12:30."

"Twelve-thirty?" Cindy asks. "Doesn't QF close at one?"

"Yeah, jeez, better not be late. See you guys later."

On the way out, I smile and nod at Adam and Cass. If only I didn't look like some kind of modified bag lady. I call Valerie's office. She's not in. I go to the dashboard on my blog. Click new entry, start typing:

If you liked high school... you'll love work!

I'm 40 and one day today, and I just had to do the walk of shame in a fucking CAFETERIA. At my job...

---

*C*ongratulations! Kara types.

We're IMing on Skype. She's just read my blog from London.

I think it's brilliant. Why on earth would you feel bad?

I'm still married?

Bollocks.

Then she goes on to tell me how she dumped Kaleem in favor of a colleague, a widower with two children under five.

If everyone is the star of their own movie, and I'm the only one who gets to see mine, why not make it a can't-miss hit?

V al invites me camping.

"I don't have any gear," I tell her, remembering the yard sale Geoff and I had held in Pittsburgh. Let's get rid of all the camping stuff, I'd said. We're surely not gonna need it.

"You can use our stuff," Val says.

We drive into the desert near the inland sea, a body of water south of Doha. As we head toward our camp through the middle of the desert— there are no roads to the inland sea— I'm impressed at her surety off road. "Outback," she grins. And then we happen upon what looks like a fortress in the middle of nowhere.

"It's an old movie set," Val's daughter Surya says. "Someone mentioned it in school."

What movie was ever made here?

"It looks like the new old souq they're building on the Corniche," Val says.

And she's right. High stone wall, with turrets and poles sticking out from the top, is apparently the modern-day vision of old Qatar. It's as good a place as any to stop and have lunch. As we sit and eat, a herd of ostriches ambles by. What the?

They are enormous and a little frightening.

"How do they survive?" I ask.

No one knows.

That night around the fire, Surya comes running toward us. "The sea, come look! It's all lit up."

"Phosphorescence," Val smiles, and looks at me. I still have no idea. We head for the water.

There, in the water, it's as if a thousand fireflies swim. When I run my hand through the water, the effect increases.

Val strips out of her clothes. "Let's get in!" And we all do.

A dam stops by my office. It's still Ramadan, and we're all enjoying a relaxed schedule. "I'm going to Shiekh Faisal's collection this afternoon," he says. "Come."

I really want to see this collection— apparently there is an Al Thani family tree that tells who's a drunk and who's gay, could they not read the English?— but I'm not so sure about spending an afternoon with Adam. Maybe it's a chance for closure, like I never got with Geoff. Or maybe he's just looking for a way to say fuck all and blow off the day during Ramadan. Why not?

"How's Cass?" I ask as we head over.

He tells me they've broken up. I will not miss this chance.

"I don't want to give it a go again, in case you're wondering," I say, pleased with myself.

"That's not why I asked you to come," he smiles.

I'm an ass.

"Why did you?" I ask, not improving on how I sound.

"Because you're leaving soon and I miss being friends," he says.

"Why did you end it with me?" I finally say.

"Me? You ended it," he says. This train is de-railing.

"Did I? You're the one who wanted to see other people. I couldn't handle feeling like I wasn't a priority."

"You have to want to make a relationship a priority, too, Lisa,"

This is the same conclusion I'd come to with Kara. Why did I always turn things against myself? If didn't want to be in a relationship with him, why wasn't it ok that he didn't want that either?

And I do want to be friends. *I have not slipped mindlessly into hating men.*

"I'm glad you asked me along," I say. *Ugh. Must I vocalize everything?*

We arrive and are greeted by a young man who disappears when we tell him we've been invited to view the collection. The sheikh never arrives and we are left to wander on our own. The villa is amazing, room after room of rare artifacts from the Bedoin culture. Tents and shoes and carpets. I even spy the family tree; naturally, I take a picture.

"I hear he has a tiger on the property somewhere," Adam says.

Qatar has been this interesting all along?

DOHA, QATAR
October 2006

Ramadan ends with a celebration called Eid Al Fitr, and though Aya is no longer working with us, she stops by. I haven't seen her since before my birthday— of course, she'd not been able to come to my party, amidst booze and men—and I'm touched she remembered and brings a present. A book. The students at VCU had put together a history of Qatari women, more design than story. I don't really understand the stories, they are snippets really, but I treasure it still. She also brings a tub of the dessert she knows I love, along with the recipe.

. . .

U MM ALI

- 1 sheet frozen puff pastry, defrosted
- 1/2 cup pistachios, chopped
- 1/2 cup almonds, sliced and toasted
- 2 tablespoons lemon juice
- 1 pint whipping cream
- 3 cups cold milk
- 3 tablespoons cornstarch
- 3 tablespoons sugar
- pinch of cinnamon rose water (dash)

Pre-heat oven to 400 degrees F. Roll out a sheet of puff pastry to spread evenly into a 9x13 inch pan. Bake approximately 15 minutes, or until lightly browned. Remove from oven, and reduce oven temperature to 350 degrees F.

Mix the almonds and pistachios with the lemon juice. Spread mixture over the pastry, reserving a small amount for garnish.

Combine cream, milk, cornstarch, sugar and cinnamon in a saucepan. Stir over medium heat until thickened. Remove from heat and let cool.

Spread the cooled cream mixture over the nuts and pastry. If desired, sprinkle with rose water. Return dish to oven for 30 minutes, or until cream becomes golden.

Serve hot, garnished with reserved nut mixture.

DOHA, QATAR
November 2006

I'm at the bank and the guy is refusing to let me close my account. I filled out all the paperwork, I waited the 45 days.

"Your husband must sign," the guy is telling me.

"But he's gone back to the States," I say. "And it's not his account. I'm the one who opened it."

The man just looks at me. He's not a Qatari, but he is an Arab male. He's not going to budge an inch. I can just drain the account, but I don't want to leave any kind of a mess behind this time. On my way out the door, I stop to let a clutch of robed women pass.

The ladies section!

I hike myself to the ladies area, where I present my paperwork.

The woman looks at me over her niqab, she can see I'm upset. "Why do you not have a signature here?" she asks.

I explain, a little more fully. "He went back to the U.S. and left me here and now he doesn't speak to me anymore."

There is a kerfuffle of robes as she swishes behind the glass wall to a manager's desk; both ladies look at me. Did she not understand? She comes back to the counter, tapping her pen where Geoff's signature should be.

"Please, just sign."

She understands completely.

I sign my own name in the slot. No one will read it. And I am one step closer to home.

Mohamed stops by my office.

"What are you doing with the Audi?" he asks.

I tell him I'm trying to sell it. He offers to buy it if I can't unload it.

Maybe he would've liked to be friends under other circumstances, too.

"I'd sell it to you for sure," I tell him. "But I'm trading with Riyaz. The car for one of his rugs."

Mohamed grins.

"I think you might've figured this thing out at last," he says, turning heel and leaving my office.

The day before I leave I get something in the mail from Hilary's office. I let it sit on the desk all day — yes, I work right up to the last day, New York City's expensive! — and open it as I'm driving home. In the roundabout between mine and Val's house, I see it's the divorce papers. I call Valerie. I expected to feel something, I tell her.

"Congratulations," she says.

At the airport there is one last snag; my exit visa has expired. I'm in stunned disbelief as the man at the counter turns me away. I phone Cindy. Can anything be done? We should have the wasta for this.

We do, except, it's 3:00 p.m. On Thursday and Cindy can't find anyone at QF.

"Sorry love," she says when she phones me back. "You'll just have to cool your jets in Qatar for another couple of days."

I'm crushed. I am so ready to go home, I can't bear the thought of waiting another week. All my worldly goods are on their way. I'm walking toward the exit when I recall a story Robert Baxter told me on his stoop. This very thing had happened to him once, and he'd simply gone to another counter.

"The majority of time they're too busy on their cell phones to check thoroughly."

But I was in a new wing of the airport, and there were only two counters, each in plain view of the other. I'd not made a scene— thank you Valerie and yoga and Victoria— but I'm still pretty sure I'd been noticed. The place is completely dead.

But I have to try.

I make my way back to the counter. The woman behind the desk looks directly into my eyes as she stamps my passport. With that, I am free to go.

THIRTY

MABROUK!

Mabrouk!:
"Congratulations!"

GOA, INDIA
March 2007

T HE SUNLIGHT FELT so perfect on my arms, I barely noticed the policeman flagging us down as we were returning from the Wednesday market in Anjuna. Of course, this was prime picking. Many of my fellow students on the yoga course had gotten pulled over and given expensive tickets for driving scooters without a license. I slowed and pulled over, letting sarah dismount first.

"Oh bollocks," she said. But I had come prepared. I reached into the compartment below my Honda Aviator's seat. Before leaving Qatari'd gotten an international driver's license for just such situations, ever the hopeless nerd.

I handed it over to the policeman proudly, but he wasn't having it. "This no good," he said. "You have to pay. One thousand rupees."

"What!" I yelled more than asked. "No way. I'm not paying. You can suck it."

"This license is not the proper license," he continued. Calm in the face of my outburst. I was angry, but didn't want a scene. We were talking about approximately $20.

"Oh no, you're wrong," came sarah to the rescue. "This license is actually better than what you require for scooters."

I could hardly believe it. For so long any conflict meant I was the bad cop, I'd lost any sense of being right to be angry. I didn't know it yet, but this was the significant beginning to being healed. I came out of my marriage believing that I was not worthy, that I was damaged, that it was my fault. What I was beginning to learn was that we all have our roles to play. I'd believed that Geoff and I never fought, but that's because for us "not fighting" meant I would try to provoke him and he would withdraw. Then I would feel terrible, swallow whatever bothered me, and carry on. I lost the distinction between suppressing the inappropriate, and leaving out the things that mattered.

The policeman stuffed my paper back in my hand and turned to his colleague. I looked at sarah and winked. "Get on! Quick, let's get away while he's not looking."

And off we rode, yes, into the sunset.

EPILOGUE

DOHA, QATAR
July 2009

I RETURNED TO QATAR to help launch a Tribeca Film Festival outpost. Martin Scorcese and Robert DeNiro in Doha? A talent upgrade for sure, but had the place really changed? The answer was a resounding yes. And no.

For one, I had no trouble staffing up my team. There were loads of talented young people anxious to work the festival, both Qataris and expats. But the dissonance of daily life—covered women in malls passing by lingerie ads—remained. Though the abayas had gone trendy.

Once plain black robes, these garments were now decorated, fuchsia flashing from Chinese sleeves, fancy beading and cuts that changed the lines completely.

Yet the summer I was there, a couple was arrested for kissing at the Ramada hotel. Beyond disapproving glares, fines were levied at people who showed their bare shoulders in public. "Public" was extended to mean, in some cases, the inside of a person's car.

I meet Jameel and Aya at La Maison, the W's French restaurant. Both sport abayas adorned with colorful stitching and beads. We order lunch specials and proceed to talk about, naturally, work. Then it gets interesting.

"If my husband only knew," says Aya. "At the Ministry of Culture we are kept separate from the men, and they treat us terribly. The men pass out their phone numbers. They're always trying to talk to us and never about work. But I will be leaving soon."

I look up from my shitakes and pasta to see Aya grinning and flushed.

"Mabrouk!" I say. "When are you expecting?"

As she gives me the due date and astrological rundown, I can't help but wonder what it will be like to have her cousin's baby.

"Do you know if it will be a boy or a girl?" I venture. Aya smiles. "That is for God to know," she says.

Jameel thinks it will be a boy. "All of his brothers have had boys first," she says.

It's not like they don't get how it works. I am confronted, once again, with the fact that this is not my culture and, by any measure, these women appear happy. It may be considered in poor taste to ask after someone's spouse, but I'm curious why Jameel's husband, one of the lesser Al Thanis, didn't seem to mind her working in a mixed environment.

"Does your husband ever say anything about working at Education City?" I ask her.

The girls pass a look between them, and then Jameel looks squarely at me.

"We are divorced now."

There are so many possible ways to respond, and I have no idea what might be proper. This means the beautiful and young Jameel has had to return to her family home. That her children may be with her husband. But she does not seem at all adrift.

"Mabrouk?" I say with a question mark.

And then we're all laughing. None of us is living the life we'd planned, but who does?

"Things are gonna have to change around here," was the constant refrain of my youth, as uttered by my mother. She could be talking about who should put away the dishes, whether my father should remember to carry money, or the fact that we weren't ready for church. But the only thing that ever did change was our address; we always took our crap with us. As I grew up, I craved constancy, not realizing I'd had it all along in the form of the crap I carried. It took living in a country in an obvious state of flux — and the unraveling of everything I thought I wanted — to discover my own immutability.

For a long while I'd thought Qatar was the problem. How could I possibly be serene in that environment — in its effervescent frenzy to become something else, the place was the exact opposite of Zen. But the whole point to Buddhism was to realize the unchanging self, not the unchanging stuff. Stuff changes all the time, and this was what I actually despised.

But stuff is empty, and has only the properties I project onto it. If I found Qatari women to exude authority and femininity, I had this capacity, too. If I found the world a friendly place, I, too, was friendly. Rather than wait for what I wanted to come to me, I realized I already had everything I needed. This gave me the courage to finally ask, and act on, the big question.

What would you do if you weren't afraid?

And I knew. I knew exactly what I'd do. I'd move to New York City and write a book.

And that's exactly what I did.

PHOTOGRAPHS

Days before leaving Pittsburgh, in the author's
Pittsburgh garden.

The skating rink at the center of Doha's three-story
City Center Mall.

Construction in Doha, ca. 2006.

L.L. hard at work at the Salmon Palace.

A Friday morning beach day on Qatar's
undeveloped coastline.

Duning in Qatar.

A typical crowd the author encountered.

Beach day with Little Bear (L) and Grandpa (R).

Beach day with Little Bear (L) and Grandpa (R).

GLOSSARY

Though I'm not fluent in Arabic, several words and phrases I use liberally in this book are included here. It would have been impossible to survive without them. These words are clues.

Abaya: Black robe worn to cover fully clothed women.

Allah: God; invoked at the beginning, middle and end of every interaction.

Aoud: Ceremonial incense

Bismillah: God is great.

Bukara: Tomorrow; an ever-shifting, Wile E. Coyote point in time.

Ghuttra: The Flying Nun-style head scarf worn by men, even while driving.

Habibi: Term of endearment, as a Baltimore waitress might use the word "Hon." (Habibti is the feminine.)

Halal: Quran approved.

Hamdullah!: Thanks be to God!

Haram: Something that is forbidden in the Koran.

Helas: Enough; finished. Used broadly to announce anything from the conclusion of a meal to a medical diagnosis.

Igal: The black rope that holds the ghuttra in place; previously the camel harness worn while riding. A physical therapist told me its weight has spawned a generation of neck problems.

Insha'Allah: God willing.

Madrasah: Islamic school

Mafi Mushkilla: No problem.

Marhaba: A nonsecular hello

PBUH: Peace be upon him; standard newspaper abbreviation for the words which must follow the prophet's name as in, Mohamed, PBUH.

Quran: The central religious text of Islam.

Ramadan: The holy month of fasting during daylight hours and feeding through the night; the month shifts through the calendar according to lunar cycles.

Salaam Oulaikoum: The peace of God be with you.

Sharia: Quranic interpretation of law.

Shayla: A scarf wrapped around the head to cover the hair. Some women use this cloth to cover their face as well.

Shisha: Glass based water pipe for smoking tobacco.

Shwarma: Pita wrapped sandwiches.

Shway Shway: Little little; used often to mean "not too much"; e.g., as a response to the question of how well I could speak Arabic.

Shukkran: Thank you.

Souq: Shopping area.

Talaq: I divorce you.

Thobe: Contemporary Gulf male dress; highly starched, floor-length white robe.

Wahhabism: Conservative sect of Sunni Muslims, established some 200 years ago to rid Islam of cultural interpretations of the Quran.

Waqf: Charity; as in keeping property in the family by gifting it.

Wasta: Influence.

Yanni: A breather word, like, "like."

AUTHOR'S NOTE

I wrote this book using journals, emails, and blog entries to recreate the world I inhabited in Qatar. To protect anonymity, some names and identifying details have been altered. But it all happened, and this is how it went down. According to me.